The Enchanted Canopy

To Bill
with best wishes

Andrew Mitchell

BOOKS BY ANDREW W. MITCHELL

Voyage of Discovery
The Young Naturalist
Reaching the Rainforest Roof

The Enchanted Canopy

A *Journey of Discovery to the Last Unexplored Frontier,* the Roof of the World's Rainforests

ANDREW W. MITCHELL

With a foreword by
GERALD DURRELL

Macmillan Publishing Company
New York

Macmillan Publishing Company
866 Third Avenue, New York, N.Y. 10022

Library of Congress Cataloging-in-Publication Data

Mitchell, Andrew W.
  The enchanted canopy.

  Bibliography: p.
  Includes index.
  1. Rain forest ecology.   I. Title.
QH541.5.R27M58   1986   574.5'2642   86-8505
ISBN 0-02-585420-8

Macmillan books are available at special
discounts for bulk purchases for sales
promotions, premiums, fund-raising, or
educational use. For details contact:
Special Sales Director
Macmillan Publishing Company
866 Third Avenue
NEW YORK
NY 10022

10 9 8 7 6 5 4 3 2 1

Printed in Great Britain

Contents

Acknowledgements

A great many people have made this book possible through the work that they have conducted in the tree tops and which I have been able to reflect in these pages. To them I owe special thanks for allowing me to see the fruits of their labours. In particular I must express deep gratitude to Stephen Sutton, whose enthusiasm propelled us both into the forest roof and for his role as mentor whose eyes, with insect precision, scanned the manuscripts; to Elliot McClure, who kindly allowed me to have access to so much of his information, gained from years aloft on a Malaysian tree platform; to David Chivers, for his help on primates; and to Bill Timmis, who helped with the birds.

I give thanks to fellow arboreal naturalists including Nalini Nadkarni and Jack Longino, Meg Lowman, Adriaan Kortlandt, Fritz Dieterlan, Francis Ng, Peter Ashton, Don Perry, Francis Hallé and Hubert de Foresta, Bernard Boutin, Van Vooren, Eduardo Santana, Gary Stiles, Joe Marshall and Elizabeth Proctor Gray, whose studies of the rainforest roof and the creatures that live there, in many parts of the world, have been an inspiration for this book.

I would also like to thank the many researchers I met at the La Selva Research Station in Costa Rica and the Smithsonian Tropical Research Institute in Panama, in particular Steve Hubbell, Paul Rich, Neil Smith, Henk Wolda and Don Winsor, for their tales of tropical trees, bees, birds and figs. To Mrs Muriel Field I am grateful for enabling me to see the work of her son Andrew; and to Mike Fogden I pay tribute for his beautiful photographs, often obtained under extremely trying conditions surrounded by the large numbers of snakes with which he shares his house.

To John Healy and Nick Payne thanks are due for their early research; also to Sue Steward for locating so many attractive illustrations. To the tireless team at Collins I owe great thanks, not least to editor Gill Gibbins and designer Ron Clark for their skill at seeing the book through all its stages. Also a special thank-you to June Hall, for her constant encouragement and enthusiasm from start to finish.

Finally, I must pay tribute to Colonel John Blashford-Snell, Jim Masters and the walkway construction teams, without whose support on Operation Drake I would never have taken a single step through the enchanted canopy.

To Anniepan and Puttha, for me. I wish they could have seen it.

Foreword

Rainforests are one of the most complex, beautiful and important of the many ecosystems of this planet. They are also ones that, primarily out of greed, we are destroying with the savage, unthinking ferocity of a troop of drunken apes in an art gallery. But whereas pictures can be repainted, tropical rainforests can't be recreated, and at the rate we are destroyng them this bodes ill for the future of the planet, for these vast forests are climate controllers, desert preventers and huge storehouses of as yet untapped natural resources. The bounty we have already received from them in the shape of everything from timber and spices to medicines is staggering, and there is obviously an enormous amount still to be discovered if we do not destroy this treasure trove.

I remember vividly the first time I entered a tropical rainforest. I spent a whole day bewildered and enchanted by all the sights, sounds and scents. The leafmould alone contained hundreds of insects I had never seen or heard of before. Roll over any rotting log and I found a world as bizarre as anything thought up by science fiction. Each hollow tree was an apartment block containing anything from snakes to bats, from owls to flying mice. Every forest stream was an orchestra of frogs, a ballet of tiny fish, and from the canopy high above came a constant rain of fruit, twigs and pirouetting blossoms thrown down by the great army of creatures — mammals, birds, reptiles and insects — that inhabit this high, sunlit, flower-scented realm. I did not know where to look next. Every leaf, flower, liana, every insect, frog, fish or bird was a lifetime's study in itself, and I knew that there was another hidden, secretive army of creatures that would emerge at night to take over. As any naturalist knows, there is nothing like a tropical rainforest for replacing arrogance with awe.

In this beautiful book, as informative as it is well-written (a rare combination) Andrew Mitchell has given us a magnificent picture of the forest from both his own experience and the experience of others, and what a vivid and fascinating picture he paints. Reading this book is the next best thing to visiting a tropical forest yourself. While reading it, however, be reminded of the fact that for future generations, their only means of experiencing this natural splendour may be by reading about it and, while they read, damning us for not having preserved their heritage.

GERALD DURRELL
May, 1986

Mist veils the Melinau Valley in
Borneo's Mulu National Park.
Beneath it exists one of the
world's richest forests.

Prologue

Dawn is never a quiet time in the rainforest. The change began as an almost imperceptible hum, punctuated by the tip-tap of water droplets, plump with night rain, splashing onto large green leaves in the forest understorey. An occasional raucous bird call, the nocturnal frogs piping their last chorus; then a new collection of sounds began to swell and fill the forest. At a quarter to six precisely the 'six o'clock cicada' started to rasp like a miniature chain saw. No need for alarms here, all thought of sleep was gone.

It was then that the calls of the wa-wa began. They were later than usual, faint like a child's whimper at first but then, increasing in frequency and power, the gibbons voiced their morning song. The males would call first, head thrown back, lips drawn into a pouting circle; the forest canopy echoed to their cries. Half an hour later a female demonstrated her great call, slow, deep whoops, building to a crescendo, gradually fading to a sound like bubbling laughter. The instant she finished, a male would hoot with apparent satisfaction and leap about the branches, swinging with unbelievable agility in circles and turns before sitting to listen for any answering voices from other groups nearby. In this way they laid claim to their part of the forest.

In the mink-blue dawn, massive green mountains, Gunung Api and Benarat, began to emerge from swirling veils of mist that slowly drifted upwards to caress the sky. My back was stiff from a night spent on saplings cut from the forest and bound into a wooden frame to make a sleeping platform. Dew dripped from the plastic sheet that served as a roof. Swinging my legs to the ground, I put on a damp, musty smelling shirt, faintly mouldy trousers and wet boots, beating the latter out first to dislodge any scorpions that had chosen to spend the night there. A wash in the river could wait.

There was no wind within the forest to disturb the smoke spiralling from the fire Leloh was blowing into. His hair was black and cut into a fringe across his forehead, a long pony tail hanging down his back. He was a Penan, a true nomad of the Bornean heartland, an encyclopaedia of forest lore and, for me, a guide whose language I could not understand, nor could he speak mine. A parang was thrust into his black woven loincloth. I nodded to him, shouldering my small pack containing notepads, water and binoculars. He picked up his blowpipe, ebony black, thrust a bamboo quiver of poisoned darts into his belt, and we moved down from the mountain ridge, through the forest and into the valley, in the direction of the calls.

From my vantage point overlooking the Melinau valley in Borneo's Mulu National Park, the undulating forest canopy had given no hint of what lay beneath its magnificent tree crowns – its unbelievable richness, its multitude of life forms, its unsolved mysteries – and now, padding quietly along the early morning trail, it appeared a dark, even forbidding place. Still damp from the night's rain and not yet warmed by the pale sun, the path wove through giant trees laden with vines and creepers but branchless until their trunks divided some thirty metres above my head, and spread into an enormous crown. No two trees seemed the same, and they weren't. A hectare of Bornean jungle may support over three hundred species of tree: a temperate woodland can boast but fifty. The largest trees in the world are found here, like the tualang tree, which can exceed the height of a twenty-storey building. But standing back and peering through the forest, the massive trees, the greenness, verdancy everywhere, seemed to press in on two very small human beings surrounded by sweeping palms, clinging vines, and gently nodding drip-tipped leaves. And somewhere, up there, were the gibbons I was searching for, listening for. But I saw nothing of them, and enveloped by the hum of the forest there was only their silence to hear. All I could discern were the criss-crossed branches laden with leaves, tangled gardens of orchids, ferns and trailing vines spotlit with occasional bright sunlight piercing the green canopy all the way to the ground where I was gazing upwards in wonder and frustration.

When the time for a close encounter came, it was brief and exhilarating. As we approached an area where the forest canopy appeared less dense, Leloh crouched and motioned for me to stop. It was now past 7.30 and we were close to where the gibbons had been calling, but they had long since stopped. Suddenly, there was a rustle of branches and leaves. Leloh pointed, I moved closer. There was a second movement. This time I knew it was not the wind moving the branches but definitely a primate, almost overhead, several of them – but where? I seemed to stop breathing, my excitement recharged as always at such times. On the ground were leaves showing bite marks. There was a sound of falling twigs and fruits. Suddenly a wild squealing and snarling began overhead and a nearby tree erupted with jumping monkeys – a fight had started and several of them began to chase each other amongst the branches. Leaves scattered down, falling on the floor not far from where I was standing with Leloh, our eyes raised expectantly. More squealing, and then silence. We moved closer.

The silhouettes high above were enough to tell me that this was a band of Hose's leaf monkeys, perhaps twelve to fifteen strong. Their brilliant white belly fur blends into a back of steel grey. They have long, elegant tails and legs, and faces of soot black sporting flesh-coloured noses, muzzles and eyelids, the whole fringed with white fur. A crest of long hairs sprouts down the midline of their head. Even with binoculars I could see little of this: the description came from museum specimens I had seen and text books. Fifty metres below them on the forest floor I could only imagine what they must look like, and could see very little of what they were doing. A loud whirring noise swept over the trees above me, followed by flapping and silence: a large hornbill had alighted in a tree nearby to take some fruits. But I couldn't see it. My arms and neck were beginning to ache from peering upwards. Then I made a mistake.

Leeches are one of the more intriguing, if unpleasant, aspects of life in South East Asian forests. They spend most of their lives on the forest floor and the lower shrubs, from where they hope to attach themselves to a passing vertebrate, so securing a blood meal which will sustain them through many months of subsequent starvation until the next pig or tapir comes within reach. They are remarkably sensitive to the presence of carbon dioxide and warm temperatures, both of which signal that a mammal, and therefore a meal, is nearby. Should the vibration of a passing step reach them, they can move with surprising agility towards it, occasionally stopping to wave their heads in the air to ascertain the direction in which to travel and then looping, with a certain desperation, across the leaf-strewn forest floor towards their target. I kept one as a pet back at the camp inside a small glass bottle, bringing it out for a blood feed on my arm whenever I thought it was looking a little thin. I would sometimes see another, more attractive, species, decorated in yellow stripes, patiently waiting on the leaves of bushes. If their vigilance is to be rewarded, they must launch themselves out into space in the hopes of landing on a passing meal. One such had landed on my neck and had already swollen grotesquely. I pinched its tail hard, and it released itself, vomiting blood onto my skin, and fell to the ground where I noticed others looping enthusiastically towards my boots. I moved my foot to avoid them, and placed it on a twig.

With a loud crack, it broke. Above me there was a harsh 'croo-crook', and the monkey troop jumped in all directions, then moved rapidly away. The hornbill permitted a glimpse of its massive black wings disappearing across a gap between two trees. But the moment was not without its compensations. Further on there was another gap and one by one the monkeys burst from the crown, arms held aloft, legs pulled up, tails thrashing the air, and with a crash of leaves they landed in the next tree ten metres below. Each followed the same route precisely, as though it were a well trodden path. A big male was the last to flee. He stood on a branch, barking defiance in my direction until, when the group was some distance away, he too jumped and disappeared into the trees.

Though the sounds of the forest can reveal a great deal, I caught only fleeting views of life in the canopy. Tree crowns laden with bright flowers, butterflies and a multitude of insects were just discernible floating in the humid air high above, and colourful birds flashed from one crown to another. But of the gibbons I saw and heard nothing. By noon the forest was quieter. Though relatively cool on the forest floor, the forest roof was now bathed in a harsh sunlight and most animals had sought shade; there was little activity. Disappointed, I signalled to Leloh and we set off up the ridge in the direction of the the camp.

Perhaps the gibbon had been asleep. It didn't notice my approach until I was practically underneath its branch and had it not moved I should never have seen its dark brown fur against the blackness of the tree bark and dark, clustered leaves. About eight metres above my head, it leapt to its feet and in one fluid movement sprang from the branch and swung up onto a bough reaching over my path. Across this it walked, nimble as a ballerina, arms almost too long for its body held out sideways, long hands hanging downwards. Halfway across, it paused, arms still held out, and looked towards where I was standing, its dark brown eyes framed by eyebrows of white hairs. Our eyes appeared to meet and then it was gone, swinging with immense speed and agility hand over hand through the branches and up into the trees.

My brief elation was tinged with a feeling of hopelessness. It takes months, even years, to habituate primate groups to the presence of a human being peering up at them from the forest floor. Too often a gibbon's caution has not been sufficient to avoid a poison-tipped dart or, more often these days, a bullet. What chance had I, with such a short time available, to gain insight into their world high above the ground? And what was that world like, tantalisingly close yet remaining out of reach and almost as unknown as the ocean depths? It needed little imagination to realize that all the interesting things in the forest, at least to me, were going on way above my head. Disregarding curious leeches and foraging creepy-crawlies, I slumped onto the decaying leaves heaped around the base of a giant tree and leaned back into the indifferent embrace of its giant buttress roots. The leaves felt damp and all around there was a musty smell of mould. I gazed up at the light filtering through gently moving silhouettes of leaves.

It seemed to me that so much of our knowledge about these intriguing habitats was based on only one part of it. Surely the discoveries made to date from grubbing about in the forest basement would pale into insignificance if only we could get up and explore the rainforest roof? It might even change our view of the forest altogether. True, much had been gleaned already by observing the tree tops across a valley or from an exposed ridge, to see what animals might live there and when trees came into flower or fruit. Collections had even been made, but mostly through blasting high limbs from trees with shotguns, or worse, from felling whole trees to get at their crowns, and seizing upon the dazed creatures that survived the shattering fall, and the tattered plants clothing the tree's torn and broken limbs. In a very few places in the world, observation towers had been built or platforms erected and though it all amounted to very little, the discoveries made from them revealed one remarkable fact: more animals and plants lived up in

It is a rare event to meet a Müller's gibbon face-to-face. Until just ten years ago, it was thought to be the only gibbon species inhabiting Borneo's forest. It is capable of moving with fluid grace and great speed.

What goes on in the rainforest roof has, until now, largely remained a mystery, since most of the trees are too tall to climb. Perhaps half of all animal life on earth may exist in the canopy, making it the richest habitat on the planet.

the canopy than in any other part of the forest, and most of them were completely unknown to mankind.

I stood up and looked at the tree against which I had been sitting. Its bark was mottled with pastel-shaded lichens. A collection of vines hung down its side from the roof above, bound to the trunk by numerous clinging ferns and other epiphytes. There were no branches for a climber to get a hold on: the first did not appear for thirty metres. The same was true of most of the other trees nearby. Any branches from which a rope might be slung were as distant as the roof of a tall building. And I knew one other thing: had I attempted to climb the trunk I would have been welcomed by a collection of stinging and biting creatures from bees and ants to scorpions and snakes, residing amongst the plants clinging to the bark. These, along with the attendant vertigo, usually provide sufficient discouragement to ensure that human feet are kept firmly on the ground. To see the primates that lived there close at hand without disturbing them, to peer into a crown of flowers to note what unknown butterflies drank their nectar, even to stay overnight in the tree tops and see what bats came to feast on fruit there under cover of darkness, was as much an impossibility for me as flying.

I turned and, with Leloh, made my way back up the ridge towards our small camp amongst the trees. As we made our way quietly through the forest I could not get these thoughts out of my mind. By the time we had reached the cool stream below the camp, the first chorus of frogs had begun the evening concert. Leloh scooped into the surface of the stream with his hand and poured the clear water into his mouth. Wearily, I dropped my pack and sat down beside the stream, watching the water trickle down the mountainside through the moss-covered rocks. A pool reflected the patterns of the tree crowns above in dark colours of brown and green. Sooner or later, I thought, a way will be found to explore that enchanted canopy.

1 | Reaching the Rainforest Roof

There are many different kinds of rainforest. On the tops of high mountains, trees tend to be shorter, their branches are often draped in moss, giving them a mysterious, elfin-like quality. Mists daily envelop these mountains and so they are known as cloud forests. The composition of the animals and plants that live there usually changes in the journey down the mountainside to lower altitudes. The forests which grow on limestone or volcanic soils are different from those found on sand. Some forests appear to stand on tiptoe above swampy ground and near the coast tall mangroves may be found. Outside the wettest regions, seasonal forests grow, deluged during certain months of the year with monsoon rains. But this book is mainly concerned with the richest of all rainforests which grow in the tropical lowlands on comparatively dry ground. As they are the most accessible, it is also these forests that are most rapidly disappearing from the world.

There are many layers of life in a rainforest, though they are rarely apparent from the ground. Shrubs and creepers fill the floor of the forest, with small saplings growing through them on their way to the forest roof. Their leafy tops are dwarfed by a region of columns, the trunks of greater trees which hold their crowns in the sun. Beneath this summit lies a network of stout branches on which the leaves are borne, creating a thick layer of limbs and leaves undulating in response to the changing shape of the land. This is the forest canopy. Above that, still greater trees emerge, spreading massive crowns of leaves, like individual islands.

Viewed collectively the world's tropical forests still cover almost eight per cent of the earth's land surface, an area as large as the United States. These forests generally grow in warm, moist places where the temperature varies little throughout the year. Rainfall can be spectacular and usually falls in torrential showers accompanied by noisy thunder and brilliant lightning. In the wettest regions, ten metres of rain may fall in a year, yet where the forests stand, the soil is not washed away and the land is not dominated by flash floods. These great forests act as a sponge and soak up the moisture in the vegetation and through their roots, releasing it slowly back into the atmosphere via their leaves, to fall as rain on parched lands elsewhere.

Almost a quarter of the remaining forests exist in South East Asia, spreading from Northern Australia, up through Papua New Guinea's knife-edged mountains, and across Indonesia's fourteen thousand islands, though not all of them are covered with virgin

PREVIOUS PAGE
Though the vast tracts of forest which still cover the earth can be surveyed from the air, no vehicle has been designed with which man can explore the forest canopy closer at hand.

forest any more. Borneo, the largest of the so-called Sunda Islands, still retains huge areas of rich, unexplored and unexploited forest, with melodious gibbons and solitary orang-utans. From there the canopy spreads north and westwards to the peninsula of Malaysia, where most of the once rich forests have now disappeared, along with the tigers that roamed them.

The winds which once took spice traders to East Africa also brought them to Madagascar and further north to Sri Lanka and the southern tip of India. Here some moist forest still remains and in Madagascar the lemurs still survive, though with each year their future is more threatened. The rainforest canopy does not begin again until tropical West Africa is reached. A tenth of the world's rainforest exists in Zaire alone. The forest here tends to be more open and fragmented than in other parts of the world, perhaps due to the bulldozing work of large herbivores such as elephant, rhino and buffalo, pushing and shoving their way through the vegetation. But lack of roads in such a poorly developed country, almost as large as Western Europe, has protected the forest here, at least compared with other regions. The forests of Nigeria and the Ivory Coast, once sources of some of the world's most valuable hard-woods, have all but gone. Spreading north and south from the Gambia to Angola they still exist, but there is growing fragmentation. All of these forests, from the Far East to West Africa, are known collectively as Old World forests.

Across the Atlantic are the tropical forests of the New World. In South America there is an unusual strip of wet forest on the eastern coast. Conflict with humans who also live there has brought many

Tropical forests stretch round the equatorial belt of the earth, where there is sufficient warmth and moisture. Those growing in the New World, the American tropics, harbour animals and plants which are quite distinct from those of the Old World forests, from West Africa to Australia.

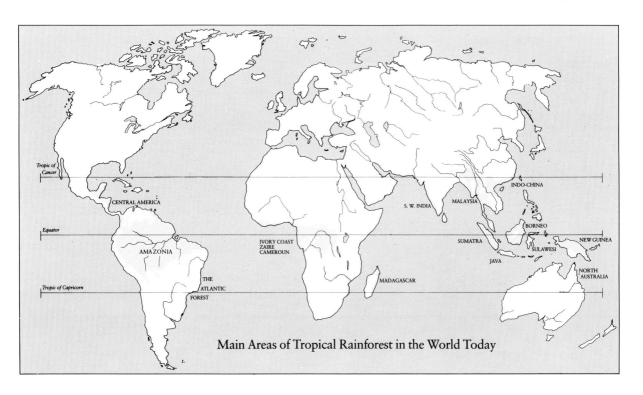

Main Areas of Tropical Rainforest in the World Today

Each year new species of insect, as extraordinary as these two moths, are discovered in the canopy. Most have yet to be given names.

The warning colours of the Australian *Lyramorpha* shield bugs proclaim that they are dangerous to eat. The sheer numbers of insects encountered in the canopy surpassed all expectation.

of its primates, such as tiny marmosets and larger woolly monkeys, to the brink of extinction. Further west the vastness of Amazonia and its magnificent jungles gives true meaning to the notion of an unbroken canopy. Thousands of kilometres westwards to the Andes and thousands more from Panama south to Brazil, account for the greatest concentration of animal and plant life in the world. The rainforest is also the land's interface between the elements and the atmosphere, through which it plays such an important part in maintaining the world in a state of climatic equilibrium. Brazil alone harbours over a third of all the world's rainforest. Enormous areas have already been cleared here but they represent less than five per cent of the whole. This should not encourage complacency, as much damage is being done and the pace each year increases.

But at least in the more inaccessible parts of Amazonia, the animals and plants of the jungle canopy still exist in relative calm. So far, not for them the sound of the bulldozer and the smell of burning – but the time is coming.

Years of study conducted in the understorey and amongst plants and animals which are easiest to reach there, have revealed the tropical rainforests to be the richest ecosystem on the planet, rivalled only by coral reefs for their diversity and the complexity of inter-relationships between their inhabitants. Yet until recently almost nothing was known of the complexity of life in the rainforest canopy. What was suspected was that life was there in much larger quantities than at lower levels. The tree crowns support a rich diversity of aerial plants which use branches for support. These epiphytes grow in huge numbers in the canopies of most rainforests. One tree may support numerous different species of orchid fern, bromeliad or philodendron, as well as innumerable mosses, liverworts and lichens. The varied habitats of all these plants provide food, drink and homes to countless creatures about whose lives almost nothing is known. The fertilization of these plants and trees fills the canopy with colourful flowers and later fruits on which come to feed a host of mammals, birds and insects, whose natural history remains a secret, glimpsed fleetingly from the ground.

As is so often the case, it is the insect world that demonstrates the depths of our ignorance. Prior to traps being placed in the canopy of tropical rainforests, it was generally supposed that there were about one million species of insect in the world. Then, in the early 1970s, a biologist named Terry Erwin from the Smithsonian Institution raised a machine high into the treetops which emitted a fog of insecticide. So many insects fell down into his collecting trays that he later revised the estimate from one million species to ten million. His latest work using similar techniques suggests a total of thirty million insect species, enough to keep all the taxonomic institutions on earth busy for decades. Few of these creatures have ever been seen by man before, let alone studied by him.

Compare these figures with the total number of mammals known in the world: just four thousand. It is possible that well over half of

all species of animal life on this planet live in the upper canopy of tropical rainforests.

With most trees as high as Nelson's column in London's Trafalgar Square, and branch-free for so many metres, it is not surprising that few humans have ventured in the canopy to study it. The first record of an Englishman climbing into a rainforest roof was in 1573. It was, surprisingly, Sir Francis Drake. Landed in Panama and preparing to raid the Spanish royal treasure road, he had been told of a high tree set upon a mountain ridge from which it was possible to see two oceans. Intrigued, he marched four days inland from Nombre de Dios on the Caribbean coast into the mountains of the Serrania del Darien. Pedro, the Cimmaron chief acting as guide, finally led the stout Devonshire sea captain up steps cut into the side of a 'giant and goodlie tree' and from the top Drake gazed out over the canopy and first laid eyes on the Pacific, praying that he:

> 'survive their present hazardous enterprise with profit and in due time be given leave to be the first man to sail an English ship upon that far-off forbidden sea.'

The idea for his great voyage to circumnavigate the globe was born.

Inadequate climbing skills and the fear of falling have kept most humans from the rainforest roof for millions of years. Only skilled tribal climbers have ventured there, whilst the explorer and the scientist remained confined to earth, incapable of learning or matching their agility. Pig-tailed macaques, trained to scale trees to knock down fruits for their masters, were sometimes used to gather specimens for the scientist. But monkeys are notoriously unreliable and may choose to eat the specimen rather than retrieve it. Felling trees, though destructive, proved a worthwhile method for early naturalists wishing to gather specimens, but few animals survived the devastating fall and those that did made their escape with remarkable speed, leaving naturalists flailing nets and waving bottles in hot pursuit. The advent of the shotgun enabled birds and mammals to be bagged, but they were dead. It was not until the 1929 Oxford University Expedition, led by Major R. W. G. Hingston to Moraballi Creek in British Guiana, that any serious attempt was made to explore the canopy by actually getting up there.

Max Nicholson, later to become one of the founders of the World Wildlife Fund, had had the idea of studying animals and plant life there, as almost nothing was known about it. With military thoroughness, Major Hingston had provided every conceivable device to effect the ascent. Rocket-firing apparatus, line-throwing guns, rope ladders, parachute slings borrowed from the RAF, scaling ladders, safety belts and spray syringes to ward off noxious insects they were convinced would try to repel the assault. They decided to make the first attempt on a huge *Morubukea* tree in the centre of the camp clearing. The guns were wheeled out and soon the forest reverberated with the sound of explosions, and projectiles

trailing lines flew skyward with impressive force. Marksmanship was, alas, in short supply and eventually:

> 'The engines of propulsion were laid aside, have effected little beyond scattering cords which stretched through the clearing from their points of entanglement like the natural ropey lianas of the canopy.'

Finally they turned to local tribesmen for help and managed to secure the services of two Indians named Jothan and Sebico from the nearby Pomaroon river; they were accustomed to climbing balata trees to tap their rubber. Hingston fitted them out with heavy spiked boots, and in a manner similar to the pygmy climbers of West Africa, with a loop of rope running around their backs and behind the tree, they slowly rose up the trunk by jabbing into the bark with their feet. In this way a number of trees were climbed and ladders placed in their crowns to enable the branches to be

The first attempts to explore the rainforest roof were made in the late 1920s. Max Nicholson took this photograph, of an 'exalted observer' clutching a large camera and being raised skywards by efforts of three stalwarts on the ground, during an Oxford University expedition to British Guiana.

explored. Even a simple armchair was constructed which could be hauled up into the canopy on pulley blocks; it was reputedly so comfortable that those using it refused to come down. However, there were some red faces when the Acting Governor of the British Colony, His Excellency the Hon. C. D. Douglas-Jones CMG paid a visit to the expedition. He was ceremoniously hauled up to gaze upon his dominions, but could not be got down again. Hurling expletives at the upturned faces below him, the Governor struggled with the ropes twisted in the blocks, and after narrowly avoiding jamming his fingers in them managed to free the pulley and rescue himself from a life of permanent suspension.

The expedition itself was enormously successful and laid the foundations for Professor Paul Richards to write his great work on the biology of the rainforest, which remains a world standard today. He is now a doyen of tropical botany but then was a mere student, renowned for wearing out both the soles and the sides of his shoes in the forest before turning to a new pair. Nevertheless, despite this early interest little of significance was done to continue the canopy exploration until 1960 when a Dutchman, Adriaan Kortlandt, engaged the help of local pygmies in Zaire to build a platform in a high tree in order to observe the behaviour of chimpanzees which regularly raided a papaya plantation below. The pygmies were marvellous assistants but built the platform sufficient for someone their own size, and when the relatively large Dutchman took to the platform there were some tense moments when it appeared in imminent danger of collapse. Modifications were made, and Kortlandt recorded some of the first systematic observations of undisturbed chimpanzees in the wild.

On the other side of the world in the forests near Kepong in Malaysia, an American began constructing a ladder up the side of an enormous meranti tree. By the time it was complete, it had reached the height of an eight-storey building. Each week for three years Elliot McClure used his platform to watch the changing patterns of flowering and fruiting in the forest below him. He saw how the trees provided food to the animals that spent their lives out of touch with the ground, and noted when branches sprouted with new leaves and what trees died and later fell beneath the green ocean to vanish and decay. Whilst placing the ladders up the tree, a native climber beat furiously at the bark to kill a small snake that threatened. It turned out to be one of the rarest snakes in Malaysia, a small tree pit viper, elegantly camouflaged in shades of brown. It was only the fourth time anyone had collected such a snake. Another shared a corner of the platform with McClure for six months. They have rarely, if ever, been found on the ground.

Around the railings of the platform large ants patrolled, and a small black-banded squirrel learned to come for a weekly offering of bananas. A flying snake sailed by one day, and each morning by 10.00 a.m. gliding lizards had flown into the tree to search the branches for insects. More than a hundred species of birds, so

difficult to observe from the ground, lived out their lives around him. He developed a great love for the forest and a respect for the animals that lived there, whose lives he was privileged to observe for the first time in their natural home. Some of the first valuable observations of the natural history of the forest roof were made by him from his platform. Numerous students were introduced to the canopy by making the heart-stopping climb up the ladder to the top to experience for the first time a view shared only by hornbills, flycatchers and monkeys. Then they would sign the visitors' book, and return to the ground. McClure made his last climb at the age of sixty-five and has outlived his tree. By the end of 1977 the forest around it had vanished in the vanguard of progress, and the tree itself came down to make way for the Trans Peninsular Highway.

A variety of steel or scaffolding towers were built to provide access to the forest roof in various countries in the 1960s and 70s, the most famous of which was the Haddow Tower at Mapanga, west of Kampala in Uganda. Built by the East African Virus Research Institute, it revolutionized the investigation of biting insects living in the forest, in particular mosquitoes. Then in 1971, a German, Fritz Dieterlan, built three short walkways out into the forest canopy in Zaire, using a scaffolding tower as a starting point and heavy wooden boards as the floor. It was a remarkable effort as no lightweight materials were then available.

Earlier another walkway, three hundred metres long, had been completed at Bukit Lanjan in West Malaysia by Illar Muul and Lim Boo Liat. It was a superb structure built directly from the side of a valley and out into the canopy of trees growing up from below. Designed by US Army engineers, it was made of aluminium ladders with timbers laid on top, and must have been of enormous weight. Without modern techniques to help them, native climbers showed remarkable ingenuity by swinging between tree crowns on lianas to get the main suspension cables across. It lasted almost ten years, during which time it proved invaluable for numerous studies; but many of the anchor trees died and fell, necessitating re-siting of certain sections. The added expense spelt its doom and it was eventually dismantled. A few other walkways have been built, one in Panama, where small animals sadly cooped in cages await the attentions of blood-sucking mosquitoes, which the walkway was designed to study. Another survived for a time in Puerto Rico. But in total these studies added up to a minute amount compared with the vast expanse of the canopy itself, and no comparative work had been done between the canopies of different countries.

Almost exactly four hundred years after Sir Francis Drake had climbed into his high tree and first gazed upon the Pacific Ocean, Stephen Sutton, a tropical ecologist from the University of Leeds, and myself were enjoying a cup of tea at the Royal Geographical Society in London, discussing the kinds of projects we could attempt on a giant expedition called Operation Drake. I was its Scientific Co-ordinator and the venture was to commemorate

Drake's great voyage around the world by using a two-masted brigantine, *Eye of the Wind*, to link a series of land-based expeditions in Panama, Papua New Guinea, Indonesia and East Africa. In addition four hundred young people aged between seventeen and twenty-four were to compete for sponsored places on the voyage, each joining for one three-month phase. The driving force behind this great enterprise was John Blashford-Snell, a colonel in the Royal Engineers and chairman of the Scientific Exploration Society, an enthusiastic collection of explorers, scientists and servicemen, all consumed with an irresistible desire to embark as often as possible on daring exploits to the furthest ends of the earth, in pursuit of scientific discovery and adventure.

As Stephen and I sat in those hallowed halls, surrounded by portraits of such great tropical explorers as Mungo Park, Stanley, Wallace and Livingstone, many of whom had set out on their adventures from that very building, we puzzled over how we could blend the enormous logistic potential of the expedition with our own scientific aspirations. Stephen had previously hung traps in the canopy of the Ituri forest in Zaire and his discoveries had fired an insatiable interest to learn the ways in which insects were using the forest from the canopy to the ground. I recalled my frustrations in Borneo at being unable to explore the canopy with the agility of the primates I was studying. To be able to walk about the tree crowns and see what was there, forty or fifty metres above the ground was a desire we both shared, and to do this in the great forests that Operation Drake would make available to us was beyond our wildest dreams. We resolved to find a method of doing it.

We decided to attempt to build lightweight, portable aerial walkways, suspended between the crowns of the enormous tropical trees, which could be constructed within weeks and which could be dismantled and moved to the next country, to save costs. We knew little about the previous attempts, save that walkways normally took months to build and could prove enormously expensive. Our desire was to provide access for the many scientists who were to take part in the expedition, and to use the enthusiasm of the young men and women who, we were certain, would find the opportunity to assist in the project irresistible.

We took the plan to the headquarters of the expedition's somewhat eccentric leader, two floors beneath the bustle of London's Whitehall, concealed in the dripping basement of the Old War Office building. It was known affectionately as 'the dungeon'. The colonel's jovial face, decorated with thin moustache and twinkling eye, belied an encyclopaedic memory and a capacity for work and brilliant organization that were at times quite terrifying. We put the plan to him. For a moment he glowered from behind the large wooden desk, jutting out an impressive rounded jaw which moved slowly from side to side as though independent of his head. He mumbled that funds were low and all materials would have to be scrounged from somewhere. Then a huge grin spread across his

face, and he announced that it was the perfect blend of science and adventure and he would put his Army engineers on to it immediately. As we hurried out, we left him standing in the middle of the room, a white solar topee on his head, shouting: 'On to Panama!' at the top of his voice, and quickly made our way above ground, into the comparative safety of the London traffic.

Almost a year and a half later I found myself on the shores of Caledonia Bay, once the site of an ancient and ill-fated Scottish colony built on the disease-ridden shores of Darien in Panama. The Scots all died of malaria or yellow fever, and those who survived were routed by the Spanish. Even the Scots' brandy supplies were lost when their resupply ship was burnt to the waterline by a careless crew member. Almost every previous project which had been attempted there had ended in disaster. Vasco Nuñez de Balboa, who had earlier discovered the Pacific, built the first European town nearby at Acla, before carrying ships piece by piece over the mountains, to become the first explorer to sail the great ocean, five years before Magellan. He returned to Acla and was later beheaded for treason. A visiting French treasure ship, the *Maurepas*, foundered on the 'iron shore' on Christmas Day 1698, with the crew too drunk to control her. An earlier American expedition attempting to cross the mountains to the Pacific lost their way, and most of them died before rescue came. The most recent colonists, a Dutch banana company, had soon gone into receivership. Now it was our turn.

An extensive base camp had been built beside the Dutch company's airstrip, now almost reclaimed by a jungle of encroaching shrubs. There was little virgin forest in the vicinity: generations of Indians had cut the trees to make their gardens, creating a mosaic of secondary jungle plants. Supplies were delivered from Colon, many miles up the coast, by landing craft and our brigantine. There were no towns or roads in this part of the Darien for hundreds of miles, only forest and scattered Cuna Indian settlements.

Our first task was to find a suitable site for our aerial walkways. The spot we chose was several miles inland, near the banks of the Aila river. The long walk there was too far to carry all the heavy equipment, so we persuaded the Panamanian Guardia Nacional to come to our aid with a helicopter.

Back at the airstrip lengths of aluminium flooring, wire mesh, ropes, jacks, nails, hammers, chain saws and food supplies were raised into the air in a cloud of dust. At the river site we waited anxiously to see if the helicopter could make a landing on the narrow, curving shingle banks. The forest almost closed over the river but there were a few gaps. The sound of the helicopter approached, and we looked skyward. Suddenly it appeared round a bend in the river, advancing just above the water and sending up clouds of spray and leaves. With remarkable skill the American pilot, a veteran from the Vietnam War, had dropped through a gap in the trees further upstream and landed right beside the camp, sending our belongings into the river.

After helping unload the equipment in the exhausting heat, he then had to turn the helicopter round in the narrow space between the two walls of trees. With a tremendous noise and downdraft of wind, the machine hovered slowly a few metres above the bank as he carefully brought the tail round. Then he misjudged the width. The tail rotor backed into the vegetation and slashed the branches, sending up a shower of wood and leaves. For a second it looked as though disaster might strike, but suddenly he spun the tail round and in a surge of power rose rapidly forwards and upwards through the trees. The huge rotor blades narrowly missed the leaves on either side of the river, and then he was out and over the canopy. Soon there was only the fading sound of the helicopter returning to the bay to collect another load.

The walkway camp was simple. We made a small leaf-covered hut to store supplies and act as a laboratory, but other than that there were no buildings. Being constantly warm in the forest there is really no need for a substantial residence to keep out the elements. A hammock easily strung between two convenient trees and topped with a waterproof plastic sheet is surprisingly adequate. The skill lies in ensuring that during the torrential downpours that almost daily drench the forest, the water runs off the sheet and does not collect in a fold. A poorly erected roof will fill and sag with collected rainfall, eventually bursting onto the sleeping occupant, filling the hammock with cold water to a depth of several fingers. I have never forgotten the experience. Personal belongings can be kept dry beneath the hammock, raised on a carpet of small logs to keep them off the damp and insect-ridden floor. Since ants enjoy patrolling along pieces of cord holding up mosquito nets, so finding their way into your sleeping bag, it is as well to coat the lines with petroleum jelly to keep them out. Now the arboreal naturalist can sleep in comfort, in readiness for the next day's toil.

It took some time to decide upon the best trees from which to construct our walkway. Round and around in the forest botanists and zoologists alike wandered, peering upwards through the leaves, discussing the merits of a span from one tree to another, and how many tree crowns the flimsy bridge would pass through, whether the trees would fall down under the strain, which species would be the most interesting. In the end a large tree not far upstream was chosen and our expert engineer, Michael Christy, a sergeant in the Royal Engineers, prepared to ascend the first trunk using metal tree-climbing bolts and a sledgehammer.

Placing the metal spike against the tree he gave it a sharp blow and the tip sank through the bark and into the wood. He gave it a second blow and nothing happened. A third, and the bolt merely bent out of shape but refused to go in. The tree was evidently not called a hardwood for nothing. Many trees in the tropics do produce enormously tough wood, which is why they are so much in demand by timber companies. Metal spikes driven into them with considerable force may be slowly squeezed out again over a period

of weeks. We returned to camp to find the rock pitons which were made of sterner stuff. These proved more successful and slowly as the day progressed the sergeant, stripped to the waist and streaming sweat, began to climb, clipping his safety harness onto the spikes as he went and balancing on spikes lower down with his feet. By the end of the day he and his team had constructed a rope ladder, disappearing into the tree crown, and I prepared to climb.

That first ascent up the ladder was truly memorable, not because of the wonders of biological life displayed around me but because of my steadily increasing fear of falling. Gazing upwards, I placed my foot on the first wooden rung. It broke. Surprisingly, this did little to dampen my eagerness, and I lunged at the rungs higher up, impatient to reach the summit. The inexperienced climber such as I was then uses his arms to pull himself up the ladder rather than his feet to push. Halfway up I was exhausted, sweat trickling down into my eyebrows and dripping, saltily, into my eyes. I noted that in my enthusiasm I had forgotten to use my climbing harness or to hitch myself to a safety line. Knuckles already a deathly white, I knew if I lost my grip there would be nothing to prevent me falling, probably to my death. Had I been less concerned with survival, I might have noticed a change in the forest as I climbed.

The clinging palms and shrubs of lower layers were now far below, the air was somewhat cooler and mosquitoes of the forest floor absent. Further up was a less dense region composed mainly of tree trunks, saplings and larger palms reaching up from the floor below, some laden with round green berries the size of plums. There were many small trees with vertically elongated crowns, and there was an occasional gentle breeze. Higher still the canopy began to close in at the level of the larger tree crowns. The neat layering of the forest into different strata, so often seen in textbooks, was hard to discern, with trees of different heights and crown shapes stretching out higgledy-piggledy in all directions.

I suppose it was at about thirty metres, just below the first enormous branches, that I realized the tree I was climbing was moving. A gust of wind, another new sensation, had gripped its upper branches and the tree, accompanied by an ominous creaking, began to lean to one side. Then, when I believed it could lean no further without breaking, it slowly swayed back again and began to lean the other way. The movement could not have been more than a few metres either way, but it was enough to leave me frozen, ant-like, to the side of the vine-laden trunk, legs quivering like jelly. Looking down was not a good idea: the forest floor, now so far below, beckoned. Telling myself that tropical trees must be designed to sway about, like skyscrapers, I continued upwards. The first tree bough reared like an overhanging cliff but once negotiated, I found myself in the crown of an enormous *Couratari* tree, a member of the brazil nut family. I later discovered that this particular species was unknown. It is not often that one comes across a new species fifty metres high and weighing in excess of thirty tonnes.

I begin my ascent to explore Nature's last frontier. New techniques using caving equipment have now made the journey much easier than on my first attempt. A platform in the branches of a rainforest giant makes a base from which to explore the strange world of plants and animals whose entire lives are lived out hundreds of feet above the ground.

Individual trees of a particular species are often separated by considerable distances, so that in any part of the forest it can be hard to find two the same. It is a measure of the great variety of tree species in rainforests that such new discoveries can still be made.

The ordeal of the climb had left me sweating profusely and clinging tenaciously to the security of the large bough on which I was sitting. But soon fear gave way to exhilaration: the view of the canopy was breathtaking. By climbing to the highest limbs it was possible to see a great distance over an undulating mass of trees, its surface like some vast fresh cauliflower stippled in green. There was bright sunlight all around, blue sky with billowing white clouds and distant, dark mountains sloping to the Caribbean. Fresh breezes blew, sending waves through the leaves like ripples on the surface of a lake. The forest roof was not uniformly flat but moulded into troughs and valleys. The crowns rubbed shoulders, joined by lianas like collections of carelessly thrown streamers, their loops rising and falling as each tree gently swayed to its own independent rhythm.

The appearance of uniform greenness is an illusion, for the canopy is a coat of many colours. In many species the youngest leaves are produced not all over a tree crown at once but as clumps, dotted about, hanging limply. These are known as leaf flushes and come in shades of bright green and yellow, or copper and even red or purple. So brightly coloured are they that it is easy to be deceived into thinking a distant tree is in flower. Other trees drop all their leaves at once and stand naked and stark in the forest, appearing dead. When conditions are right, new leaves appear all over the crown in a matter of days. These too stood out boldly against the dark green mature leaves on trees near me. On other crowns nearby, bright yellow inflorescences of *Swartzia panamensis* hung in chains of delicate blooms and violet pea-like blossoms belonging to the vine *Dioclea* threaded through my tree. In the distance there were other trees really in flower, great upwellings of colour in the otherwise continuous green. Mere silhouettes from the ground, these trees were here transformed for me into islands of lilac or red, contrasting with the virtually flowerless depths below.

There, on the forest floor, was a veritable carpet of brown, leathery leaves in various stages of decomposition, most as large as my hand. Like tropical plankton they had fallen into the depths and now nurtured those that lived there and depended on decay. A few short weeks of work by millipedes, sow bugs, springtails, nematodes, bacteria and fungi would reduce them to a skeleton as fine as Breton lace. Eventually, this too would be taken into the mulch that thinly covers the floor. Here and there rain gullies wash away this mulch, exposing a thin layer of red soil and beneath this, rock. On this changeable foundation the huge trees of the rainforest depend. There is no deep soil here for anchoring roots, only a solid floor on which to build massive trunks often buttressed fit to prop up a cathedral wall. Atop these giant wooden columns, great

crowns are held, some as big as a football pitch, and all laden with life which has evolved to exist high above the forest floor, all depending on an unseen root system through which must be drawn water, nutrients and minerals.

To reach into the rainforest roof is not an easy task either for man or for the giant trees which give birth to such small offspring. Life begins for a potentially giant emergent as a tiny seedling, poking its soft green head through the tangled mass of leaves, twigs and forest detritus that has fallen from the roof. Prior to germination, the seed may have remained dormant for a few weeks to a few years, depending on its species; but by far the majority of forest giants must germinate within a short time of descending to the floor. The period of dormancy is not without danger from seed predators. Insects, particularly weevils, bore into the seeds and destroy them. Rodents and many other larger mammals, such as tapirs, also find seeds and feed on them. Then again, the seeds may just dry out, and die. But a few out of hundreds of thousands will remain and when conditions are right they will germinate and begin the first stage of an upward journey that may take perhaps a hundred years. On the forest floor the seedling will not be alone; many others also grow here, some similar to itself, most of different species. Most will have a common aim – to seek the energy-giving light of the forest roof; only a fraction of them will survive to reach it.

Light on the forest floor is at a premium. It filters through from the world above as rays of brightness, flickering across the dark green leaves of the forest understorey and ending, burning-white, on the leathered leaves of the floor. Small insects patrol these shafts of light and courting butterflies tumble upwards through them. Palms and ferns dominate this shrub layer; there are few flowers to relieve the monotonous green. In between the massive trunks of mature trees stand numerous younger saplings, not yet weighed down with the lianas and other creepers that cling tenaciously to their larger neighbours. Looking upwards, it is scarcely possible to see a gap into which one of these younger saplings could grow.

A lattice-work as detailed as a church window screens the sky, creating silhouettes of interlocking leaves and branches held up to the sun to capture as much of its energy as possible and so shading out those that live below. Virtually all the light which falls on the rainforest roof is absorbed or reflected and lost before it reaches the leaves of the plants that live below. Starved of light, a seedling's progress into the canopy can be interminably slow. Most are unable to compete with plants better able to survive in the low-light conditions or to withstand the insect onslaught that seeks to devour each new and tender leaf the seedling can produce. Just one or two leaves sprout per year at first, but even before they have unfurled they are shot through with holes bored by caterpillars. In the first ten years of its life a hardwood seedling may remain less than a metre tall, marking time, waiting for an opening in the canopy.

Occasionally a great event occurs which dramatically alters con-

ditions on the forest floor. Perhaps a landslide removes the soil round the root system, or a tree is old and rotting. A fierce storm is enough to end its life. As the clouds darken and fierce winds begin to swirl across the forest roof, rain splashes onto the leaves and trickles down the branches, soaking into the mosses and epiphytes clinging to them. The beating of the wind and the great weight of the waterlogged plants in its branches prove too much. The sound of a large tree falling close by in the forest is electrifying; at first an agonisingly slow tearing and creaking, then loud pistol shots as its roots part and the tree's flanks burst open, unable to take the strain of the wind buffeting and twisting its crown. Moments later comes the deafening noise of the huge tree toppling, bringing down perhaps twenty other smaller trees in its headlong rush to the ground. With a massive boom that reverberates through the forest it hits the floor, and huge boughs, laden with lianas, orchids and ferns, once home to hundreds of creatures, are wrenched from the trunk to lie shattered alongside. But when the screeching of the birds has died down and the leaves have settled, there is stillness in the forest and life continues unchanged – save for one thing. There is now a huge tear in the green canopy and light floods the seedlings.

With the canopy gone, the emerald twilight of the understorey is replaced with harsh sunlight. The temperature of what was once the inside of the forest now soars, chemical reactions work faster, and the conversion by chlorophyl of the now abundant light into sugar feeds the seedling's slender stem with energy for growth. To grow the seedling also needs nitrogen to make proteins and many other chemical compounds. There is much elemental nitrogen for it in the air, but this is beyond the reach of all but the blue-green algae that grow upon its leaves. Still, there is plenty in the soil from organic material decomposed by a host of termites, earthworms and bacteria, as the debris of the crash rots down. Root nodules containing bacteria help to fix nitrogen from the air and mats of fungal threads may help to transfer phosphorous direct from the decomposing leaves to the seedling's roots, so minimising wastage to the soil.

But the growth of others is also rapid. The seeds of pioneers, such as balsa trees, that can outgrow the seedling, now also begin to germinate. Before the clearing had been created, the green light which illuminated the forest understorey had an inhibiting effect on seeds of these pioneer species. Such seeds can remain dormant, close to the soil surface, for ten years or more. Specialists given to occupying sun-splashed river banks and storm-created gaps, they must wait for large amounts of light to reach the forest floor before they can grow efficiently. For them, the conditions are now ideal and they soon out-distance the young canopy tree.

As the young tree struggles to survive in such intense competition, climbing plants, themselves too weak to stand in the canopy on their own, seek to hitch a ride there by clinging to its trunk; they save on energy by doing without a trunk themselves, and must borrow one to reach the sun. A host of climbing plants send out

Light floods into the gap where a canopy giant once stood. Its energy fosters an explosion of growth on the forest floor, through which a tree seedling may eventually find its way to the forest roof.

tendrils which, if they caress the bark of a growing tree, bind the climber's stem tightly to it, so carrying it upwards as the tree grows. In the abundant light of the clearing, passion flowers, morning glory and cucumber vines scramble over the growing trees, but their time is short as the trellis of young branches on which they depend soon spreads leaves above them, and once shaded they will die. *Monstera gigantea* is attracted at first to the dark places at the base of a trunk, then changes its behaviour to seek light, and climbs. When light is scarce its leaves are small and cling tightly to the bark, but as it grows into a pool of light filtering through the canopy, its leaves change and become gigantic structures, well over a metre long, clustered together like a collection of huge, drooping green hearts, projecting outwards from the trunk. Their attractive leaves and ability to survive on little sunlight make them a favoured occupant of many corners in our homes and offices.

Young trees suffer greater danger from the largest woody climbers, the lianas, which attain the thickness of a man's leg and reach over three hundred metres in length. Almost all the world's woody climbing plants are tropical; ivy is one of the few lianas which grows naturally in cooler temperate regions. Lianas exist as small treelets on the forest floor, often growing as suckers from their parents, but should the right conditions arrive, the lianas bind themselves to growing trees with hooks and tendrils which may even glue themselves to the bark. Some lianas wind their stems around their host's trunk, growing tissues plaited like ropes to provide flexibility. Their added weight can slow a tree's rate of growth considerably, and so cause it to lose the race to the forest roof; some trees may shed their bark in an effort to be rid of them. Once established, a liana may outlive its tree. Should its partner fall, the liana will seek another and begin again its rise into the canopy. In this way they can attain an age measured in centuries.

Though its growth may be slower, the young canopy tree lives longer than the fast-growing pioneers. After about eighty years the *Cercropia* trees which first dominated the clearing begin to die. The maturing tree, destined to fill the canopy gap, may be better able to withstand insect attacks on its leaves, which are tougher and less palatable than those of many pioneers. It is a more enduring competitor and like a long-distance runner, it succeeds where the sprinters fail. Eventually it will grow above all others in the gap and as its branches spread, blotting light from the clearing, the surface of the green ocean will be complete again.

Such a beginning would be true of many canopy trees. Throughout the vast area of the forest gaps are constantly being created through treefalls, landslides and even cyclones. Gradually these in-fill, creating a mosaic of young, maturing and ancient trees which is constantly changing but on a timescale that is hard for us to imagine. A hundred years may see a hardwood tree take its place in the canopy, yet its life will only just have begun.

My expectations of branches sprinkled with gaudy toucans and

Woody climbers borrow sturdy tree trunks to reach energy-giving light, but their presence is a threat to young trees also on their way to the canopy. Some trees may shed their bark to be rid of the climbers' vice-like grip.

brilliant orioles in a teeming circus of bird life were not well founded. As is so often the case, the tropical forest only gives up its secrets slowly. Initially there seemed to be few birds in the canopy but as I waited and watched numerous species entered the stage. Raucous calls announced a band of macaws in blue, green, yellow and red plumage long before I could see them. They burst from behind a tree crown and sped down through a 'valley', their absurdly colourful plumage standing out against the dark green of the canopy, their calls fading as they vanished behind an emergent. Then I became aware of yellow-crowned euphonias hopping about in the branches; Pacific caciques, shiny black with brilliantly golden eyes, probed epiphytes with their bright yellow beaks for insects and fruits; emerald coloured hummingbirds flitted from flower to flower, reaching in with curved beaks and great precision to search for nectar. Many of the smaller birds appeared unafraid of man in the trees, moving about regardless on branches only a few metres away. Enormous bees and flashing dragonflies cruised the canopy, along with iridescent blue morpho butterflies. Colourful spiders cast webs to snare insects that were probably new to science. In my tree teams of leaf-cutter ants carried small green crescents, neatly snipped from selected leaves, on a long and winding trail down to their nests under the ground.

William Beebe, a distinguished American naturalist and explorer who was later to become famous for plumbing the ocean depths in his 'bathy-sphere', found the canopy beyond his grasp. In 1917 he wrote: 'Yet another continent of life remains to be discovered, not upon the earth, but one or two hundred feet above it . . .' I had at last begun my own personal exploration of that strange place, and since then numerous other arboreal naturalists have begun theirs, in many parts of the world. This book is about what they have found.

A pair of scarlet macaws makes a spectacular and noisy sight, flying across the roof of the forest.

For many creatures, the canopy is
a network of arboreal highways
as familiar as any favourite walk.

2 | Highways in the Trees

I wonder if monkeys have a fear of falling? Humans occasionally dream about plunging to the earth and after a day spent suspended in the canopy, I would occasionally wake at night in the grip of just such a vision.

The speed with which primates leap through the trees seems to defy the danger inherent in their tree top way of life. Monkeys are occasionally found with broken limbs, having crashed to the ground, but it is a comparatively rare event: when they do miss their footing they are adept at making a quick recovery. The American biologist, Elliot McClure, told me of such a fall which he had observed from his tree top platform in the primary forests, east of Kuala Lumpur in Malaysia. From this construction, over forty metres above the forest floor, he could see through his telescope more than two square kilometres of canopy. Nearby was an old and dying tree, and though its branches were lifeless and had lost their leaves, many primates would use them whilst foraging through the forest. One day he saw a lone male siamang, a large relative of the gibbon, passing through the tree. Perhaps the siamang was not paying enough attention to where he was going, but as he swung onto a dead limb it snapped, dropping him into the green abyss below. He uttered no sound, showed no concern, made no frantic struggle – just watched as the canopy passed until a limb offered itself, then reached out and took it in his grasp, swinging smoothly back on course to continue in his original direction.

On another occasion a Malaysian giant squirrel, resplendent in its coat of cream and brown entered the old tree, using the same trail as the siamang. These squirrels can weigh up to three kilos, and on reaching the rotten limbs, this one also misjudged their strength and suffered the same fate as the siamang. Unlike some other squirrels, it had no flaps of skin with which to glide but still it stretched itself out flat, almost as if it was trying to do so. Down it plunged, even further than the ape, at last gripping a small branch and scampering along it as though nothing had happened. These large squirrels and their larger relatives will occasionally make prodigious leaps across wide gaps in the forest, sometimes dropping the height of a four-storey building in the process.

Most human newcomers to the canopy are at first consumed with a strong desire to cling determinedly to tree trunks, firm platforms, or perhaps another human. Suggestions that a walk along a branch to inspect an epiphyte is a must, or that being suspended beneath a tree platform is a delight, are met with blank stares of incredulity.

Our ancestors were accomplished climbers. Our primate origins were believed to have been in the tropical forests, when, as small, shrew-like creatures, we pursued an arboreal existence similar to that of modern tree shrews. Unlike squirrels, which they superficially resemble, they possess long noses on which they depend to sniff their way around, viewing their world through small dark eyes placed very differently from ours, on either side of their head. The need to cross from branch to branch led to powerful limbs for leaping and clinging. Today's lemurs, found in Madagascar, are a good example of such evolution. Also amongst these prosimians, or first primates, are the lorises. They adopted a more sedentary gait, continuing to walk along branches rather than leap between them. As the pace of movement in the tree tops quickened, dependence on sight increased, so eyes grew larger and moved to the front of the head where, with stereoscopic vision, distance could be judged accurately. Depth perception also aided them in capturing insect prey, or grasping fruit and leaves. Claws gave way to nails on dextrous hands with sensitive fingers. Large, quick-thinking brains, and powerful gripping hands on long arms and legs, added up to a new age of intelligent primates that spread through the New and Old World forests, forebears of today's monkeys and apes.

More than thirty million years ago, in the lush forests of North Africa, lived a small, agile, tree-dwelling ancestral ape. Its generic name is *Aegyptopithecus* and it enjoyed a diet mainly consisting of fruit and leaves. Though it may have had a tail, it probably lived in a similar way to some small tree-dwelling monkeys today. *Aegyptopithecus* is believed to be the last evidence we have for a common ancestor between humans and the apes; the ancestors of ground living apes abandoned the trees about fifteen million years ago evolving into the gorillas and chimpanzees of today whilst the hominids moved out of the forest to seek a new life in the open plains. Meanwhile, monkeys, other apes, and a host of arboreal species continued to evolve high in the canopy. Thus we lost the art of climbing, though some forest peoples can still ascend vines and small tree-trunks with great skill. I sometimes wonder whether those dreams of falling so many of us occasionally experience are a reminder of those distant times.

To move from place to place without ever touching the ground would, to us, be an extraordinary experience. Yet to the animals of the canopy such a life is perfectly normal, travelling a network of routeways, fine tendrils, stout columns, and open aerial spaces. They simply do not need to come down to earth.

The huge crowns of tropical trees provide an ample stage for some of the world's most dramatic acrobats. From the ground our impression of the rainforest roof is of a tangled mess of twisted, interlocking branches and gripping vines, thick with obscuring vegetation, a seemingly impenetrable jungle of leaves with unaccountable open gaps, through which a simple slip would mean a horrific, rushing plunge to land broken-boned and lifeless on the

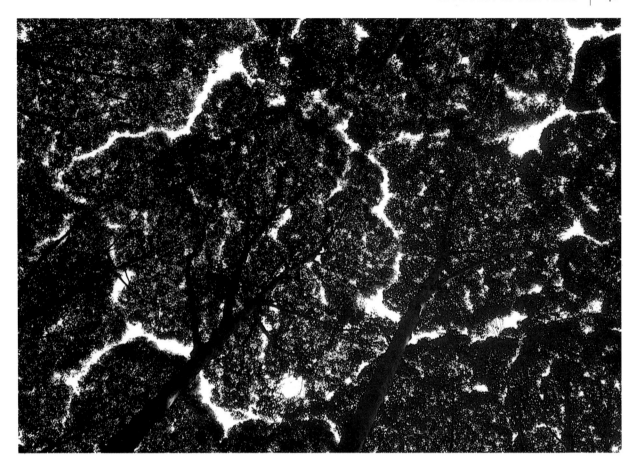

Far from interlocking, the tops of rainforest trees stand a little apart from each other – known as crown shyness – perhaps in order to avoid incursions by leaf-eating caterpillars from neighbouring trees. To cross such gaps, many animals evolved to glide or fly.

forest floor far below. Those animals we can see from the ground appear to move in a random way from branch to branch, leaping into space and grabbing the nearest limb available to help them on their way. Birds twist and turn in an apparently desperate effort to find some route through the density of branches above.

But in fact to the mammals and birds that live there, the canopy is shot through with routeways and trails as familiar as any favourite walk is to us. Having clambered up a rope ladder into a tree I would occasionally sit back in the stable comfort of a tree platform and imagine, if I were a little smaller, what it must be like to make a journey through the tree tops. The main boughs of the tree would provide excellent highways, sturdy as a horse's back, reaching ten metres or more in several directions. Without gripping toes, how-ever, it would be hard to balance on smaller branches and on reaching the smallest twigs at the edge of the crown I would need the skills of a lightweight circus tightrope walker. Stepping into the branches of the next tree on my route should present no problems – but here a strange thing becomes apparent. The branches don't interlock. The crown of each canopy giant stands as an individual, quite separate from all its neighbours, the leaves merely whispering to each other across a gap of about a metre. This phenomenon is known as crown shyness. Why the crowns do not interlock is not

Both tarsiers and tree frogs have gripping pads on fingers and toes to enable them to grasp branches, and powerful back legs allow them to spring. The South-East Asian tarsiers will leap through the region of vertical columns beneath the forest roof, whilst tree frogs generally prefer to clamber and can be found even in the topmost branches.

known; perhaps it enables them to rotate freely in the wind with minimum damage to each other. Another reason might be to prevent leaf-eating caterpillars from gaining easy access from one tree crown to another, so cutting down the risk of 'infection'. Then again, light may be the reason. The creepers and vines which do link them are coiled like springs or grow in loops so that they can extend without restricting the trees' movements during the occasional severe storms that blow over the forest roof. So to continue my journey, I would either have to creep along a liana, leap the gap or drop into a tree below and hope the route could be continued there. If no way across could be found, then I could try gliding, or better still spread wings and fly. Clearly it would be a good idea to know where the gaps between trees were smallest, where bridging vines existed and which were strong dependable boughs, so that I may move with safety and speed should danger threaten. In addition a short cut to a favoured fruit tree or an easy route over a hill would be worth remembering. If I had to fly, tunnels through the trees, free of obscuring vegetation, would be useful to know. The animals of the canopy have evolved ways of using all of these means.

Like any landscape, the forest roof is composed of simple and difficult terrain, and favoured routes are travelled often. A network

of forest highways exists, intimately memorized by the many animals that use them from leaping primates to creeping ants. The rainforest roof is the realm of clingers, leapers, gliders and fliers each of which has evolved remarkable methods of moving about in this most complex of environments. As I had discovered in Borneo, when watching primates fleeing from danger in the canopy it is possible to see how each member of the troop uses the same branches and often exactly the same spot on the branch on which to alight or launch out to another. A close look around a tree crown soon reveals whether or not a commonly used route passes through. Most limbs are covered with a thick growth of clinging vegetation known as epiphytes, but those which are travelled regularly have only a carpet of moss on their upper surface, providing a soft footing to any passing primate. On either side the epiphytes grow thickly, leaving a traffic channel along the branch. Primates are not the only creatures to use these highways in the trees. Small mice, many squirrels and the occasional loris or anteater follow such routes; even tiny ants maintain their own miniature motorways high in the trees, neatly pruning away any epiphytes that may germinate in their path. These are climbers and clamberers that spend their lives picking their way over branches and leaves. Tree frogs in the canopy are equipped with hooked adhesive pads which must make it feel as though they have strips of velcro on their feet. This enables them to walk skilfully over the surface of leaves. In some areas even kangaroos have taken to the trees. In Northern Australia and Papua New Guinea, the tree kangaroo is the largest mammal in the forest. They have shortened back legs and long claws, lead solitary lives and primarily eat leaves. Without much competition from other leaf-eating mammals, the tree kangaroo appears to have found a vacant niche in the tree crowns, and so lumbers about there, albeit in a rather cumbersome way. They have not altogether lost the art of jumping and will occasionally leap great distances down to the ground before making their escape, hopping over the forest floor.

The way larger animals use the forest is often determined by their ability to reach the foods they seek, whether leaves, fruit or insects or a combination of these, but the techniques each employs for getting about the forest is largely governed by the architecture of the trees. The shape of rainforests in different continents varies greatly. The South East Asian forests are dominated by large dipterocarp trees, so named for their two-winged seeds which spin their way to the floor like those of many maples and sycamores. These trees grow tall, phallic-shaped crowns, whilst the primary forests of Africa show a preponderence of umbrella or funnel-shaped trees. From the air the forest canopy appears quite closed in some areas, with just the occasional emergent tree standing above it, whereas in others the trunks can clearly be seen, particularly in parts of West Africa where many large herbivores play an important part in opening up the forest, creating a mosaic of habitats.

The gibbons are by far the fastest canopy-living primates. Within seconds they can disappear into the concealing vegetation leaving only the sound of their departure. From the high ridge near my camp on Mount Mulu in Sarawak, I was once fortunate enough to witness a Bornean gibbon moving at speed through the trees. I could see across the Melinau valley from my vantage point and with binoculars had been searching for the group I had heard calling earlier. I don't know why this gibbon was fleeing, but it appeared suddenly from a tree crown and moved hand-over-hand through the branches down the slope with incredible agility, whipping itself from one bough to another, covering more than ten metres in prodigious leaps. Occasionally it would appear to ricochet off a branch with its feet out into space, only to curve a long hand over another branch from which to flick itself out into space again. So fast did it move that its hands and feet barely seemed to touch the branches.

Short of flying, this method of hand-over-hand movement, known as 'brachiation', is the fastest way of getting about the forest. Leaping with their hind limbs is rare for gibbons as far greater distances can be covered using their arms. Unlike monkeys, their chest is broad rather than deep and as a consequence their shoulders have a great range of movement and immensely powerful muscles. Hanging on one arm, a gibbon can rotate through 360 degrees, a valuable asset when reaching for food. When brachiating, each new handhold results in a 180-degree rotation of the body, so that as the right arm moves forward the body faces to the left and vice versa. The body acts as a pendulum and to maximize power on the down-swing, the gibbons hang their legs down, pulling them up on the upstroke, much like a child getting the most out of a fairground swing.

There are some seventeen species of gibbons, as well as the larger and less mobile siamang, in the forests of South East Asia, scattered in distinct populations throughout Malaysia and the islands of Indonesia. They live in small, monogamous family groups of an adult male and female plus two to three offspring, and will often be found high in the emergent trees of the upper canopy, perhaps seeking fruit or perhaps a place to sleep at the end of the day. But to move long distances they must drop into the continuous canopy layer, where they can move more easily from branch to branch. Gibbons enjoy a diet of pulpy ripe fruit, though they will supplement this with leaves. Their ability to hang from the smallest branches to reach for food is a great advantage to them and may have evolved before their abilities to swing with such breathtaking speed through the trees. But whilst leaves can be found all over the forest throughout the year, succulent fruits are only available from individual trees or perhaps from a fruiting vine at certain times, and gibbons must range widely to locate a ripening crop. Having done so, it pays them to prevent other gibbon families from gorging themselves, so they defend these territories vigorously to ensure a

good supply of food for themselves and their own youngsters.

It is rare for the ranges of different gibbon species to overlap, but occasionally a variety of primates can be found living in the same area. They manage to avoid competition with each other by feeding on different foods, or by feeding on them in different parts of the forest. In certain areas of Sumatra and Malaysia the booming call of the siamang and the delightful whoops of the lar gibbon can be heard together. The former is an impressive beast covered in dense black fur and weighing about eleven kilos, whilst the lar has a variable coat of dark chocolate or creamy blond and is about half that weight; a lar gibbon's hands are always covered in white fur and white fur also encircles the face. For the last seventeen years, the relationship between these two species has been the subject of intensive study by David Chivers and his students from the University of Cambridge. These men and women are specialists at getting a crick in the neck, for most of their observations must be carried out from the ground, staring upwards into the canopy, as they desperately try to keep track of their charges moving about the obscuring tree crowns.

By following the various families round each day, they found that the lar gibbons occupy territories of about fifty-five hectares, covering about one and half kilometres in a day, whilst the siamang's is smaller, at thirty-two hectares, and it tends to cover about half the lar's daily distance. All gibbons have well-formed fingers and thumbs, and with these both animals pluck a diet of ripe fruit plus the odd flower or spider from the trees; but the bigger siamang eats more leaves than the lar and can spend more time sitting in trees eating them rather than searching for fruit. On the other hand, the lar is lighter and so can hang from fine branches and reach less accessible fruits, but it still must move further to find them as they only grow on scattered trees. Nevertheless the fruits supply a higher energy than leaves, so the benefit to the lar is greater, even though it must travel further to find them. The subtle differences in diet allow these two species to co-exist without too much competition.

If the lesser apes of Asia are amongst the fastest of all 'land' animals, the great ape of the canopy in that region must be one of the slowest. Not for this creature is the energetic existence of its nearest relatives, nor does it aspire to their monogamous family life, preferring a solitary existence in the forest, shunning for the most part the attentions even of its own species. Despite its being one of the world's largest and most interesting apes, our knowledge of the orang-utan, the 'man of the forest', remains pitifully inadequate. A large male orang-utan is an animal of enormous bulk, up to a hundred kilos. Somewhat baleful eyes are set in a bearded face surrounded by great discs of fat. Huge, powerful arms rather longer than its legs, support a body possessed of a rather obese appearance. The whole is covered in copious amounts of shaggy, orange hair. Their great weight precludes any attempt at leaping through branches with the agility of a gibbon, but despite their size orang-

utans do spend much of their time high in the trees, the only really large animals to do so, and only rarely come to the ground. There are two races of orang-utan, one confined to parts of Borneo, the other to northern Sumatra. The males of the latter tend to grow a rather more conspicuous moustache and beard than their Bornean counterparts, and their faces are also longer, but they are otherwise very similar.

To the orang-utans, the greatest danger in the canopy is from branches giving way under their great weight. They solve this problem by quadrumanous, or four-handed locomotion, distributing their bulk between all four limbs. There is little to distinguish hands and feet – thumbs are reduced – and on these they proceed in a very considered fashion, first one hand then another gripping tightly. Most horizontal or diagonal movements are carried out in this way, though they will hang from both arms beneath branches, and it is also the favoured method of crossing small gaps. Occasionally they will reach out to grasp the small branches of neighbouring trees, pull these towards them to shamble across. Adult males may be twice as heavy as the females and so cannot reach the branch extremities that would enable them to cross the larger gaps. To do this they use their great weight to good advantage and swing backwards and forwards, swaying the tree in increasing oscillations until they can grasp the next. Tree trunks are scaled efficiently by reaching their long arms round the bole and pressing their feet against the bark. In this way they gain access to all strata of the forest. Descending a trunk, when they do it at all, is always feet first.

I imagine an orang-utan is happiest sitting in a tree top, gorging fruit. They consume vast quantities of fruits that we ourselves enjoy, such as figs, mangoes, lychees and rambutans, but they will also pluck young leaves and shoots and, to provide a little protein, consume insects and even raid the nests of birds and squirrels. Being large and slow, they cannot range as far in a day as gibbons and usually manage no more than a few hundred metres. They compensate by memorizing where large fruiting trees are situated or watch for others using them, such as pigeons or hornbills, and then cash in on the feast. Orangs have an uncanny ability to arrive at a tree just as its crop is ripening, even though they may not have visited the area for over a year. No one knows how they do this. On finding their tree, they may remain in it all day before retiring, bloated, in the evening, perhaps to seek a small tree hole where some water is trapped, into which they will dip a hairy hand. Holding it up, they let the sparkling droplets trickle into their mouth before curling up in a simple nest for the night.

There is another policy for getting about the trees which involves the expenditure of even less energy than the orang-utan's. That is to spend as much time as possible doing as little as possible, and only move to eat when absolutely necessary. The delightful canopy creature whose name is synonymous with its way of life is the sloth. There are two genera of sloths, both widespread in the rainforests of

Central and South America. Both are covered in coarse, shaggy grey hair and both have highly modified feet equipped with claws for clinging to branches. *Choloepus* has two claws on each foot and is larger than *Bradypus* which has three.

My first encounter with a sloth was not high in the canopy but in the back of a motor car. The unfortunate creature had been rescued from some local villagers who were taking it to Panama City to sell as a pet. Ten dollars secured the beast and her clinging baby and both completed the journey into town sitting in the back seat of the car with that look of uncomprehending contentment that only a sloth can muster. Sloths have always suffered from a bad press owing to their apparently lazy way of life. But books tell of their ability to bite and claw with startling speed when aggravated so before transferring the couple from the car I donned a large pair of leather gloves – at which point the parent gave me her version of a 'right hook'. This devastating blow was delivered at such a leisurely pace that the most slothful of humans would have had no difficulty in avoiding it. Convinced of her good intentions, I then decided to drive the pair to an out-of-town nature reserve. By this time the mother, with her baby, had taken to sitting on my chest, her shaggy arms wrapped firmly round my neck, obscuring most of my face, a position from which she genially refused to move. I was forced to drive through the city enduring the startled expressions of passers-by under the impression that they had just seen a sloth driving a car. On reaching the forest several miles beyond the city boundary in what was then the Canal Zone, I gently prised the mother's arms from my neck, released the sloths into a tree and waited to watch their escape. With her small youngster peeping out from under her arms, the mother sloth showed no interest whatsoever in making a wild bid for freedom and it was only after some minutes that she began an unhurried climb up into the rainforest roof.

Far from being a disadvantage, the sloth's leisurely existence is a perfect adaptation to life amongst the leaves. Though not often seen, sloths are one of the most common large mammals in the New World forests and account for two-thirds of the weight of all living mammals, or biomass, in some areas. They have become so success-ful by uniquely adapting themselves to a diet of leaves, consuming large quantities from perhaps fifteen to thirty different trees, though they will spend much of their time in just a few of them. Many rainforest leaves are indigestible, so sloths have large, compartmen-talized stomachs containing cellulose-digesting bacteria. Food may remain up to a month inside the sloth so that the maximum value can be extracted from it. Such a diet means the sloths have little energy for seeking food but with a wide range of leaves near at hand they needn't go far to find those they prefer. Moreover, they con-serve what energy they have by dropping their metabolic rate to about half that of many other mammals. Their body temperature is lower, too, and unlike most mammals it varies according to their environment. Rather than use energy to keep themselves warm,

sloths solar-regulate by climbing into open trees, like *Cercropia*, in the early mornings, to heat themselves in the sun. For a large animal like a sloth hanging beneath a branch uses less energy than balancing above it, so they have evolved vice-like claws lock that onto branches – so much so that when they die, they hang there until they are quite decomposed. So efficient are sloths at this mode of life, they can afford to spend up to eighteen hours of their day suspended almost motionless from a chosen branch. As they are incapable of running away should danger threaten, it obviously pays not to be noticed, so they adopt a disguise. Their coarse hairs are grooved and are filled with algae, lending a green colouring to their coats, enabling them to blend perfectly with the forest where they hope to remain invisible to any predatory eye.

The two-toed sloth, like most other canopy creatures, takes little interest in where its dung should fall, but the three-toed sloth takes much greater care over its lavatorial arrangements and once a fortnight embarks on a journey that seems quite out of character, all the way down to the forest floor, to deposit its pellets in special middens at the base of a tree. At this moment something unexpected occurs. Moths fly out of the sloth's coat and down onto the dung heaps to lay their leggs. Larvae will hatch there and feed on the dung before flying up into the canopy as adult moths to find other sloths in which to hide. The significance of these dung heaps, territorial or otherwise, has so far eluded scientists, though there must be some, since the journey for a sloth, is a lengthy and potentially dangerous affair.

Sloths are not the only mammals in the canopy to thermo-regulate by using the sun. Leaf-eating howler monkeys inhabit the same forests and in the early morning they too move into open trees to warm up after the night's cold. Yet others also favour these sunbathing spots, and howlers may have to compete with turkey vultures, spreading their wings to catch the warming rays. Like sloths the howlers spend much of their day at rest, digesting their bellyful of leaves, and only need to cover about four hundred metres in a day to find sufficient food.

When walking in the forest the animals I most like to see are monkeys, but even if you walk quietly they often find you instead, and have an unfortunate habit of urinating or dropping twigs onto the head of an unwitting observer – experience quickly determines the difference between the sound of wind-rustled leaves and those moved by monkeys.

Monkeys have evolved to use all parts of the canopy, each species occupying a separate niche by virtue of the food it eats and the area of the forest in which it does so. In some forests as many as eight species live sympatrically or in the same area, and the story of how they all co-exist is the subject of Chapter 6. As far as moving around goes, monkeys specializing in the upper canopy must travel from tree crown to tree crown by running along branches and hurling themselves out into space using their powerful back legs. Of all

Powerful claws keep a three-toed sloth aloft. Their locking grip makes all sloths almost impossible to dislodge, and by hanging beneath the branches they are difficult for predators to reach.

these, the most spectacular leapers are the sakis of South America and the leaf monkeys of South East Asia.

In Colombia, sakis are known as *monos voladores*, or flying monkeys, but wherever they are found their ability to jump through the canopy is renowned. Like all monkeys, they can run on all fours along tree boughs using their well known routeways, but when pressed they can also gallop in leaps and bounds and even hop on their back legs kangaroo-like through the trees, covering ten metre gaps with ease, their thick bushy tails probably helping them to balance. Bearded sakis are accomplished arborealists and cover three kilometres or more in a daily search for nutritious seeds and fruit. They live in large groups of thirty monkeys or more, with several adults of both sexes co-existing. They specialize in unripe seeds that other monkeys avoid, but must cover large distances to find them. Trees often defend their seeds by encasing them inside hard shells – the brazil nut is a good example – but the bearded saki has teeth designed to crack them: the front incisors project forwards above the lower set and can crush most hard seeds in a similar way to parrots. Pithecine sakis live in small family groups, usually an adult pair and their offspring, and find all they need in small home ranges of nine to ten hectares. They live lower down in the forest, although they probably feed on fruits and seeds as well. Until recently little was known about the natural history of either of these groups of monkeys, but what is certain is that their very existence is severely threatened by destruction of their forest, and it seems likely that at least one variety, the southern bearded saki, may soon cease to exist in the wild.

Similar groups of high canopy specialists occur in the great forests of West Africa and South East Asia. Black-and-white colobus and red-tailed guenons favour the canopies of African trees, and in the East a range of leaf-eating langurs dominates the crowns of the Malaysian and Indonesian forests. A selection of smaller species exists such as the tamarins and marmosets of the New World, which occupy a range of niches from the high canopy to the ground. All of them are accomplished climbers, generally moving about the canopy by a combination of running on all fours and jumping and leaping with their powerful back legs. But to hang beneath a branch either involves a hand which might be better employed in searching for food, or a foot which is better designed for walking along a branch than hanging below it. Only in the New World forests have monkeys come up with a solution which leaves both their hands and legs free and still secures them to the branches – the prehensile tail.

Many monkeys of the New World from tiny titis to the surprisingly intelligent capuchins have prehensile tails, though they do not all use them in the same way. Capuchin tails grope at vegetation as they move, titi monkeys often grope at each other with their tails as well as the branches. But there is a difference between groping and grasping. Only howler monkeys, spider and woolly monkeys really

With four gripping limbs and a prehensile tail, Geoffroy's spider monkey is beautifully equipped to explore the rainforest roof.

grasp with their tails. They all belong to a mixed bag family of monkeys known as the Cebids. Spider monkeys inhabit the high trees in the forests of Central America and Amazonia and favour a diet of ripe fruit: their prehensile tail, the tip of which is strongly muscled and bare on the inside like a furrowed finger, enables them to reach into all conceivable parts of the tree crowns. By curling their tail round branches they can hang from the trees leaving their hands and legs free. Like gibbons they often swing through the branches hand-over-hand, and have powerful shoulder joints to enable them to do this. Usually they forage singly but occasionally, if an abundant food source is found, they will gather in congregations of up to twenty animals. Woolly monkeys also have prehensile tails but are not so widespread as spider monkeys. Rarest of all is the muriqui, or woolly spider monkey, of Brazil. This is the biggest of all South American monkeys covered in soft, pale orange fur. Only a few hundred exist in the wild.

Surprisingly, no monkeys in the Old World evolved prehensile tails, but other animals have done so and use them to good effect. The termite-eating tamandua and the silky anteater of South America have prehensile tails, and this helps keep their front legs free to tear open nests. So does the long-tailed pangolin, which explores the canopy of West Africa's rainforests in search of columns of arboreal ants or the hanging nests of termites. Some ringtail possums found in Australian and Papuan forests have them too, but

A nilgiri langur leaps across the gap between two tree crowns. Such monkeys are capable of prodigious leaps and use their tails to help them balance. A missed footing may plunge them earthwards, but fatal falls are few.

for these smaller creatures, and for squirrels and marsupial possums, to flee an enemy or to cross large gaps in the forest in search of food presents enormous difficulties. Descending to the ground would be laborious and equally dangerous, so in the evolutionary past those that could leap farthest survived to exploit a wider range of food sources. Poised on branch-tips and stretching their arms out over the drop, they evolved to glide.

A squirrel gliding through the forest is easily noticed by those that might choose to eat it, so most confine their flying activities to the hours of darkness. As dusk falls over a clearing in the Bornean forests and the sky becomes tinged with copper and orange giant squirrels occasionally gather near the tops of high trees. During the breeding season males seem to try and attract females with their gliding prowess, repeatedly floating backwards and forwards across a clearing. As they run up and down the tree trunks they appear to be wearing a fur coat several sizes too large, but as they turn and leap into space their limbs stretch out pulling the folds taut as a parachute, and in a long curve they glide perhaps one hundred and twenty metres to another tree. A cartilaginous spur extending from the wrist stabilizes the furred membrane or patagium during flight and enables them to cross valleys with ease. The giant squirrels are nocturnal masters of gliding. At take-off they will plunge downwards before their speed picks up enough for their membrane to fill with air, so they usually prefer tall emergents from which to launch themselves into an unobstructed glide above the canopy. Using their flattened tails as a rudder, they travel at about fourteen metres per second and at the point of landing pull themselves steeply upwards and backwards so that the patagium acts as a brake.

Many of the smaller mammals have taken to gliding as a rapid and economical way of getting about the forest. They range in size from the elegant sugar glider, a marsupial which specializes in tapping eucalyptus trees for their sweet sap, to leaf-eating gliders, the greatest diversity of which are to be found in the wet forests of Northern Australia and New Guinea. Pride of place must however go to the extraordinary flying lemur which, interestingly, is not a lemur – and nor does it fly. There are two species, one from Malaysia and one from the Philippines, belonging to an order of mammals all their own, the *Dermoptera* or skin-wings. Launching itself at dusk from a high tree, the flying lemur, or colugo as it is sometimes known, resembles a flying cat, though with a smaller head, with a thin membrane stretched between arms, legs and outstretched tail; it is even webbed between its fingers. To glide it climbs a tall tree trunk in a rather ungainly fashion, encumbered by the folds of its patagium. Turning its head round, it will search for a target tree and then leap off into the air, flying anything up to a hundred and thirty metres through the forest in a shallow glide to land low down on the next trunk. Then it must climb again before making the next glide. In this way it can cover large distances

through the forest. On reaching a feeding tree, it moves into the crown and pulls leaves towards its mouth using its arms, nipping them off with strong tongue and teeth. A remarkable feature of all these gliding mammals is that they carry their young in flight, often clinging firmly to their bellies. At rest the colugo hangs beneath the branches with its single youngster snug in a furry hammock.

Mammals are not the only creatures of the canopy to have learnt to glide: reptiles and amphibians have also taken to the air. Perhaps the most extraordinary of these is the Malaysian flying tree snake, *Chrysopelea pelias*. From the tops of tall trees this species will launch itself out into space, perhaps to avoid an attacking bird of prey. As it does so it raises its ribs up and outwards, so flattening its body and increasing wind resistance. With lateral writhing movements, it makes a passable 'flight' into trees as far as fifty metres away. I have never witnessed this but I have often enjoyed watching the antics of the flying lizard *Draco volans*. On tree trunks in the forest, this small brown lizard looks like any other, but it has a loose membrane of skin attached to its ribs. Prior to flight it too pulls the ribs out laterally, creating a stiff 'wing' on each side of its body, and leaps; in a shallow glide, it travels expertly to a neighbouring tree.

It is to the famous Victorian naturalist Alfred Russell Wallace that we owe the discovery that frogs can fly. In March 1855, whilst collecting in Borneo, he canoed up the Simunjon river in Sarawak province. Arriving at a small Dayak village, he determined to remain there for some nine months. With the inducement of a cent for each insect caught, the villagers soon had Wallace's collecting boxes bulging with specimens. Then one day a 'Chinaman' arrived

These Australian sugar gliders are expert at foraging for nectar at night. The membrane of skin stretched between their limbs acts like a parachute, enabling them to glide remarkable distances.

with a large green frog that had, he claimed, flown from the trees. In disbelief, Wallace took it and:

> 'On examining it, I found the toes very long and fully webbed to their very extremity, so that when expanded, they offered a surface much larger than that of the body. The fore legs were also bordered by a membrane, and the body was capable of great inflation ... This is, I believe, the first instance known of a "flying frog".'

The amazing flying frog leaps from branches, holding its limbs out so that each foot acts as a small parachute. By moving its left-hand limbs in, it can glide to the left and by altering those on the right, can steer itself the other way. Gaps twelve metres wide are not beyond its abilities. Since Wallace's discovery several other frog species have been found in South East Asia which use membranes to glide short distances. *Hyla miliaria* and *Agalychnis spurellii* are both tree-living frogs in Central America which, though they have less obvious membranes, are also believed to be gliding amphibians.

As gliding proved so advantageous in forests, it was but a short step to furnish the body with the necessary muscles to flap, and fly. No amphibians do this, but reptile gliders probably evolved into birds and likewise the gliding mammals gave rise to bats. Nevertheless, to fly through the canopy is no easy task. Leaves obscure vision, a collision with a branch could break a wing and tangled vines lined with thorns threaten to snare the unwary. Yet birds have colonized all parts of the forest to exploit its food supply. Many fly only short distances and are also well equipped for climbing: woodpeckers have two toes facing forwards and two backwards to help them

Draco volans, the flying lizard, also uses a skin membrane to glide, but stretched on ribs extended from its belly.

creep about the trees, and numerous other small creepers can be seen working their way over tree bark in search of insects, beetles and grubs. The birds of the canopy are often those also seen at the edge of forests and in open areas: the rainforest roof has similarities to open fields full of flowers and fruits, and colourful groups of birds range over both in noisy mixed species flocks.

The larger and highly coloured species, such as macaws and toucans in the New World and hornbills and parrots in the Old are canopy specialists, often nesting in holes high in tree trunks amid much competition for those with a clear flight path leading into them. West African gliding squirrels also use such holes and will gnaw through branches as thick as a man's arm to clear a flyway to their nest. Large birds which hunt in the forest, particularly hawks and eagles, have short, broad wings to give manoeuvrability through the tree crowns, but it is the hummingbirds of the American tropics that have mastered the art of flight to perfection. Most flowers, being delicate, are difficult to perch on: by hovering in front of them, hummingbirds, and sunbirds of the Old World have no need to land to obtain nectar. But their darting, hovering mode of flight is exhausting – as many as a hundred beats in a second in hummingbirds – so they must take on high energy fuel at regular intervals throughout the day. Even at rest during the night, hummingbirds are almost at starvation point by dawn. In cooler mountain areas some species will shut down their metabolism and pass the night in a state of torpor to conserve energy.

No mammals have mastered flight as expertly as hummingbirds but bats flying at night are just as marvellous. By evolving an elongated forearm and stretching the gliding membrane over long, spindly fingers bats have created wings, a great improvement over the kite flying arrangement of gliding mammals. With powerful chest and arm muscles, bats can flap wings like birds and many of the smaller species fly as expertly. All bats have a clawed thumb on the leading edge of their wings, and the hind feet have claws also, with which to hang upside down from branches, under leaves, in caves or hollow trees where they have their daytime roosts. The thumbs of large flying foxes of South East Asia are also elongated to help them move about tree crowns and manipulate the fruit on which they feed. Flying foxes do not occur in the American tropics, but are found from West Africa all the way to the Pacific Islands. Some may have a wingspan as wide as a man's outstretched arms but others are much smaller and some are minute, like Kitty's hog-nosed bat from Thailand's forests, with a wingspan of fifteen centimetres and weighing just one and a half grams; it is the world's smallest mammal. Flying foxes cannot manoeuvre well and prefer to forage over the canopy of the forest, rarely entering it. Their day is spent in large tree-top roosts of several hundred snarling, growling bats, gently flapping their wings to keep cool in the sun. Large bats are the only ones to roost in such exposed sites. Smaller species often reside in caves in huge colonies numbering millions. The sight

of them emerging at dusk to forage in the forest is unforgettable.

Deer Cave in the Gunung Mulu National Park in Sarawak, Borneo is the most breathtaking natural phenomenon I have ever seen. It must be one of the largest caves in the world: St Paul's Cathedral in London would fit into it not once but five times. Millions of free-tailed bats live in its roof, producing a deep layer of thick, dark guano on the cave floor. Wading knee-deep through this in the gloom is an unnerving experience since numerous small creatures scuttle across its surface, feeding on the guano and on each other. Large parasitic earwigs, several centimetres long, which live on the bats, would occasionally fall and land in my hair. Others, eager to regain the roof, crawled rapidly up my legs as soon as I stopped moving. As dusk falls, bats start to fly in ever-increasing numbers inside the cave in whirlwind formation, producing a cacophony of twittering cries. Then, as if at some unseen signal, hundreds of thousands of bats stream from the cave and like a wheeling vortex swirl out over the canopy into the indigo sky.

Little is known about the birds that specialize in living up in the canopy, and even less is known about the bats. The traditional way of trapping them is to place nets in the forest understorey, but this has revealed little about the high fliers that rarely come to the ground. Man is as yet confined to ignorance through his ineptitude for a life in the trees. Even having hauled himself up to a platform laid between the giant branches of a canopy tree, man is but a helpless castaway in an ocean of green. All around are tantalizing tree crowns, harbouring all kinds of creatures – still out of reach. If only it were possible to stroll about in one to see what was there, or suspend a net across a flyway: who knows what might be caught?

It was with these thoughts in mind that I had contacted Dr Stephen Sutton in 1977 to discuss the chances promised by Operation Drake to visit the rainforests of Panama, Papua New Guinea and Sulawesi in Indonesia between 1978 and 1980. And it was then that we determined to build our walkways through the canopy in each of the field areas. The first was built near the banks of the Aila river deep in the Darien jungles of Panama, an enormous task but highly successful.

The construction of the walkway was not without adventure; few of us had any experience of building bridges under such trying conditions, yet everyone worked with enthusiasm and tireless energy. The walkways were built with help from the Royal Engineers, the first by Sergeant Mike Christy, and subsequent ones by Sergeant John Rimmer, now possibly the most skilled walkway builder in the world. The young people who joined the expedition proved invaluable too, and agile as monkeys in the trees; no doubt scrambling around the ratlines above *Eye of the Wind*'s heaving deck on the Atlantic crossing had helped. Timbers cut from the forest had to be carefully fashioned and hauled up from the ground to make sturdy platforms on which to stand. Once these were nailed and roped into position, a crossbow was pulled up to fire a light-

weight line across to a platform in a neighbouring tree. This could then be used to pull across the main cables from which the walkway would be suspended. At first the crossbow fired with such force that the line immediately snapped and the bolt disappeared into the forest. After several attempts it was abandoned in favour of a shampoo bottle weighted with water which, with apparent total disregard for the laws of gravity, Sergeant Mike Christy insisted on throwing with great force from his perch high in the branches. Surprisingly, this worked rather better, although we later perfected the use of the crossbow.

Then it was necessary to climb the tree – a laborious process – into which the line had been thrown, in order to pull the main suspending ropes across. Once these were hanging in place between the two anchor trees it was a simple matter to tension them with heavy duty jacks – once these too had been heaved up into the crowns. Then sections of flooring, assembled on the ground, had to be raised into the canopy on pulleys. Each one was connected to strong nylon fibre tapes which would slide along the ropes to which they were attached. By pulling on the flooring from the platform in the second tree, the walkway slowly inched out across the gap, and another section was added at the first platform, rather like a chimney sweep adding sections to his brush. After five weeks, three sections of walkway were complete, creating a Z-shaped bridge, one hundred and twenty-five metres long and about thirty metres above ground. It was a triumph of engineering skill for the construction teams, many of whom had had to spend hours aloft, suspended in a harness from climbing ropes.

At last it was possible to wander past a flowering tree crown and note how many bees were taking nectar that day, or compare the lilliputian life of one tree-leaf with another further on. The sensations experienced walking amongst these giant tree crowns are hard to describe. Where the walkway passed over a gap, its frail structure seemed as though it could spring apart at any moment and plunge me into the abyss; yet where it touched the tops of trees round about the fear of falling evaporated, dispelled by the illusion of a thick-piled carpet of green close beneath, an illusion as false as the apparent solidity of clouds seen from a plane. As warm breezes blew over the canopy, the trees gently groaned and creaked, moving slightly from side to side. The giants from which the walkway spans were suspended moved too, one minute stretching the lightweight bridge, the next releasing it, the changing strain on the main cables causing the walkway alternately to rise and slowly fall, almost as if the forest breathed, or as if we were afloat on a gentle swell.

As dawn was breaking over the Panamanian forest one morning, I climbed into the canopy and gazed along the walkway. To my surprise, I discovered someone else already using it: a tamandua, or arboreal anteater, was making its way in determined fashion along one of the main cables. Apparently unconcerned by my presence, it ambled along after its night's feast, diverting onto a nearby branch

just before reaching me, and I was left helplessly fumbling with my camera – which had neither the right lens on nor any film in it to capture the moment.

Aerial walkways provide a powerful tool with which to explore the rainforest roof. Traps to lure unknown insects can be suspended in different parts of tree crowns, or probes placed in flowers to measure how much nectar a bee might be offered to drink in reward for its pollinating services. Discovering how hummingbirds defend their territory as they sparkle between the blooms, or toucans choose which fruit to eat as they hop about the canopy is the daily bread of ecologists seeking to elaborate the complex workings of the forest. Surprisingly, birds seem less afraid of humans in the trees and will hop about on branches a few metres away; once I saw a hummingbird land on the binoculars of the person observing it.

Leaves belonging to a wide range of trees were at arm's length for the first time and a long pruning pole gave access to those further away. Here there was a chance to see who was eating them and what damage the trees sustained, but as fast as scientists could tie labels onto flowers or leaves, teams of leaf-cutter ants would remove them, and carry them like captured banners through the branches and, where these touched the walkway, onto its suspend-ing ropes. Marching in resolute lines, they clambered along the ropeway before branching off into a tree, to proceed to their ground-level nest. It was a simple matter to recover the labels. Outside one of the main entrances of the nest, an impressive heap of fine, granulated soil several metres across, all the labels would be piled up. It seemed that here a rigorous quality control department threw them out, along with any sub-standard pieces of leaf, allow-ing only those ants with perfect produce to disappear beneath the mound.

As is so often the case, much of the knowledge we have gained from studying rainforests at ground level is proved to be wrong once biologists get up into the canopy. Some surprising discoveries were made when mist nets were first raised there to catch bats. Mist nets had been invented by ancient Japanese peoples for catching birds to eat. Many bats fail to sense the fine mesh of the nets' loose folds with their echo-location system and become entangled. In parts of the American tropics, the most common bat caught in the understorey is a fruit-eating spear-nosed bat called *Artibeus jamaicensis*. Another closely related species, the great fruit-eating bat, had hardly ever been caught and was believed to be much rarer. Now for the first time, using a system of ropes suspended in the trees, Charles Handley, Curator of Mammals at the Smithsonian Institution, was able to catch bats high in the tree crowns. He caught large numbers of the great fruit-eating bat near Belem in Brazil. The bat wasn't rare at all, but merely lived in the canopy, so it had not been caught as often as its ground-living relative. Sixteen of the twenty-five species of bat caught in this way were found almost exclusively in the canopy; of those, many were considered

rare and almost nothing was known about their habits. Another species, *Carollia perspicillata*, generally thought to be the most universally abundant bat in the American tropical lowlands, was hardly ever found in the canopy. Thus, identifying an animal as rare or common in the rainforest largely depends on where you look for it. No doubt many other supposedly rare creatures will be found to be commoner than the common ones, once the abundance of the canopy is more fully explored.

Already the use of the walkways has increased our knowledge about tropical forest bats. In some regions fruit bats were ten times as abundant in the canopy as at ground level, no doubt in search of the canopy's rich pickings. On occasions great rarities were found, such as the harlequin fruit bat of Sulawesi, only five of which had ever been discovered before. This enchanting bat is the only one known to possess white eyebrows, with which it signals. Males of the nectar-feeding blossom bat, also in Sulawesi, were discovered to fly down from the canopy during the night and patrol the under-storey. Here, with testicles swollen in full breeding condition, they staked out territories into which they hoped to lure females from the forest roof by uttering high-pitched cries and emitting attractive odours from special armpit glands.

Panama was merely the beginning of what has become an inter-national effort, using exactly comparable techniques, to compare the canopies of forests in as many different countries as possible, in particular to study the abundant flying insects. Over subsequent years several of these lightweight walkways have been built; in the forests on the eastern coast of New Guinea at Buso, one still remains. Another was completed at Morowali in eastern Sulawesi in Indonesia in 1980, and more recently in 1985 two small walkways were built near La Selva in Costa Rica for the Organization of Tropical Studies, which has a research station there. This was part of Operation Raleigh, a follow-up expedition to Operation Drake, though of a much larger size and scope, but also involving thousands of young people and once again organized by the Sci-entific Exploration Society of Great Britain. Other walkways are planned in the forests of Northern Australia and West Africa.

The world through which these walkways pass is to be found amongst these pages, as well as much that has been discovered by other means. Elsewhere, whilst we were struggling to build our first canopy bridges in the forests of Panama, naturalists were experi-menting with new techniques for entering the rainforest roof which surprisingly had their origin deep beneath the ground. So effective was this borrowed technology that all the means necessary to explore the crown of a giant tree could be carried on a single person's back. Its simplicity and low cost has led a growing number of naturalists the world over, equipped with a taste for adventure and a desire to pursue creatures amongst the trees, to leave the safety of the forest floor and creep up into the canopy like so many looping caterpillars on threads of silk.

As though suspended on a thread of silk, arboreal naturalists are inchworming their way upwards to explore the forest canopy.

A russet-backed oropendola
leaves its curious nest.

3 | The Hanging Gardens

One of the aspects of tropical rainforests that make them so frustrating to understand and so exciting to be in is that the animals living there are not always what they seem. They have a remarkable ability to surprise us. An attractive pink bloom sprouting from a branch may suddenly get up and walk away, revealing itself to be an ingeniously disguised preying mantis. As if such disguise were not enough, many species enter into an alliance with other animals and even with plants in a form of evolutionary 'you scratch my back, and I'll scratch yours' – so much so that their lives become intricately entwined. How these remarkable interactions could be brought about merely through the moulding of time seems to stretch Darwin's theory of evolution by natural selection to its very limits.

The extent to which these interactions occur is in some cases unimaginably complex. Our present knowledge of them is a tribute to the tenacity of certain biologists who have carried out such exhaustive detective work that much is now known about the way some species co-habit in an almost communal existence, to the satisfaction of at least some of the partners, if not all of them. As the canopy has been so little explored, the extent of these sorts of interactions there remains a tantalizing subject for future arboreal naturalists, but one remarkable interaction has now been well studied with the aid of a large truck fitted with a hydraulic arm. This is the story of the basket-weaving oropendola, a parasitic cowbird, a bad-tempered bee and a flesh-eating botfly.

Compared with many birds, those in the tropics make far less successful parents than their temperate counterparts. Far fewer of their young survive to adulthood, though if they do they will often live much longer than most of the birds that we are familiar with: some parrots may live for thirty years or more. In the rainforest birds do not have to contend with the harsh winters which account for so many deaths elsewhere, nor are they likely to suffer seasonal shortages of food as the canopy table is very rarely completely bare. The single most important factor for many of them in the survival stakes is the loss of their eggs and young to marauding predators. Many birds seek to camouflage their nests behind twigs and leaves within dense tangles of vines amongst the branches. Others prefer to build their nests hanging from the tips of branches or leaves, so that larger predators such as possums and kinkajous may find it difficult to reach into them. Yet others have sought to avoid danger by apparently courting it.

Most of us know about wasps. They sting. It is easy to recognize them in their striking yellow and black stripes. Most of us are also easily fooled by harmless hoverflies, which pretend to be wasps by adopting their livery, though they are not equipped with their sting. Because the wasp's sting is so painful we remember their colours and are loath to give them a second chance, avoiding all such creatures with equal fear. Or we should do. During an Operation Drake project, whilst climbing a steep slope encumbered with a heavy pack on my back and sweat in my eyes, I noticed a couple of large wasp-like creatures hovering on guard, outside a hole in the base of a tree. Directing others to avoid the spot I, for some reason I still cannot fathom, blundered past within arm's length of the nest. The hornets' colourful warning had been clear, my thinking was not. A flash of yellow followed by searing pain in my forearm ensured that I would cause them no further trouble. The hornet had a sting like a sabre which pierced my tough shirt and drew blood, causing my arm to swell painfully for two days. I still bear the scar.

I have never been stung by a bee in the rainforest, though many exist there. The reason is not my hard-won wisdom but the fact that most do not have stings. However, though they cannot sting, they can bite. Some colony-living species are very easily irritated, particularly trigonid bees, and their jaws are often powerful, being designed for mining resin from bark or cutting through tough flower bases to rob nectar. One of our walkway builders was resting on a branch after climbing a tree in Costa Rica when a mass of black bees suddenly clouded round his head, buzzing angrily. In seconds his whole face was enveloped, with bees biting his skin, crawling into his ears and hair. He could not see. In a panic he leapt from the tree, and slid rapidly on his safety rope to the ground, where, thankfully, most of the bees dispersed. To continue construction whilst the colony controlled the crown was impossible. It is easy to see why primates, or other arboreal mammals, seeking to plunder bird nests, may avoid crowns shared with wasps or such bees. Oropendolas have found that sheltering beneath such a fearful umbrella is a convenient way of avoiding trouble in the jungle.

Walking along the banks of a river or through an open clearing in the rainforests of Panama or Costa Rica, I would occasionally notice a tall tree which appeared to have a collection of perhaps forty slender string baskets hanging from its branches. They were in fact the suspended nests of chestnut-headed oropendolas. These delightful birds nest in colonies and may return to the same crown year after year to weave their intricate nests. The female oropendolas build their nests using grass-shaped leaves plucked from the open ground nearby; the males prefer to court them from tree branches, with deep bows and extraordinary gurgling noises. The top of the nest is attached to a thin branch tip and the nest entrance is just below this, leading into the hollow chamber. Here the female will lay her two eggs, safe from most predators.

Unfortunately for the oropendolas, the position of their nests is no defence against a much smaller enemy which has no need to climb past the wasps, because it has wings. This is the botfly. The males of these large flies gather in noisy buzzing swarms near the oropendola nests in order to attract female botflies. Having copulated, the females go in search of oropendola chicks. Flying into the nests, they deposit their eggs on a tender young oropendola nestling. Maggots will soon hatch and burrow into the chick's skin to feed on the tissues below, growing grotesquely. The chick can withstand a few of these but a heavy infestation of ten or more will result in death. Against these small predators the oropendolas themselves have no defence, so they have managed to enlist a little help, from very bad-tempered bees.

Neil Smith, a biologist at the Smithsonian Tropical Research Institute in Panama, wanted to know why it was that oropendolas sometimes abandoned the branch tips on which they habitually chose to build their nests. As these were sometimes thirty metres above ground, access to them was not easy, so he chose to study colonies to which he could drive the truck with the hydraulic arm. By raising himself up on this he was able to get a close look at the oropendolas and their neighbours. He found that the birds ideally looked for trees in which there were trigonid bee colonies. These bees will attack intruders ferociously both during the day and in total darkness, and unlike wasps which tend to guard only their immediate vicinity, trigonid bees will defend quite large parts of the tree crown. They fear only other insect predators, such as carnivorous wasps and ants, and to avoid them often locate their colonies inside termite nests whose soldiers can repel their enemies – the termites tolerate the bees as they prevent anteaters from attacking them. Some smaller birds, such as trogons, will actually nest inside the bee nest inside the termite nest to gain their protection, and the larger oropendolas abandon branch tips in trees colonized by the trigonid bees, to place their nests as close to the bee colony as possible.

The oropendolas do not escape the bees' attention entirely but their feathers seem to afford them special protection. Other birds, even large toucans, beat a hasty retreat when confronted by the irascible bees but oropendolas are unaffected by them, though they will not lay eggs until the bees have got used to them: their young hatchlings would have no protective feathers to ward off the bees' attacks. There is some evidence that these colony-nesting birds, as well as others which use the same tree, such as caciques, develop a compatible colony odour which the bees might be able to recognize so they will refrain from attacking them. But what of the botflies? For some reason which remains a mystery, they do not swarm in trees occupied by bees, and so, by nesting there, the oropendolas manage to avoid their maggots.

The chicks occasionally have another very unusual bed partner, however, a giant parasitic cowbird looking rather like a raven

clothed in iridescent purple neck and shoulder feathers. With beady red eyes, the adults search out oropendola nests and enter them, cuckoo-like, to deposit an egg or two, they hope without the oropendola noticing. The resulting chick is stronger than the oropendola's own and rapidly grows at their expense.

Neil Smith discovered something very odd about the cowbirds. In some trees the cowbirds were very furtive in the way they entered the nests, only doing so when the oropendolas were absent; whilst in others, they were quite brazen and would even boot out the sitting oropendola. In the former they would lay only one egg, almost identical to the oropendolas, whilst in the latter several undisguised eggs would be laid. The oropendolas acted differently, too. The eggs of furtive cowbirds were clearly not wanted and were often thrown out if detected; those of brazen cowbirds were tolerated, but only when the oropendolas nested in trees where there were no bees or wasps.

It seems the oropendolas find cowbird chicks useful when their nesting trees lack protection to ward off the botflies. Inside the nest a cowbird chick will hatch first and, being precocious, will snap at any insect entering the nest, including botflies. Oropendola chicks are weak on hatching and unable to protect themselves against the botflies, so the cowbird effectively does it for them and will even gobble up maggots wriggling beneath their skin. This enables more oropendola chicks to survive than would be possible without the cowbird's help, so the lodger is allowed in. But if there are no botflies anyway, because of protective bees, then it is no longer worth the oropendola's effort to feed the gluttonous cowbird chick, and its egg is ejected.

With such relationships apparent between just a few animals, the prospect of unravelling how the forest and its inhabitants exist together remains a daunting task. Yet it is one of absorbing interest, for the special way in which these interactions occur in tropical forests is one of their great attractions. In the canopy there is ample scope for new discoveries of equal complexity.

Amongst the branches of rainforest trees there are gardens full of creatures rarely glimpsed from the ground whose lives have only recently begun to be explored. The trees themselves display many flowers either direct from their trunks or from branch tips which are visited by numerous bees, wasps, birds or bats. The climbing plants which sprawl through them also put on a show of colour at intervals and in some cases can almost dominate the tree crown. But the most striking feature of the canopy garden, and one that is possibly responsible for the richness of its animal life, is the epiphytes.

As their Greek name implies, epiphytes, or air plants as they are often called, grow above ground on other plants, not as parasites draining sustenance from their hosts, but as botanical hitch-hikers that have abandoned all need to root in the earth, and colonize branches instead. About twenty-eight thousand species are known worldwide, in sixty-five families. Of the great rainforest regions of

Epiphytes cling to the bark of a pine tree in Sierra Madre, Mexico.

The numerous plants colonizing rainforest branches give the trees an appearance quite unlike those of the temperate world.

the world, America and South East Asia are by far the richest in epiphytes and Africa the poorest, though quite why this should be so remains a mystery. Only in America are bromeliads to be found, perched in the branches with magnificent orchids and arboreal cacti as well as lower plants, such as ferns, mosses, liverworts and lichens. As the exploration of the canopy is just beginning, the list of species is sure to be expanded. Epiphytes are not just of interest to botanists, however: the numerous niches they provide within their leaves, roots or flowers are often the chief and in some cases the only habitat of certain animals which play an important part in the rainforest ecosystem.

To reach these tantalizing canopy gardens has long been the goal of many an aspiring arboreal naturalist. In 1870 Gary Hartwig wrote:

> 'No botanist ever entered a primitive forest without envying the bird to whom no blossom is inaccessible; who, high above the loftiest trees looks down upon the sea of verdure and enjoys prospects whose beauty can hardly be imagined by man.'

Since the study of rainforests began, the possibility of exploring the epiphyte-laden branches within the canopy, rather than their remains once they had been brought to the ground, had been but a dream. But now the rainforest roof is at last accessible to all who choose to venture there through a new technique borrowed from cavers. The days of laboriously beating metal pitons into the side of suffering trees to erect ladders or pulleys into the world above have gone. Now the naturalist is equipped with climbing ropes, harnesses and mechanical ascenders fit to scale a tropical Everest.

Potholers and cavers have no difficulties dropping into their chasms on ropes, but climbing up again using hands alone is much harder. Humans, as we have seen, are poorly equipped to climb.

With technology borrowed from cavers, the extraordinary world of the canopy is accessible to all who choose to venture there.

They are less agile than tarsiers and have no sticky pads to their fingers like tree frogs to pin themselves to a rock face or a tree trunk. Technology comes to our aid in the form of a sliding clamp: attached to a climbing rope, they grip with the tenacity of a three-toed sloth.

Known as ascenders, or jumars, these clamps provide the arboreal naturalist with a unique way to enter the rainforest roof. Having first chosen a tree to ascend, a climbing rope has to be pulled over a suitably strong tree limb. This is no easy matter, as the branch may be a great distance above ground and obscured by vegetation. A thin nylon line attached to a projectile provides the answer, as of old. Each arboreal naturalist favours his or her weapon to hurl the line aloft. Some swear by crossbows, others prefer catapults or line-firing guns; one angling enthusiast insists on casting a lead weight into the branches with a fishing rod, disregarding the looks of puzzled onlookers, who find it hard to believe that fish are to be found in the tree crowns.

Often the weight refuses to come down again, impeded by epiphytes, and dangles frustratingly out of reach. Even when it does fall to earth, it is surprising how invisible a fishing line becomes amongst the greenery of the forest and many exasperating minutes can be spent searching vainly for the landing point. Once found, the other end of the nylon line can be used to pull over a strong climbing rope, which is then secured. The clamps are fixed to this and slide up the rope, but lock if moved downwards. The climber attaches himself to them by means of a harness and stirrups, and by alternately moving first one clamp then the other, it is possible to inch-worm up into the canopy.

My first chance to use the technique came at the La Selva Research Station in Costa Rica, some years after Operation Drake. Confronted with the complicated set of ropes and clamps, I was immediately thrown into a panic, imagining that in minutes I should be suspended upside down high above the forest floor, swinging helplessly with little prospect of recovery. The first, surprising sensation was that the climbing rope stretched more than expected and on placing my full weight on it to begin the momentous climb, I sagged ignominiously to the forest floor and lay sprawled amongst the leaves. These days, less stretchable climbing ropes are used. The second sensation was one of severe pain in the groin. I was sitting the wrong way in the harness. Once rearranged, I began to climb and soon mastered the technique, which proved less arduous than it looked, since one expended no energy in hanging on, only in moving the clamps. As I rose above the forest floor I experienced none of the fear associated with my first ascent in Panama. At any height I could pause on the rope and watch the surrounding scene, spinning slowly round. On the nearby trunk splendid lianas coiled their way to the roof, and two-way columns of leaf-cutter ants kept up a constant come and go. Being on the rope, away from the trunk, kept me free of any undesirable creepy-

crawlies I might otherwise have encountered. Epiphytes growing from the bark and the occasional orchid were just at arm's reach. Looking up, I could see blue sky through the branches and a hummingbird flitting from flower to flower.

I soon found myself in the crown of a large almendro tree. Clustered along its branches was a collection of plants resembling pineapple tops, all spiky-leaved and serrated with no apparent stem and only a simple root system with which to claim a foothold. Moss and lichens grew thickly in between them and small orchids sprouted, some with delicate strings of white blooms. The tree limbs themselves were almost completely obscured by a thick covering of colonizing plants which spread from the trunk out towards the very edge of the crown, though the covering appeared less dense there. Leaning over towards a branch I prised off one of the largest plants. I knew it to be a bromeliad, closely related to the pineapple, and lifted it down to the large platform built in the crotch of the tree. There I placed the plant on a plastic sheet and set about exploring its contents. It was shaped rather like a flask, the serrated leaves close to its base overlapping tightly, creating a watertight chamber. The tops of the leaves were bright green and almost half the length of my arm, leathery to the touch. The base of many of them appeared brown, and rotten inside. There was some water in the bottom of the leafy flask and some leaves from the branches above had been trapped there. As I gently pulled the bromeliad apart, I discovered that all kinds of animals had chosen to make it their home.

After an enjoyable hour, I had found four harvestmen with long spindly legs supporting black bodies brightly streaked in yellow; a tiny brown spider brooding over some eggs; three different kinds of woodlice; a centipede; a millipede that jumped; a pseudo-scorpion just a couple of millimetres long; numerous small, inconspicuous beetles as well as others that shone in the water with metallic colours; earwigs; a tree seedling in an advanced stage of germination; a nymphal cockroach; the aquatic larvae of various sorts of chironomid fly; a nest of minute brown ants complete with eggs and larvae; a collection of small seeds resembling those of dandelions; an earthworm with a brightly iridescent blue nose; mites galore; a small, mottled brown frog; and *Peripatus*. I was particularly startled by *Peripatus*. It is a primitive creature somewhere between a millipede and a worm, and is capable of narrowing its body to an eighth of its diameter to help it squeeze through tiny spaces. It hunts by moving around on pudgy legs and spitting sticky threads at its prey which, once snared, is devoured. *Peripatus* has a clever way of avoiding being eaten itself by playing possum. I removed this apparently dead specimen from the leaves and placed it on the wooden floor of the platform, determining to photograph it later; only to discover when I returned that it had miraculously reanimated and made its escape. All this life, and no doubt much more that I had missed, had been in merely one bromeliad growing high on a branch in the canopy. And all the branches here were full of

OVERLEAF
Vast numbers of bromeliads colonize a tree at Chiapas in Mexico. Different species colonize branch tips as opposed to the shaded interior of the tree, and their own interiors are home to literally hundreds of tiny creatures. Rainwater trapped in these plants after a storm may be heavy enough to cause a tree to fall.

Many orchids are epiphytes and brighten the hanging gardens with complex and beautiful flowers. They are often designed to attract a single species of insect to act as their pollinating agent.

them. The variety and numbers of different animals they must collectively contain are mind-boggling.

Many epiphytes are orchids. For centuries man has been entranced by the beautiful colours and extraordinary shapes of orchids but it is only recently that he has learnt the true purpose of the flowers belonging to certain tropical species.

The efforts of canopy trees and vines to attract pollen messengers and harness their services in the pursuit of sex are totally eclipsed, as will be seen, by the extraordinary interactions between orchids and the bees that pollinate them. Enslaved by these epiphytes, the bees are deceived, drugged and clubbed in a variety of floral gymnastics which, when first discovered by early naturalists, were deemed too incredible to be true.

For example, male flowers of Neotropical catasetum orchids fire small packets of pollen, called pollinia, at bees which enter their flowers: the bees on landing trip a spring-loaded catapult which hurls the pollen packet at them with such force it may knock them out of the flower. A sticky disk on the pollinia adheres to the bee in just the right spot for it to be transferred to a female flower of the same species the bee may later visit. Another tropical American orchid, *Gongora maculata*, attracts particular species of bees with intoxicating fragrances. When a bee alights, upside-down in a special receptacle formed by *Gongora*'s petals, it is quickly overcome by the heady fumes and falls senseless onto another waiting receptacle beneath. In so doing the bee transfers small packets of pollen which have been carefully positioned by the orchid to coincide with its drugged movements.

Another extraordinary example involves the interaction between euglossine bees and the orchids they pollinate in Central America. I would occasionally see these highly coloured bees flying at great speed through the forest from our walkway in Panama. Many of them are solitary foragers and reflect brilliant iridescent blues, bronzes or greens or sport striking orange or black hairs. It is the males the orchids are after.

These bees attract females with dancing flights in patches of sunlight within the forest which will best show off their colours. But first they must collect a cocktail of fragrances from the orchids to act as a seductive perfume. These orchids provide no nectar, settling instead for a selection of oily substances placed on particular surfaces of their petals. The male bees are attracted to these oils and land on the orchids to gather them with brushes on their legs. The oils are placed in special pockets and the particular combination of fragrances required from specific orchids limits the numbers of bees visiting the flowers to a select suite of pollinators.

Once they are smelling to perfection, the bees fly off and mating can begin. But the smell of a suitably perfumed bee does not at first attract females, but other males of the same species and fragrance. On its own, a single male seems unable to bring females in, but the swarm of males which crowds around him, buzzing noisily and

flashing brilliantly in the sun, certainly does. It is while the males are collecting their perfumed oils that the orchids have their chance to donate pollen to them, and receive it. It now appears that the bees may range very widely over the forest, visiting some parts for nectar, others for orchid fragrances, and still other parts to search for females with which to mate, dividing up the forest in a way we would more closely associate with birds but which, with their excellent flying capabilities, presents no difficulties for bees.

The main purpose of these elaborate measures is to ensure that the orchids' precious pollinia is received only by its own species. Other orchids visited by bees may be closely related and hybrids could result which may be infertile and are therefore of no use in perpetuating a pure species. Orchids have evolved an increasingly sophisticated lock and key process whereby their pollinating bees are almost manhandled around their flowers in an effort to make best use of their services. It is not the bees which exploit the orchids but the reverse, and those bees landing in bucket orchids may certainly get much more than they bargained for.

There are about twenty species of epiphytic bucket orchid in tropical Central America. Their mottled yellow flowers are extra-ordinarily complex and resemble a small thimble with a knob growing out of one side and a pair of wings out of the other. At dawn the flowers open and a small gland near the rim of the bucket drips fluid into the bottom, filling it to a depth of about half a centimetre. Male euglossine bees are soon attracted to the flowers by their soapy scent and land on the knob to gather the oils they need. The surfaces of the flower are waxy and very slippery and some bees will fall into the fluid-filled bucket below, quickly sinking beneath the surface.

Sensing that it is drowning, the bee desperately scrambles about inside the bucket and eventually finds purchase on a conveniently placed step at the mouth of a small tunnel leading out of the side of the bucket. It is the only way out and up the bee scrambles towards light and freedom; but the orchid will not let it escape so easily. As the bee's head emerges from the tunnel the orchid snaps down a locking device and traps it. At the same time a small packet of pollen is glued onto the bee's back. After some minutes the locking mechanism is released and the bee can fly off. Had it already been carrying a pollinia from another coryanthes orchid, this would have been collected from its back by a hook in the ceiling of the escape tunnel, leaving its dorsal surface free to have another pollinia glued in its place further up.

For the sun-loving epiphytes the shady world of the forest floor is no place to live. Being of small stature they would be unable to outgrow giant trees and consequently must find some other method of ensuring that their species continues in the prime area for growth. Most have lightweight seeds that can be borne on the wind and, unlike other parts of the forest, the wind is available in the canopy as a transport medium. Other epiphytes rely on birds to deposit

Euglossine bees poised to fly into a bucket orchid, attracted by its scent. Should they enter they will get more than they bargained for: the bucket contains a fluid into which they are likely to fall.

A half-drowned bee makes its escape from a *Coryanthes* orchid's bucket. A small packet of pollen has been glued to its back in the confines of the exit tunnel; it will be removed only when the bee visits another similar *Coryanthes* flower.

their seeds in the trees as they hop from branch to branch, having fed previously on their succulent fruits. A sticky coating to the seed gives it a better chance of staying put, even during heavy falls of rain.

To survive, epiphytes must be opportunists and germinate where their seeds land, if conditions permit. Some seeds may land in a branch crotch or in other epiphytes, some require nursery patches of moisture-retaining moss or lichen to give them a head start. That they are successful is self-evident. In a relatively short time a bare branch will become coated with a thin green layer of rapidly growing epiphytes. A hundred species have been counted on one tree, each appearing to have a favoured position in the crown. Some species prefer sunlit branch tips, others the shady interior. It may even be that certain epiphytes will only grow on one or two tree species, failing to survive on others. It is not just the branches that provide a home: even the surfaces of leaves are ripe for colonization. In especially wet forests, miniature epiphytes known as epiphylls spread over tree leaves in such profusion that they appear to be covered in palm green upholstery.

It is not just to obtain energy that epiphytes have evolved to borrow branches for a place in the sun; there are other benefits. Without the need to expend energy on growing a huge trunk to get into the light, epiphytes save resources and can put greater energy into reproduction. Roots are largely redundant except as anchors, so they can be dispensed with too, as in many orchids and *Tillandsia*. But these advantages come at a price. Having jostled for a position in the canopy, epiphytes face a hard time getting something to eat and drink.

The part of the forest which epiphytes colonize presents conditions which are at times particularly harsh. Though much rain may fall, there is no soil on branches from which roots may absorb it. There is also little opportunity to extract nutrients released through decaying detritus that falls to the forest floor. High in the canopy, plants and the animals in them are exposed to strong sunlight and heavy rain, so they must exist in an almost perpetual famine, in constant danger either of drying out or of drowning. Consequently, many of the plants which live there have similar characteristics to those found in deserts, despite growing in the wettest regions of the world. To survive they have evolved a range of adaptations which are some of the most remarkable in the plant kingdom.

Some epiphytes are capable of shutting down their metabolism in times of drought until the next deluge, when they miraculously return to life and begin to flower. Many have leaves toughened with waxy coatings to cut down water loss. Some orchids have gone one stage further, reducing their leaves and roots to small strands in order to cut down the surface from which water can evaporate. But with fewer leaves they have less chance to trap the sun's energy, so they invest their roots with chlorophyl, giving them a green appearance and enabling them to photosynthesize as well. When the air is

dry and the sun bright, a layer of dead cells contracts about the roots and becomes reflective, protecting them from the burning sun; when humidity returns the process reverses, allowing the roots to trap energy again. Some epiphytes have roots like sponges which they dangle beneath their branches to soak up moisture directly from the air.

Green plants need a good supply of carbon dioxide during photosynthesis to make carbohydrates. Most open their stomata, small pores in the leaf surface, to the atmosphere and sip it from the air during daylight. However, through these pores a great deal of water evaporates, so many epiphytes have sensitive hairs which close over them and reflect sunlight when conditions get too dry. Some epiphytic orchids only open their stomata at night, when it is more humid and when the chance of losing moisture is much lower. The carbon dioxide they need enters their pores during the hours of darkness, is chemically stored until the following day, and only then released.

Of all the epiphytes in the world it is the bromeliads that have the most unusual method of trapping moisture in the canopy — they have evolved into water tanks. By closely overlapping the leaves at their base and channelling raindrops into their centre, they create a perfect arboreal chalice which will hold water for weeks or even months, as much as a bucketful inside a large bromeliad. Within small hollows on the inner leaf surface are tiny scales shaped like open, inverted umbrellas. When wet the edges of the umbrella curl upwards, letting water in under the rim to absorbent cells hidden beneath. In dry conditions the umbrella is pulled down, sealing off the pore and preventing water loss. Crowded together on a tree limb, bromeliads can create a veritable swampland of small arboreal ponds and marshes, a valuable airborne water supply that has not gone unnoticed by the animals of the forest.

A host of tiny creatures take advantage of this miniature wetland and lead their lives, or part of them, within the hanging gardens. Snails chew their way over the decaying compost of leaves trapped in the bromeliads, and even small crabs have been found amongst the leaves, thirty metres higher than we might normally expect to see them. Earthworms, which we generally think of as being soil-bound creatures, have taken to the canopy and burrow their way through this aerial mulch. Within a bromeliad's pool micro-organisms flourish and provide food for the larvae of many insects. Numerous mosquitoes will breed there, some confined only to these airborne pools, as arboreal naturalists find to their cost. Predatory midge larvae prey on the mosquitoes and may in turn be eaten by the voracious larvae of a dragonfly, attracted up there in the first place by tadpoles in the pool. Small snakes may curl up in a bromeliad to snatch an unsuspecting mouse or lizard stopping to quench its thirst. A spider monkey, hanging from a branch on its prehensile tail, may pause to drink from a bromeliad, a valuable water source when moisture, otherwise found in moss or licked from fur after rain, is in short supply. The microscopic carnivorous

bladderwort, normally found in ground-level ponds, also lives in bromeliad pools and can even be found clinging to strands of damp moss in wet montane forests, waiting to snare tiny water fleas in the film of water that surrounds them.

The weight of all these epiphytes can run to several tonnes per tree, and after rain the water trapped in epiphyte gardens greatly increases the burden, so much so that whole branches may break off and plunge to the forest floor. The presence of these hangers-on appears of little benefit to trees and many of them have evolved strategies to be rid of them. Some, such as the Neotropical *Terminalia* and *Bursera*, have flaky bark which they slough off at intervals in great sheets perhaps to dislodge any clinging epiphytes. It seems likely, too, that some trees may impregnate their bark with toxic chemicals to prevent epiphytic germination, but a recent discovery has revealed that far from being a nuisance, epiphytes may in fact provide an unsuspected benefit to the trees that support them.

When Nalini Nadkarni first suggested to her Department at the University of Washington that she should study epiphytes by suspending herself from the tree tops, she was viewed with some scepticism; there were dark mutterings about 'Tarzan' and 'fancy' climbing gear. Undaunted, she eventually travelled to the cloud forests at Monteverde in Costa Rica and began climbing trees with

An alligator lizard pauses for a drink at an arboreal filling station. Moisture trapped in bromeliads provides an oasis for numerous creatures in the otherwise dry canopy: a very large plant may contain a bucketful.

enthusiasm. What she found dramatically altered scientific opinion about the relationship between tropical trees and their epiphytes. Peeling back the tangled mats of decaying vegetation, she discovered a complete hidden root system; but it didn't belong to the epiphytes, it belonged to the tree. Nalini had previously found canopy root systems emerging from the branches of temperate rainforest trees in the Olympic National Park near Washington, trees that also had thick epiphytic mats owing to the high rainfall there. She has now discovered canopy root systems in Papua New Guinea and New Zealand, and it seems to be a regular phenomenon where large numbers of epiphytes occur. But why should trees need to grow roots out of their branches? It is not just water that roots seek, but minerals needed by the trees to build their giant frames. Surprisingly, in the canopy there is a rich supply.

The watery home bromeliads provide is not designed to be of benefit solely to the animals that live in them. Many mosquito and other insect larvae in fact die before emergence, and their carcases, along with those of countless micro-organisms, fall to the bottom of the pool and decay. The nutrients thus released provide these epiphytes with the other resource so lacking in their aerial existence – nitrogen. Without roots to suck goodness from the soil, epiphytes must obtain minerals from elsewhere and they solve this difficulty by absorbing nutrients from all the animal matter that breaks down within them, though surprisingly none has become truly carnivorous as have the pitcher plants of South East Asia. The droppings of birds and animals that visit bromeliads to eat and drink provide an additional nitrogen source, enabling epiphytes to cling to life and do without the soil. But animal enrichment is a chancy affair for most epiphytes, so many must look to other methods of obtaining the minerals they need.

Unlike mistletoes, which grow rootlets into the tree's tissues, epiphytes gain little from their host tree's tough bark. Falling leaves are a valuable source of organic material and some epiphytes, like the giant stag's horn ferns, and some bromeliads, have evolved basket shapes to trap such leaves which rot down into a fertile compost. The bird's nest fern retains its own strap-like leaves when it dies to make a nest of rotting vegetation held below the plant.

But perhaps most remarkable of all is the ability of some epiphytes to pluck goodness from the atmosphere simply by sieving the air. The winds that swirl over the canopy contain large amounts of nutrients in dust particles or dissolved in rain. In either form, the epiphytes are remarkably efficient at retaining them in their aerial colonies.

Almost half of all the nutrients in the rainforest canopy foliage may be pirated out of the air and locked up by epiphytes. With their remarkable ability to retrieve particles from the atmosphere their role in maintaining the forest ecosystem appears to be much more crucial than was ever thought before. Trees have turned this form of 'piracy' to their own advantage and tap the epiphytes as their own

special airborne food supply. By growing roots into the mineral-laden gardens, trees intercept nutrients before the epiphytes fall, and thus prevent neighbouring tree roots from benefiting. So finely balanced is the arboreal scramble for nutrients that some trees have taken to growing roots into their own trunks in order to survive. Many solid-looking canopy giants in fact are hollow, and may even rot their cores deliberately in order to recycle the organic material locked up in them. Through openings in the tree trunk animals such as bats and owls enter to roost, along with possums, lizards and a host of small insects and spiders, and the nutrient value of their collective compost of guano and prey adds to the tree's meagre diet, giving it a competitive advantage over its neighbours, and helping it to outgrow them.

The way in which animals and plants interact in the forest to mutual advantage is nowhere better demonstrated than the associations between trees, epiphytes and ants. At almost every level in the forest, from the canopy to the ground, there always seem to be ants. There are ferocious army ants which patrol the forest floor, devouring any insects unfortunate enough to be grasped by their terrifying jaws; they will even scale trees and enter wasp nests, carrying off helpless larvae despite the preventive efforts of their stinging parents. Even more fearsome to the arboreal naturalist are the giant bolsas ants, the largest ants in the Central American rainforests, almost three centimetres long. They have powerful jaws to deliver a nasty bite and an excrutiatingly painful sting. Unlike other ants they forage alone, seeking out medium-sized insects even in the topmost branches where the unsuspecting naturalist may be enjoying a siesta amongst the crowns. Jumping from a sting from a bolsas ant is enough to make a fall to the ground a dangerous possibility.

In West Africa it was once customary to tie an unfaithful wife to a certain tree and leave her there to suffer fierce punishment. The tree was *Barteria fistulosa*; its branches are hollow and filled with *Pachysima* ants. Disturbed by the struggles of the unfortunate wife, they would emerge from their chambers and swarm over her body, stinging mercilessly. Understandably, after this experience, wives were rarely said to be unfaithful again.

Outside the tropics interactions between animals and plants in which both parties benefit, such as in the pollination of flowers and the dispersal of seeds, are relatively scarce. Where they do occur only one group of animals is generally involved – the ants. For plants in the rainforest roof, ants provide two major benefits – defence and food – and it is in return for these that plants furnish them with something to eat and a secure home.

Perhaps the simplest ant-plant relationship of this kind is that of the South East Asian weaver ant. Their football-sized nests of leaves can be found hanging from tree branches at any height. I once came across such a nest in a shrub beside a river bank in Papua New Guinea and spent a fascinating hour watching the ants make improvements to their home. First the leaves on the tips of adjacent

Weaver ants grip larvae in their jaws and stimulate them to exude silk, with which they can stitch their leafy home together; inside, chambers house the growing brood. Ants will fiercely defend the plant on which they reside.

branches were gradually pulled together by workers, forming bridges of ants across the gap between the leaf edges. Once the edges were a few millimetres apart, plump white larvae were carried onto the scene in the jaws of adult ants. Straddling the gap, the adults gently squeezed the larvae, stimulating them to extrude silk from their salivary glands. As nimble as a tailor, the ants 'stitched' the leaves together, silken strands glistening as the larvae were zig-zagged across the gap. Eventually several leaves were sewn together in this way, creating a closed chamber.

Inside these nests, there is intense activity. There are incubator rooms to which new-laid eggs are carried by the worker ants from a large green queen. Brood chambers house plump larvae which are fed on predigested food, regurgitated by the workers. Black males wander apparently aimlessly about, tending the queen and copulat-ing with the occasional young female. The other adult ants are bright tan colour and very aggressive. If I touched the nest with my finger numbers of them would rush out, jaws agape, standing on their hind legs and looking about determinedly, with their antennae erect. They are capable of delivering a painful sting and the effect is obvious: not only protection for the ant colony, but also for the tree. The presence of weaver ants excludes most birds, colony-nesting insects and squirrels from choosing that tree as their nest site and source of food. So the weaver ants illustrate the beginnings of the ant-plant relationship. But it goes much further than this.

Elsewhere in the forests that stretch from New Guinea to the Solomon Islands is a tree with similar occupants to the African wife tree. It does particularly well in open spaces in the forest, growing fast to reach light ahead of other pioneer species nearby, and for this reason it is known as the king tree. Remarkably, it is usually totally free of epiphytes and lianas cluttering its branches that might slow its progress up towards the canopy. Like *Barteria*, its hollow

branches are occupied by ferocious red *Camponotus* ants, that snip through the growing tips of any vine or epiphyte that tries to get a foothold on the tree, so the branches appear uncharacteristically smooth and their leaves bear few signs of damage by leaf-eating animals. The benefit to the plant is obvious, but how do the ants profit?

Both *Camponotus* and *Pachysima* ants gain an easily defensible home but their real object is to make a desirable residence for another lodger which they bring in to live with them. Most of us are familiar with the way ants 'milk' aphids to obtain honeydew. The aphid's stylet pierces the external wall of a plant, such as a rose, and removes sap from the tissues beneath. Unwanted sugars are exuded in solution from the aphid's anus, and ants collect this mixture and feed it to their young. The bark of the king tree is too thick for sap sucking bugs to pierce, so *Camponotus* carries its stock into the hollow chambers, to attack the plant from the inside. These are scale insects, resembling small warty discs about the size of a drawing pin head. They have become highly specialized for their task. Their legs no longer exist, so they are totally dependent upon the ants for movement, husbanded by them like miniature cattle. Honeydew exudes from a special pore on the insect's back and worker ants gently stroke this when they wish a drop of the precious liquid to be released. This is then quickly drunk by the ant, stored in its crop and carried off to feed growing larvae.

As the tree grows, its wood expands around the scale insects which become embedded at the bottom of small pits inside the branches. To prevent them from becoming trapped, the ants must move them to the extremities of the branches; conveniently, it is also easier for the scale insects to suck sap through the softer walls there. In this way, the ants and their livestock generally occupy the tips of the branches, so providing the tree with protection where it is most needed, near to its growing leaves.

In this relationship the tree provides no food directly to the ants in return for their defensive services. But other ant trees ingeniously reward their servants, and in so doing can more effectively control ant activity around their branches. Such a generous benefactor is the *Cercropia* tree of Central America. The *Azteca* ants which protect *Cercropia* trees do not sting but they do make good gardeners. As they patrol the tree's branches they too groom it of germinating epiphytes, enabling it to outgrow its competitors more quickly. The *Azteca* ants chew their way through thin patches in the tree bark and establish colonies inside the hollow branches. Sap-sucking bugs are introduced and husbanded as before, but the tree has more to offer. On its leaves small pores ooze nectar upon which the ants also feed, and where the leaves join the trunk pinhead-sized white capsules, called Müllerian bodies, grow out from the bark in small clusters, like miniature juggler's clubs. These are rich in protein, forming compounds which are essential to the ant colony's diet. The ants therefore have no need to forage away from the tree for

their protein, so they can spend more time on sentry duty. By providing two important constituents on the *Azteca* ant's menu, the tree ensures the loyalty of its protector.

Such co-evolved systems as these are not unique to the rainforest. Neither the plants nor the ants are dependent upon this mutual back-scratching for their survival, and both can be found living successfully in the absence of their partners. But the manufacture of complex poisons to render leaves unpalatable would be far more demanding on the plant's resources than the provision of a few drops of nectar or sap to secure an ant's protection. So when the association does occur both parties are given a competitive advantage, which in the case of the plants can be adjusted seasonally by the provision of nectar and food bodies on those occasions when protection is required most, such as when new leaves are being formed. Once again, it is high in the forest canopy that the most intriguing ant-plant relationships are to be found; there it is not stinging and defensive ants that are in the plant's employ, but diligent and attentive gardeners whose purpose is quite different from their ferocious counterparts elsewhere.

Before the rains came in April 1980, I was walking along a forest trail near Mount Tambusisi in Sulawesi, when I noticed one of those gifts from the canopy lying on the forest floor. It was a broken branch. Clustered on it was an assortment of ferns and other epiphytic plants, one of which was particularly strange. It was unlike anything I had ever seen before, covered in spines, rather like a grey, somewhat balding, hedgehog with leaves sprouting out of its nose. I split the end off and discovered an interior full of small chambers with purple-coloured walls. Nothing seemed to be living inside and the purpose of the strangely swollen tuber remained a mystery to me until I climbed the mountain.

Climbing mountains with a heavy pack on my back is not generally my idea of fun and in the tropics especially the whole thing becomes an exhausting endurance test, one of those experiences which are looked back upon with mild pride but are not attempted again too quickly. But the tops of high peaks in the tropics are an irresistible magnet to naturalists, since the animals and plants living there are often very strange. Mount Tambusisi rises out of what is now the Morowali Nature Reserve on the eastern coast of Sulawesi. As part of Operation Drake, I had the task of co-ordinating efforts to draw up a management plan for what was then a large area of unmapped and poorly explored mountains, forests, and rivers which tumbled to the coral reefs of Tomori Bay.

Mount Tambusisi, rising to 2400 metres directly from the coast, and a sister mountain, Tokala, dominated the whole region planned for the future nature reserve. Tokala remains unclimbed and Tambusisi had only been climbed once before our expedition. We set off from our base camp by canoe across the bay, and a day's trek with porters followed through the foot-hills. No forest existed here: ill-planned agriculture and the attentions of loggers had removed it

all. Now only tall alang-alang grass remains, with leaves sharp enough to cut tender skin and too tough for many animals to eat. There are now some twenty million hectares of such grassland in Indonesia alone, a strangely green wasteland. Entering the welcome shade of the forest we journeyed past the forest gardens of the Wana tribe and, further to the east, of the secretive Kayu Merangka who maintained a fierce reputation to discourage intruders from the coast. They had not seen European visitors since the Dutch had left, some forty years earlier.

We left camp next morning to begin the climb. There was no food to be had on top of the mountain and rain vanished through its porous rocks, so everything had to be brought on our backs. The porters carried the water supply: long bamboos with the chambers inside knocked through to make a hollow tube. At our next camp, halfway up, the forest was much cooler and the canopy was closer to the ground as the trees became more stunted by altitude. Here the mountain began to reveal some of its secrets. Two new species of rats appeared in traps we set for small mammals; new species of silk moths came to our light traps at night; and a unique visitor from the canopy flew into camp. It was an enormous butterfly, light creamy yellow with a distinctive lattice-work of black markings, suggesting that it was poisonous. We had previously only seen them flying through the forest roof, frustratingly out of reach, but this time, with the trees being lower, one fluttered through our clearing at head height. Everyone grabbed a net if they could and advanced. As the butterfly dipped towards me I swiped at it with a large net and missed completely. My enthusiastic efforts almost caused me to overbalance but the subsequent air turbulence sent the poor creature spiralling to the ground. It turned out to be a new species and the largest *Danaeid* butterfly caught for ninety-seven years. It is now named after the mountain where it was found. Next day on the climb to the summit we ran out of water: it is not as easy to know how much is inside a bamboo tube as you might think. Rocks and tangled roots had made the steep climb exhausting and cold sweat dampened our clothes. My rucksack snagged in the moss-laden vegetation as I scrambled on my way, determined not to be outdone by mere lack of water. We would be sure to find some somewhere. The trees were now comparatively elfin-like, perhaps a few metres tall but growing thickly. Fingers and feet tore and slithered on rocks hidden beneath in a thick layer of sphagnum moss. Veils of damp moss hanging from branches clung to our faces. Climbing a steep ridge-top we emerged onto a rocky outcrop and for the first time obtained a magnificent view.

The blue waters of Tomori Bay looked a great distance away. The dark green flanks of the mountain stretched down into the lowlands to the south. We could see the Morowali river, reflecting silver in the sunlight as it wound its way through the coastal plain to the seas, spilling a brown silty stain into the ocean, reaching out to the small, steep islands of Nanaka and Tokobae. In the distance were more

mountains and to the east a huge mountain, flat like a tabletop within the centre of the planned reserve. The rivers which passed near its base flowed in an entirely different direction on our ancient Dutch colonial maps and the mountain itself was simply not there. There was an eerie silence save for a light sound of wind passing through the trees and shrubs nearby. There seemed few birds at this altitude to brighten the air. I wondered that there were still such unexplored lands in our diminishing world. Hardly anyone had gazed on that magnificent mountain before. I knew then why I should climb more mountains.

I was startled to see the distance we had covered in those few days, and just on our feet. We were, however, becoming a little dehydrated with the effort and I debated whether it was wise to climb right to the summit as we should certainly have to spend the night there. As it happened, the plants around us were able to donate an ample water supply: the thick moss festooning the cloud forest acted as a sponge in the morning mists, and from it we squeezed brown liquid into our water bottles. Boiling it with a teabag and some sugar improved the taste somewhat. An alternative water supply could be found inside the curiously sculptured pitcher plants which hung from the vegetation. The fluid inside the plants contains insecticide and enzymes and a mulch of insect remains but by pouring the contents through a handkerchief a large tumblerful of clean water could be obtained from many of them, a valuable reservoir for thirsty climbers. The decaying insect mulch provided the link to the strange canopy epiphyte I had found in the forest below.

The pitcher plants solve the problem of food shortage in the thin soil of mountains such as Tambusisi by trapping water and then digesting the insects which fall inside them, thus carrying both their food and their water supply. Then I noticed the same hedgehog-like plant growing on the side of a small tree trunk and saw that there were lots more on the trees round about. This time when I looked at one I noticed numerous tiny ants scurrying over its surface and running in and out of small holes in its leathery skin. Splitting it open, I found it full of chambers, many of them occupied. It was clearly another ant plant.

In fact it belonged to an extraordinary group of plants known as the *Myrmecodia* which, rather than destroy insects to obtain food, have evolved to employ ant porters to go out and find it for them.

A far greater diversity of epiphytic ant plants is to be found in the forests of South East Asia and Papua New Guinea than anywhere else. There, a range of plant structures has evolved through selective pressures fostered by attendant ants. The vine *Dischidia* creates small hanging apartments, similar to pitchers, which tiny *Iridomyrmex* ants colonize. Many of these apartments are full of decaying debris brought in by the ants, and into this mulch the vine sends fine roots to obtain sustenance. But the vine makes use of its tenants in a yet more intriguing way. The external surface of the

pitcher has only small pores through which to breathe, to keep water loss to a minimum. Inside the pitcher the pores are much larger to sip the high concentration of carbon dioxide there, needed by the vine for photosynthesis. It is the living ant colony and decaying debris which provide it with the carbon dioxide it needs.

The little black *Iridomyrmex* is of a very different disposition from its more ferocious, larger, defensive counterparts, but what it lacks in valour it gains through numbers. Various species of *Iridomyrmex* can be found all over South East Asia, and it is often these that occupy ant plants. *Myrmecodia* plants especially find them ideal porters. Perhaps ten or twenty plants in a single tree crown may be occupied by one amorphous ant colony composed of many queens and countless workers. Throughout the night, these workers search the forest floor for beetles, flies, aphids, thrips, any carcass that may have fallen in the constant rain of death from the canopy. They cut and snip tiny morsels and bear them up the giant flanks of the forest trees.

Through the small holes in the skin of the myrmecodia, the ants gain entry to its many purple rooms; some of these are interconnecting, like flat horizontal shelves. Here the ants rear their brood. Some rooms may be designed to provide oxygen for the colony by exchanging gas with the exterior; others are tube-like, a dead end, with their inner surface covered in warts. The ants use these chambers as deposits for the organic material they have collected and as graveyards for dead members of their colony. The ants are thought to feed from the fungal gardens which they cultivate on the decaying midden. This they infect with fungal spores, and it rots. The nutrients so released are absorbed through the wart-like rootlets and feed the plant, helping to satisfy its need for nitrogen.

Myrmecodia are not the only plants to do this. In the Neotropics there are ant ferns whose rhizomes are invaded by *Azteca* ants. Bromeliads also form ant associations: in some species of *Tillandsia*, the rosette of leaves which normally forms a water-filled tank is tightly closed near the top, so that a dry, hollow flask is created, which ants colonize. Pseudo-bulbs of some orchids are occasionally occupied by ants, and some epiphytes may have evolved to germinate only in ant nests. These create what are known as ant gardens. It may be that the plant's seeds are especially attractive to ants, who then carry these to their nests where they sprout in a rich compost. Bromeliads and orchids can germinate on bare surfaces, but many other epiphytes require some organic matter to root in. The kind made of 'carton' by ants in their covered runways and nests is ideal, and it is possible that if the 'carton'-building ants are not present, few epiphytes will grow. Thus indirectly ants may control the distribution of many epiphytes within a tree's branches.

Hydnophytum, or the truffle plant, is a close relative of *Myrmecodia* and also grows as an epiphyte. It, too, has chambers which are occupied by ants in the same way, but larger entrance holes allow it to be occupied by many other animals as well. Centipedes

A slice through an epiphytic *Myrmecodia* plant reveals numerous hollows colonized by *Iridomyrmex* ants. Some hollows contain eggs and larvae whilst others are miniature graveyards for nutritious insect carcases scavenged from the forest floor: the ants get a secure home, the plant obtains nitrogen from the decaying midden.

and spiders also lodge there, their prey adding to the carcasses which the ants may obtain for their middens. Flatworms and sand-hoppers live in the moist interior, along with the occasional primitive *Peripatus*; worms and nematodes can often be found slithering through the ant compost.

In the uplands near Mount Shungol in Papua New Guinea the truffle plants are given to croaking. A small frog, *Cophixalus riparis*, lays strings of eight white eggs inside the plant and the tadpoles presumably hatch within the water it occasionally collects. This small frog is never seen at ground level and probably spends all its time in the canopy, forsaking the need for ground-based pools in which to rear its young, thanks to *Hydnophytum*. Many frogs have been found to use bromeliads as breeding grounds as the next chapter reveals, but none have been found to use ant plants before. Though so far *Cophixalus* has been discovered only in this locality, no doubt they will be found elsewhere as the canopy is explored. Such discoveries often come from the most unexpected places. As the water rose behind the Monsavu Dam on Suva in the Fijian islands, scientists took to boats to cruise between the canopies of slowly drowning trees. Pausing to collect an interesting truffle plant they discovered a beautiful yellow gecko living inside, a new species which had never been seen before, despite a century of scientific collecting on the island.

Scientific study of ant plants is only just beginning and new discoveries of this kind may become more common. But there is one new and chilling discovery which suggests that plants such as *Myrmecodia* have had to pay a heavy price for their co-existence with ants. Many insects are used as pollinators, yet despite their vast numbers, ants very rarely carry out this role. Recently it has been found that ants smear themselves with a deadly substance called myrmicacin, which is probably a powerful antibiotic designed to prevent disease breaking out in the colony. Its effect on pollen grains is equally deadly: those which have been in contact with it die within minutes. Myrmecodia, whilst enjoying the benefits of ant occupation, must therefore prevent them from reaching its flowers or suffer potential sterility. Thus its small white flowers are hidden and rarely open to the world, and without wind or animal agents to pass pollen to a neighbouring plant, it is forced to pollinate itself. The pollen grows directly from stamen to style, and so the plant is denied the genetic diversity that sex would bring, and seems to be locked into an evolutionary dead end.

4 | A Place to Live

What must it be like to be born in the trees? Creating a fixed home in the trees is something that few animals seem to do, though many birds such as hornbills, toucans and larger birds of prey may return to the same nest site year after year: the inside of a tree trunk makes a fine, secure bedchamber in which to rear young, though not always inaccessible to a marauding snake. But almost nothing is known about the breeding habits of most animals occupying the forest roof. What arrangements a primate mother may make for the birth of her offspring remain a mystery, as most give birth under cover of darkness. A newborn human child would be helpless in their arboreal world of flimsy branches and swaying boughs – without a mother's caring hand it would drop into the green abyss. Even now our babies are born with a strong grip to protect themselves from a fatal fall, a legacy from our primate ancestry.

Where each animal lives in the forest is dictated in part by what it needs to eat, as we have already seen, and in part by where it needs to breed; yet far from being a disorderly crowd moving through the trees at will, each species, from the smallest insect to the largest primate, appears to have its own address. That so many creatures are able to live together in the forest is a testimony to their success in not treading on each other's ecological toes.

The micro-climate of the forest also determines where animals choose to live. To a small insect a gentle breeze may seem like a storm, so that a life in the tree crowns for a mayfly, say, would be at the mercy of the wind; for these, the still air within the forest may prove kinder. Tropical nights can, in comparison to the day, feel surprisingly cool. While a pair of warm-blooded titi monkeys can gain warmth huddled on a branch, tails entwined, an iguana would find little comfort in clutching its cold-blooded friends on the forest floor, and so may clamber up into the canopy to warm itself in the first rays of the sun.

At dusk the moist air in the canopy quickly loses heat to the cooler night above, enveloping the leaves in a foggy dew. This moisture waters the epiphyte gardens and renews life for the tiny insects living within them. Below, the air is insulated within the forest and remains a little warmer and clearer. At dawn the position is reversed in minutes. The sun draws the mist from the branches on rising currents of warm air, spiralling into the zone above the forest. The harsh solar radiation of the daylight hours threatens to burn tender skins, and the change in humidity and temperature then can

A tiny mouse lemur peers from its arboreal nest in a Madagascan forest. Inside, two or three young may be born. It is the smallest lemur in the world.

make the difference for many water-conscious insects between the ability to fly and seek food, and the need to find shade and rest.

Perhaps there is an imaginary surface which joins all the points at which these huge forest trees branch. Below this boundary, dividing the canopy from the lower forest levels, a calmer world exists in which temperatures vary little, wind is slight, and the weaker insects move as though in a still, twilit ocean of warm air. Above it the canopy is flush with leaves; insects there bathe in life-giving sunlight but subject to turbulent winds, lashing rain and great changes in temperature. Like the outer edges of a coral reef, pounded by ocean waves bringing rich planktonic pickings for its tiny inhabitants which in turn supply the appetites of a multitude of larger creatures, so the canopy is the rich fringe of the rainforest.

The changing conditions from the forest floor to the canopy create a multitude of apartments, corridors, sunny patches, dark corners, dry hollows and humid havens at varying levels above ground, layers of life in which different creatures have their being, slicing leaves, pursuing prey, courting mates and rearing young. To discover where these animals live and what level they occupy in the complex of forest tenements is an absorbing pastime, but there are few elevators or stairways to gain access to the different floors, and

Tree holes for nesting sites are at a premium in the forest. Some are natural, many are made by woodpeckers. This chestnut-mandibled toucan has been successful in obtaining a fair-sized hole in which to rear its young.

Dozing on a tree branch, an iguana takes the morning sun. It may climb to a considerable height to sprawl amongst the leaves: the extra warmth it finds high up speeds the rate at which it can digest its food.

as yet little is known about who lives where. Access to the right kind of food and nesting sites may be the deciding factor – or avoiding predatory jaws, or finding the right microclimate. More likely it is a combination of all these: arboreal naturalists of the future will have some fascinating discoveries to make.

What is already known is that whilst some animals prefer to remain at the same level in the forest for much of the time, others move between them at different times of the day or year. Some beetles commonly swarm on bushes in the lower levels of the forest, then simply vanish during other months of the year. Where they go is unknown, but perhaps it is to the canopy. Other animals, as in the case of the patrolling bats we found in Sulawesi, separate their sexes by flying at different heights in the forest. In the jungles of West Africa there is a very rare swallowtail butterfly of which the males appear to be a hundred times more common than the females. Somewhere the females must be flying and must mate with them. Eugène Le Moult, a notorious French butterfly collector who used prisoners from Devil's Island to search for specimens, was so anxious to have one of these elusive females that he offered millions of francs to obtain one. Their 'rarity' is almost certainly because they spend the majority of their lives out of human reach, in the canopy.

Scrambling amongst the tree boughs, encumbered with climbing

ropes, one occasionally comes across an unexpected home. It might be the moss-lined hole of a small marsupial possum, snarling and showing an impressive display of pointed teeth as it pokes its furry head out; inside may be a young family. Possums were popularly thought to mate through the nose, with the young later being sneezed into the mother's pouch, a bizarre misconception ascribed to the male's two-pronged penis and the female's frequent tendency to lick her pouch. As many as seven possum species may be found in the tropical rainforests of South America, but each lives at a different level to avoid competing for insects, worms and spiders: the woolly opossums and the ashy mouse possum inhabit the canopy, the common mouse possum uses the lower branches, and southern and grey possums live on the ground, occasionally climbing among the branches closest to the floor; only the short-tailed possums appear to spend their lives entirely on the forest floor.

In the forests of West Africa, fruit-eating pottos and insect-eating pygmy bush babies patrol the tree crowns at night. A few levels below them, the sharp nails of the needle-clawed bush baby enable it to spring between the tree trunks, clinging to the bark in search of fruit. Beneath this, in the understorey, Allen's bush baby hunts insects, whilst the golden potto or angwantibo picks its way slowly amongst the leaves to find poisonous caterpillars. When she leaves her nest to feed, the mother bush baby carries her tiny fluffy young in her mouth. Having chosen a good spot, she will 'park' it on a branch nearby, returning to collect it every time she moves to a new feeding place. Pottos and the similar lorises do the same, though their youngsters cling to the mother's belly fur during the journey. As dawn breaks the bush babies head for their nests and the pottos curl up in the branches, leaving the fruit- and leaf-eating primates to take over with a similarly stratified lifestyle. A group of red or black-and-white colobus monkeys may wake the pottos from their slumbers as they forage in the topmost branches; the needle-clawed bush baby may be surprised by a chimpanzee heaving past its tree hole on a climb to the forest roof; on the ground the mandrill grunts and pokes its colourful nose amongst the understorey shrubs.

Feeding on different foods at different levels in the forest is just one of the ways in which the animals separate their lives. They divide it up into separate courtship grounds, too, and sometimes the two combine. A common bird in the canopy of the Monteverde cloud forests in Costa Rica is the fiery-throated hummingbird — common here, but found nowhere else in the world. Its feathers are glossy green, its tail dark blue, countered by a shortish, straight bill above the glittering coppery-orange throat. As the bird flies, iridescent violet hues flash from its chest and brilliant blue from its crown. Throughout the year it feeds from different plants as they each come into flower, so it is never short of food. Some flowers, however, are too deep for the fiery-throated hummingbird's beak to reach the nectar inside, as they are designed to be pollinated by the larger admirable hummingbird, with a bill a third as long again.

But the fierce little hummingbird is not to be outdone. Another neighbour, the small slaty flower-piercer, has a beak adapted to cut into the base of large-tubed flowers, creating a small hole through which it inserts its long tongue to lap nectar. The fiery-throated hummingbird knows this and when its own usual flowers are in short supply, it will follow the slaty flower-piercer from flower to flower, inserting its own beak into the piercer's holes to feed.

But why is the male fiery-throated hummingbird so noisy, so aggressive, frequently chasing other birds from his patch? Unlike most birds here, which breed in the dry season, this hummingbird breeds during the wet season between late July and November. It is only then that the flowers of the large epiphytic shrub *Macleania glabra* become available, with their specially rich nectar supply, and with these the male woos his mate. He sets up a showground amongst the colourful clumps of flowers, noisily defending as many as he can from all other hummingbirds, reserving their nectar exclusively for the females he wishes to attract; during this court-ship he will not even drink it himself. Only females of his own species are allowed into his territory amongst the epiphytes, and there he will mate with them. The females are thus provided with a guaranteed food supply near the nesting site, and the male ensures his paternity.

Raising young in the canopy is not just the prerogative of the animals that live there. Ground-living species have also found a safe haven amongst the branches and will go to great lengths to make use of a hidden nursery amongst the arboreal marshlands the epiphytes provide. Their humid atmosphere makes tropical forests an ideal place for amphibians. Far from being restricted to ponds and streams, as in the temperate world, frogs in rainforests abound all over the place, hopping amongst leaves on the forest floor and along the topmost branches. Their bright colours and varied calls make them some of the most enchanting of the forest's inhabitants. All amphibians suffer from the fact that their skins are permeable to water, so most must live constantly in touch with moisture and many must seek pools in which to breed.

Most of us are probably familiar with what we regard as the 'normal' way in which frogs breed. Males peep and croak at ponds to attract females, who are then somewhat unceremoniously grab-bed in a loving embrace known as 'amplexus'; the eggs are fertilized as they are laid in water. Frogs do not lavish a great deal of parental care upon their offspring: those which are not eaten by fish or other predators hatch some days later into tadpoles, feed on rotting vegetation and algae, and the continuing survivors eventually trans-form themselves into froglets to emerge onto land and begin the cycle again. Breeding in streams and ponds has a number of disad-vantages, however. Firstly a long journey may be necessary to find suitable breeding grounds, during which many adults may fall foul of predators or, in the developed world, of speeding cars: frogs and toads still hop their way along time-honoured migration routes

now criss-crossed by our modern highways.

In tropical rainforests, the humid environment has enabled frogs increasingly to abandon open water and its threats for the land, where they pursue far more wide-ranging lives. Though most of them still need water in which to breed, they find it in extraordinary places, and some may almost do without it altogether. No longer do they produce numerous expendable tadpoles but put all their resources into bearing much smaller numbers of offspring. Some go even further, and take good care of them too.

In Central American frogs, each step in the evolutionary march away from water is illustrated by the various breeding strategies they adopt. Some frogs climb into the trees to lay their eggs in balls of moisture-retaining foam on low branches over temporary pools or streams. There the eggs are at least safe from fish until they fall. On hatching, the tadpoles wriggle out of the foam and drop into the water, and must take their chances there. Such branches near streams deep in the interior of the forest are the haunt of a family of tree frogs called Centrolenids; four or five species may breed along a single stream. As the female searches for a leaf under which to lay her clutch of eggs, her tiny heart can be seen beating furiously beneath translucent skin; they are thus known as glass frogs. No fearsome water beetles or scavenging freshwater prawns will find the eggs here, but there are other dangers. They may fall prey to small wasps, grasshopper-like katydids and even fruit flies. Against these foes the little glass frogs stand guard through the night and often the day as well, chasing off would-be predators or snapping them up with their sticky tongues. Valiant though they are, however, they can do little against a marauding cat-eyed snake slithering along the branches. Should it find the eggs, it will gobble them up like so much tapioca, defending parent or no.

Occasionally in the forest it is possible to hear frog calls coming

Beneath a leaf, a cat-eyed snake finds a cluster of developing frogs eggs. To protect their young, many frogs have moved into the canopy to find a more secure home for the tadpoles.

from underground. These may belong to species of Leptodactylids that have left streams altogether and chosen to take up residence in small burrows excavated by the male. Before the onset of rains he calls to attract a female and, if successful, mates with her in the burrow. Using his back legs he whips up a foam from air, water and mucus as he rides on her back. Into this the eggs are laid, ensuring that they will remain moist underground. Tadpoles develop protected by the foam and when the rains come, the burrow fills. Soon young froglets emerge to paddle out into the forest. Another genus of Neotropical frogs, *Eleutherodactylus*, has gone one stage further. They lay just a dozen yolk-rich eggs, also in a burrow; but the entire tadpole stage takes place within the eggs, from which small froglets eventually squirm. This completely avoids the need for water in which to lay eggs and mimics reptiles in that respect. But unlike reptiles, these eggs have no membrane or leathery protective shell to prevent them from drying out, so they must still be laid in damp places.

But there are groups of frogs which have surpassed all others in their efforts to find a safe place for their tadpoles: it is to bromeliads high in the trees or to other small pools trapped in tree hollows that these frogs go to rear their young. Some species' habits are well known, as they are generally ground-living frogs and easy to see, but of the others little is known, since they pass their whole lives high in the tree tops and only very rarely have been found on the ground. Almost nothing is known about the natural history of the Costa Rican flying frogs which are assumed to breed in water-filled tree cavities, as is *Anotheca spinosa*, whose tadpoles are carnivorous and feed on mosquito larvae in bromeliad pools. The tadpoles of *Hyla zeteki* have highly modified mouthparts for eating frog's eggs and even other tadpoles. Marsupial frogs carry their developing eggs under a small flap of skin or in a small depression in their

The pygmy marsupial frog carries developing tadpoles under a flap of skin on her back. When these are ready, the female frog will search for a bromeliad pool in which to release them to mature into froglets.

With a single tadpole clinging to her back, a female red-and-green arrow poison frog embarks on an exhausting journey into the rainforest roof. From the forest floor she will carry her young up into a bromeliad and leave it there, returning later to the ground. Each day she will return and deliver a parcel of food, a single unfertilized egg, to the tadpole. Such parental care gives her young the best possible chance of survival.

back. When the tadpoles are ready to hatch the female searches out a suitable bromeliad up in the canopy and crawls down into it. There the young tadpoles wriggle from her back and into their arboreal pool. Those in the genus *Gastrotheca* retain their eggs in their pouch right through the tadpole stage, a wriggling mass under their skin flap. Eventually tiny froglets emerge and begin to explore the branches on their own, like *Eleutherodactylus* avoiding the need for water altogether.

However, the ultimate in amphibian parental devotion is shown by the arrow poison frogs, highly toxic creatures that spend most of their time in the moist leaf litter on the forest floor. The parent frogs lay a small clutch of large eggs under some damp leaves, then the male, or in some cases the female, stands guard near the eggs until they hatch. That done, the guarding frog approaches the young tadpoles and allows them to wriggle onto its back. The parent may

then carry the tadpoles for some time before advancing towards a tree trunk to begin an arduous climb up into the branches in search of a suitable place for the next stage in their lives. Exposed during the climb, the tadpoles could be in great danger from predators were it not for the fact that the bright colours of their parents are a message to all that they are unpalatable. After what may be a considerable vertical climb, the frog searches for a bromeliad growing from the trunk or on a branch. It will climb inside and walk down to the water trapped in the base of a leaf, where it will release just one of its offspring. Moving to another leaf base, it will deposit one more, but not all the tadpoles are placed in the same bromeliad. Soon the frog will climb out and search for another, and so spread its family between a number of pools. By not placing all its eggs in one basket, where the larvae of a predatory damselfly may lurk or where food may be scarce, the arrow poison frog provides the best chances of survival for at least some of its offspring. But the arrangements do not end there.

As the young tadpoles grow they may devour all the available mosquito larvae and other food in their pond, so some species of devoted arrow poison frogs prefer to feed their young with special daily food parcels. Having deposited their charges, the adult frogs return to the forest floor, but each day the female will make the climb again, returning to each bromeliad where young are stationed to deliver a small quantity of unfertilized eggs, valuable protein packets with which the growing tadpoles can supplement their diet. But the intriguing question is how does the parent frog remember which bromeliad houses her young? As the frog climbs down into the bromeliad, she turns around and completes the last part of the journey backwards until her rear is just touching the water. A tadpole, if present, somehow senses the adult's approach and rapidly vibrates the tip of its tail, sending pressure waves through the water which the adult frog can feel. If she does not feel these vibrations she will not release any eggs, and moves to the next plant.

The giant Central American damselfly also rears its nymphs in these tanks. Male giant damselflies often flutter in light gaps in forest clearings, perhaps to attract a female. The adult female has an enormous ten-centimetre pencil-thin abdomen, making it one of the longest of all insects. She has almost the largest wingspan of any insect, too, sometimes reaching the width of an open hand. Bluish purple bands colour the otherwise clear wings, etched with a dark stiffening framework as delicate as the finest leaded glass. After mating, the female flies up into the canopy to search for a bromeliad pool, reversing into it with her very long abdomen to explore its depths for a suitable place in which to deposit her eggs. These will hatch into carnivorous larvae which feed on the tank's other inhabitants, even tadpoles, eventually emerging and transforming themselves into beautiful damselflies. Once their four enormous wings have expanded and hardened they take to the air, each wing beating independently of the others, giving the damselfly the

appearance of a miniature helicopter slowly beating through the forest. Their unhurried flight and fragile appearance bely their nature, for they are adept predators, and treat the huge webs of the *Nephila* orb-weaving spiders as a favoured site for prey.

Nephila silk is enormously strong – it is used as a fishing lure by some tribes in New Guinea. The spider uses it to spin a yellow web over half a metre in diameter, and sits in the middle to snare her own insect prey. But she is not the only spider to cling to the web; others, much smaller than herself, sit unnoticed on the silken threads. These are klepto-parasites which make a precarious living by darting in and snatching entangled insects too small to be of interest to their larger neighbour. It is on these parasitic spiders that the giant damselfly may choose to feed. Hovering in front of the web, it too darts in and snatches its prey, retiring to a nearby twig to consume them. However, some giant damselflies will even attack the huge *Nephila* itself. The spider seems unaware of the damselfly's translucent wings hovering before it. In an instant the damselfly seizes the unsuspecting spider and tears it from the web, severing the succulent abdomen from the rest of the body, and sends the legs, thorax and jaws flailing down to the ground.

The superabundance of insects in the tropics is obvious to all who have been there. At the turn of the century the explorer and naturalist Henry Bates collected more than seven hundred species of butterfly within an hour's walk of his home at Pará in Brazil – about twice as many as in the whole of Western Europe. A glowing lamp in the rainforest attracts such a bewildering array of large beetles, tiny flies or highly coloured moths that the night becomes a collector's dream and a taxonomist's nightmare. But where do all these insects live? Do they exist as a jumbled-up mass floating or crawling about at random, or does each tree harbour its own collection? Do different types of rainforest play host to different kinds of insects, and are there whole groups that are never seen on the ground, acting out their lives entirely within the canopy? Are there particular heights above ground at which certain groups prefer to move, so that the different species live on top of each other rather like the layers of a cake?

Top of the list of six-legged residents in the canopy comes as no surprise – ants. There are millions of them up there, crawling along epiphyte fronds, inside branches, and into the arboreal naturalist's pants. Certainly in South America they are present in the greatest numbers and possibly outweigh all the other insects combined. Among beetles it is weevils and leaf-eating *Chrysomelids* that dominate; ladybirds and rove beetles appear to be the main scavengers, with fireflies being the most common large predators. In the forests of Morowali in Sulawesi in Indonesia, we found mosquitos to be a thousand times more abundant in the canopy at night than on the ground. Perhaps they fly up there to seek a blood meal from a sleeping mammal. Certainly their attentions are enough to drive the most determined nocturnal naturalist from the tree crowns into the

safety of a mosquito net on the ground. During the day whilst working on the forest floor, the mosquitos perversely fly down from the canopy and the position is reversed.

Even species which specialize in feeding on leaves or carrion on the forest floor can live equally well in the canopy, on the leaves and dead bodies lodged in the epiphyte gardens. A great surprise to us was that predatory carabid beetles, often known as 'ground' beetles, are much more common in the canopy than amongst the floor litter where they are 'normally' found. It seems that the insect 'centre of gravity' has shifted to a position thirty metres above the ground, and with it the interest of the bug hunters should follow. Cicadas and other sap-sucking bugs and frog hoppers all seem to fly in the canopy in much greater numbers than at ground level, but this is, after all, not surprising since the leaves whose sap they wish to tap are there in greatest numbers too. Far from being isolated islands of distinct insect populations, the trees' inhabitants seem to move freely between them. To be reliant on just one variety of tree for food when another offering the same leaves may be so far away would be a dangerous policy for many insects, particularly those ill-equipped to fly long distances.

Graceful orange butterflies, and often bright blue ones as well, are a common sight in the canopy in the American jungles, but I have less frequently found them flying near to the ground. In Peru Christine Papageorgis has found that different coloured butterflies do fly at different levels in the forest. Near the forest floor a group of transparent butterflies lives, their wings merely etched in dark lines, a signal many butterflies use to indicate that they are poisonous. Above them butterflies coloured like tigers predominate to a height of about seven metres. Between seven and thirteen metres high, a group of predominately red-coloured butterflies occupies the forest, and higher still those with orange or blue iridescent wings.

Butterfly colours vary at different heights within the forest. In South America, transparent Ithomids roost near the forest floor. Zebra butterflies, with striking yellow-and-black patterns, are found above them and higher still orange and iridescent blue butterflies fly. The colours each employs are a ruse to avoid being eaten.

Butterflies are high on the list of tasty morsels on many bird menus and evolution has conjured numerous schemes designed to give them a measure of protection. Colour patterns are one of the most important, either to lend concealment through camouflage or to advertise a poisonous taste. Non-poisonous species will mimic the toxic varieties, knowing that a predator, having once had the misfortune to try eating a poisonous variety, will remember that image and so avoid it in future. Such mimetic associations are known as Batesian mimicry, after Henry Bates, who discovered it. It may also be that the colours adopted relate to the amount of light penetrating the forest at each level. In the understorey, the gloomy background favours a transparent wing which blends well with the vegetation but which, once spotted, still displays the black warning framework. Slightly above the forest floor, where more sunflecks penetrate, the yellow-and-black butterflies perhaps find their stripes as effective a disguise as those of a prowling tiger. Higher still, the red-and-black butterflies are hard to follow in the mosaic of large patches of light and shade, and in the full glare of the sun in the canopy, the eyes of predatory birds are confused by colours which brilliantly contrast the vegetation: one moment they pursue flashing blue or orange which suddenly disappears when their prey enters shade. The bird's eyes cannot adjust to the change in light intensity fast enough, and the butterfly makes its escape.

It is not only animals which take advantage of this evolutionary camouflage. Plants too have at their disposal a wide range of defences which they use to protect themselves, from tough leaves to poisons and even ant guards as we have seen. Where insects have been cunning enough to circumvent these defences, the plant must evolve a new strategy to avoid being eaten. The resulting action and reaction of these species to such selective forces is a recurrent theme in the tropical forest ecosystem, and is the basis of extraordinary co-evolved interactions between different animal and plant groups.

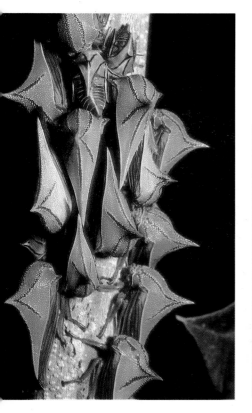

Camouflage plays an important role in staying alive in the forest. These thornbugs, which must spend much of their life exposed on bark, sucking sap from plant tissues below it, adopt an effective disguise.

Plants mimic another's painful reputation just as animals do: nettles in our hedgerows are a good example. Not all of them sting; some are imposters. In the rainforest roof there is a vine which is also remarkably clever at pretending to be something else. A stroll along the aerial walkway in Panama would bring me into contact with a wide variety of leaves. Most of these would belong to trees whose crowns were within arm's reach or overlapped the hanging bridge, but sprawling over the edge of the tree crowns I would also find the leaves of vines whose woody stems and coiling tendrils reached up from the forest floor far below. In flower such vines are easy to see, lending bright colours in a cascade of red or perhaps purple against the supporting green crown, but when merely in leaf it is much harder to distinguish them from the tree's leaves. There is even a group of vines which actually copies the leaves of trees growing in the canopy in order to make its own leaves less recognizable to one particular butterfly whose caterpillar hopes to eat them: the *Passiflora* or passion flower vines. There are about five hundred species of these vines in the Neotropics; many of us are familiar with the magnificent spiky flowers of domestic varieties grown in our gardens. Their leaves rarely suffer damage as they are poisonous to insects, and in the tropics where they normally grow this affords them special protection.

Gazing over the forest roof in Central and South America you might be lucky enough to see some highly coloured butterflies streaked in black and yellow or occasionally splashed with red. Some of these may be Heliconid butterflies, and they have a very special relationship with passion flower vines that has evolved over millions of years.

These butterflies flutter along canopy flyways in search of a variety of flowering plants from which they take nectar – and pollen. Adults may live as long as six months, which is unusual for butterflies, and they are able to do this by extracting proteins from pollen. Most butterflies cannot eat hard pollen, as their proboscis is designed to suck fluids. The Heliconids get round this difficulty by squirting a mixture of nectar and enzymes onto the pollen in flowers they visit, and then gathering up the pollen-rich broth which forms on the surface. The extra nutrients they obtain in this way mean that they can afford to lay a large number of eggs, and when they wish to lay, they search for passion flower vines.

Heliconid butterflies have turned the chemicals which make passion flower leaves unpalatable to all other insects to their own advantage. Only their caterpillars have cracked the poison code and evolved enzymes capable of digesting the poisons the leaves contain. In so doing their bodies become infused with them, rendering them inedible to birds which might otherwise prey on them, a fact they advertise with bright colours. When they metamorphose into adults they carry their poisons with them, hence the butterflies are brightly coloured too.

To complicate the interaction still further, other poisonous but-

The impressive colours of the Hercules caterpillar advertise the fact that it is unpalatable. It feeds in the forest roof and will metamorphose into the largest moth in the world.

terflies have evolved a similar shape and colouration to the Heliconids, a special advantage in the battle to avoid being eaten. This kind of mimicry is known as Müllerian mimicry, after the German zoologist who first noticed it. Even the poisonous males and females of *Heliconius nattereri* have different colour patterns and each therefore has different mimics. *Aeria olena* is a non-poisonous, Batesian, mimic of the male.

All these imposters are benefiting from the Heliconid caterpillars' ability to eat passion flower vines. Those vines which were best able to survive the caterpillars' jaws have gradually evolved into new species with new toxins, and in response, new species of Heliconid butterfly capable of digesting them have evolved alongside. This has resulted in a whole range of passion flower species with their attendant Heliconid butterflies, each of which is dependent on its particular variety of vine for its caterpillars to feed on. But the passion flower has more evolutionary tricks up its sleeve than poison alone.

Some passion flower vines attempt to make themselves invisible to the egg-laying females. Apart from mimicking both the shape and texture of leaves belonging to totally unrelated plants growing in their vicinity, they even adopt different leaf patterns in the canopy from those they grow near the ground, so that in the rainforest roof their leaves resemble those of trees whilst smaller immature vines near to the ground mimic those of shrubs. It all makes life a little harder for the searching butterfly.

If egg-laying butterflies still manage to find its leaves, as of course many do, the passion flower still has a *pièce-de-résistance* it hopes will yet confuse them. On landing, the Heliconid butterfly tests the qualities of the vine's leaves by drumming on their surface with specially sensitive front legs. Satisfied that it has found the correct passion flower species to which its caterpillars are tuned, it searches for an egg-laying site. Young leaves and growing shoots are best suited, being the least poisonous and the most tender for the emerging caterpillar to eat. The females will rarely deposit their yellow eggs on vines where eggs have already been laid: the subsequent overcrowding would be of no benefit, and in any case the first caterpillars to emerge would cannibalize the rest to give themselves a better chance. The passion flower has seized on this behaviour and evolved a remarkable ruse: it grows imitation Heliconid eggs.

Even the pattern and distribution of the yellow spots can follow the egg-laying pattern of the particular butterfly which uses the vine. But the duplicity doesn't end there. Some vines produce tendrils which attract the females to lay on them, only to drop the tendrils soon afterwards, sending the eggs to their doom. *Passiflora adenopoda* also has sharp hairs which pierce caterpillar feet, snaring them to a slow starvation. Many vines employ ants to guard their leaves and remove young caterpillars, ensuring the ants' loyalty by providing them with additional nectar outside their flowers from small glands growing on their stems. And the story still has not

come to an end. It will continue to evolve as long as the forest exists.

The butterflies seek to make use of the passion flower vine's poisons to avoid being eaten, but not all insects have that capacity and most which lurk amongst the canopy branches are vulnerable. With their skills at camouflage they can nevertheless be extremely hard to find, so many of the birds of the forest that enjoy eating them don't go about their business alone but gather together in flocks, to get a little help from their friends.

One morning after spending the night on a platform on top of a Costa Rican tree I was woken by a strange croaking noise. Mistakenly, I believed it to come from some tree frogs in the branches nearby. I crawled out from under my makeshift roof and looked with binoculars out over the brightening forest. I could see six toucans hopping about an open-branched tree, waving their beaks left and right as they searched in bromeliads and tree holes for frogs and lizards. It was they who were making the noise. A group of shiny black caciques hopped about some epiphytes in another tree not far away, probing and shaking the leaves with long yellow beaks, searching out insects and spiders with their bright yellow eyes. I find these amusing birds. They search with great intensity through the canopy roof gardens, all the time making a curious warble in the back of their throats, like water dribbling from a tap. If nothing is found they seem to shake their heads in disgust, make their dribbling call, and then hop to the next plant. On arrival they will peer round it, first one way then the other, closely inspecting the surface for any moving insect. If this is empty too they will seize on a leaf or flick out trapped dead leaves to see if something is there.

As I sat on the platform looking out at the brilliant yellow sun rising over the trees and these individual hunters, the forest nearby was suddenly filled with a cacophony of chirping and twittering. Scanning the trees I could see numerous small birds, calling and bobbing, flying from branch to branch, probing orchids and ferns and crevices in the bark. There must have been at least a hundred of them in just a couple of tree crowns, spilling down into the lower layers of the forest where only their sounds filtered up to me from the understorey. Birding is not my strong point and in the tropics the vast range of species leaves me desperately flicking the pages of a guide book, if one even exists for the area I am in. However, I could spot a few brightly coloured tanagers and woodcreepers, plus some antwrens scurrying about the leaves. As they searched, small moths flew out and were instantly snatched by a waiting jacamar. All around was intense activity as birds came gliding in from nearby trees to join the flock. Some flew over the tree's topmost surface, others scurried along its branches. The woodcreepers occasionally found a juicy katydid in a curled-up leaf and instantly bashed it senseless on a branch, breaking the insect's legs off. Another small bird battled for several minutes with an enormous beetle almost a third of its own length, beating it against the branch on which it was standing, but still the beetle continued to struggle. The tree crowns

Superb flying skill enables the rainbow bee-eater to pluck fast-moving insects from the air; its long beak protects it from flailing wings or stings. Such birds are found in all the rainforests from the Lesser Sunda Islands and Bismarck Archipelago to the Solomons.

were filled with darting birds, snatching insects disturbed from their daytime lairs, swooping down to catch those that fell from another bird's grasp. Then just as suddenly as they had arrived, some of the birds began to fly away and the entire flock moved on, flowing through the forest like a wave, leaving only their sound slowly fading as they themselves were swallowed up within the forest.

Such bird waves, of as many as fifty different species hunting together, are a common phenomenon in the tropical forest. Why they should flock together has for a long time been something for debate, but it seems that the competition for food between individuals is out-weighed by the benefits of a joint foraging effort. To begin with, many insects are expertly camouflaged or small and hard to find. Not all the birds feed on the same things and whilst one bird is finding its own particular delicacy it may disturb some other insect, ideal for another. The effect of a whole flock feeding together is to provide blanket coverage of any particular tree they are in and cause such a disturbance that all will benefit from the scatter of escaping insects. They avoid direct competition with each other by operating at different levels within the forest and by searching in different ways on the tree. It may even be that there are separate canopy and understorey flocks which, though they forage together, overlap very little in their species composition.

In South American forests there may be up to fifteen different species of beige or grey tit-sized antwrens and vireos. Some antwrens prefer to operate in the topmost branches, with other species dividing up the forest between them all the way to the ground. Crevices in the bark of tree trunks provide the feeding ground for up to twenty species of woodcreeper and oven bird, whose brown or cinnamon plumage blends well with the woody surfaces on which they search for food. They particularly look for nocturnal creatures, such as spiders and katydids, which hide behind loose bark during the day. Jacamars position themselves on branches and quickly scan from side to side, looking out for butterflies, dragonflies and even wasps which other birds are too slow to catch.

These birds provide the core of the flock. Numerous other species will join in the feast but will also eat fruit, or even a lizard or a frog, and are less permanent members, teaming up for just a couple of hours as the flock passes nearby. Tanagers, woodpeckers, manakins and orioles belong to these temporary members.

One disadvantage of so many birds noisily feeding together is that they may draw the attention of birds of prey, but fortunately the flock posts its own sentries to guard against just such an incident. In the centre of the flock there may be a few birds that do no gleaning themselves but rely entirely on other birds' efforts to flush insects out for them. These birds, perhaps a specific tanager or antshrike, almost appear to parasitize the flock, but by not having their eyes down amongst the bark and leaves, they are in a better position to play lookout. Should they catch sight of a hawk or forest falcon rushing through the trees, it is always these 'sentinel' birds

that are first to give the alarm. The instant the flock hears their high-pitched notes, the numerous small birds dive for cover under leaves or amongst the epiphytes. The swooping bird of prey may go away hungry, but not always, especially if the sentinels are playing a double game. In Peru the canopy sentinel is the white-winged shrike-tanager, and in the understorey it is the bluish-slate antshrike. Both can be surprisingly crafty. Occasionally a foraging bird will flush an insect from cover and several birds, including a sentinel, will go for it. The sentinel then gives an alarm call and the other birds dive for cover, leaving the insect to the 'sentinel' alone.

These mixed feeding flocks fly on surprisingly regular routes. Elliot McClure could almost set his watch by the bird wave that flew past his canopy platform above the Gombak forest in Malaysia, and got to know them well in his years there. As the first birds shook their feathers in the early morning and set out over the forest to feed, others would join in and so the flock would swell as it moved. An hour after sunrise it was at its maximum. Flycatchers, cuckoo-shrikes and minivets would lead the wave along its route, spreading through the forest like some giant ornothological amoeba. Bringing up the rear, malachoas would run squirrel-like along the branches then glide from tree to tree, and below them a pair of trogons would be last of all, picking off the remaining insects falling to the ground. By mid-day the flock may have travelled some distance along a semi-circular route and would lay up in the shade to avoid the oppressive heat. After their rest they would set off again for home, and individuals would gradually drop out along the way so that by evening most would be back where they started from. In this way the various flocks divide up the forest between them, and only occasionally come into contact.

Many of the species which join these tropical flocks abandon the forest at a particular time of the year and embark on much greater journeys, to fly north and take advantage of the abundant insect life of our temperate summers. Though they return to the warm tropical sun whilst we endure the freezing winter, we still tend to regard them as 'our' birds. In recent years there has been a noticeable decline in the numbers of such migrants flooding into the United States, particularly the delightful singing warblers. Olive-sided flycatchers and grey vireos have dropped about four to eight per cent every year since 1966. It seems almost certain that this is due in large part to the destruction of forests in South America, currently estimated at over four million hectares annually, an area the size of Massachusetts and Vermont combined. Bird enthusiasts should be getting apprehensive. The American experience is a warning of impending tragedy which will strike other areas of the world. Mankind, the greatest predator, is consuming not just a few species but whole forests of them as the price for a better world. Each year Americans, and perhaps Europeans too, will notice their disappearance more. We don't yet have silent springs, but each year they are getting just a little quieter.

5 | Treetop Voices

To keep in touch with your own kind in a rainforest is not very easy. The dark greenery has the rather disconcerting and sometimes sinister effect of swallowing up people, until suddenly you realize that you are on your own and have lost your way. Even a walk of only a hundred paces into thick jungle can have a disorientating effect, as I have learnt to my cost.

Having paddled a dugout canoe up-river from a camp in an area of lowland forest in Sarawak, I can remember tying it to a tree root and stepping ashore into squelchy mud, scattering small mudskipping fish and freshwater crabs which scuttled into their burrows. I only needed to go a short distance into the forest, to see if there was any evidence of primates having eaten fruit there. As I walked in, the light from the open riverbank was soon obscured by tall trees, hanging creepers and a mass of bankside vegetation. Daydreaming a little, I didn't take adequate notice of my direction.

I inspected various trees, collected a few fruits with bite marks, and decided to return to the canoe. Normally it is possible to keep an eye on the route home by looking for leaves that have been disturbed by your passage, either on the decaying compost of the forest floor or on bushes that you may have brushed. Small snicks in the bark of trees with a machete also help, or you can bend and break small branches in the direction of travel which then hang like dull flags to guide you home. But it is easy to make mistakes.

After a short time I could see the light of the riverbank, and soon cut my way through the vegetation and out into the open. There was no sign of the canoe. Looking at the small river I noticed it was flowing the wrong way. It was a different river.

I couldn't understand it. I had been certain this was the right direction and inwardly rather prided myself on being able to find my way around the forest. Confused, I started back into the trees, stumbling about in the apparent darkness until my eyes gradually grew accustomed to the change in light levels from the bright riverbank. It must have been a tributary of the first river, I thought, the canoe can't be more than a few hundred metres away.

There was no slope or hill to give a clue to the direction from which I had come: the forest here was uniformly flat. I walked on. My shirt became snagged in the sharp barbs of a 'wait-a-while' rattan, so-called because of the length of time it takes to release yourself from its hooked tendrils. There hadn't been so many of them where I started before. A little further. No river, no canoe. I was lost.

It is easy to lose your way in the forest. The jungle quickly mops up any cry for help, but there are windows through which certain sounds will travel. Animals use them to stay in touch.

108 | THE ENCHANTED CANOPY

Standing alone in the forest, I looked around. Each direction seemed the same: no change in light to indicate where a riverbank might be, just tall buttressed trunks, reaching high to the light above, and jostling vegetation loosely filling the understorey. A mosquito settled on my cheek. Sweat trickled down my temple. It was mid-day and the forest was relatively silent.

Animals of the forest canopy, and humans better versed in the art of forest lore than me, rarely lose their way, but they are faced with similar problems when surrounded by trees. In the forest it is not possible to see very far, and it is rather gloomy, so signals to friend or foe need to be especially eye-catching for them to be seen at all, and even then are not much good for keeping in touch over long distances. Sound would seem a much better way of drawing attention to yourself, but within the forest, unless you have a loud voice, sound does not travel far. Since it also bounces off the trees, it seems anyway to come from several different directions at once; so even that is not always the best method of letting others know where you are. Some birds of the forest understorey appear to make excellent ventriloquists, so that it is almost impossible to be sure from which direction their voice is coming, a quality which may confuse predators but keeps mates informed that they are there. So, unlike a human lost in the desert, I could neither wave to a searching plane nor shout across a valley for help to a passer-by.

I could turn to the earth's magnetic field for guidance, had I not foolishly left my compass in the canoe. Radio is another source of communication we humans exploit that animals do not, but to cover any distance an aerial must be raised above the canopy, since radio waves bounce better through the air than they do through trees. The markers I had placed would have led me home had I watched them more carefully, but for the inexperienced, markers are often difficult to see. Animals, too, place markers in the forest but theirs are designed for their nose, not their eyes. For short-distance communication, scent can be ideal, particularly for revealing a territorial boundary without gesticulating and shouting, an activity which could just as easily attract an unwelcome visitor who might be hungry.

Like many other group-living primates, I was anxious to keep in touch with others of my group, for they offered security from danger and, as I didn't know all that well how to seek food in the trees, they also offered my best chance of getting a square meal. All in all, as evening approached, I was not looking forward to spending a night alone. Having done with cursing and swearing, I sat down to make a small fire. Away to my left a chorus of frogs, stirred to song by the approach of night, began to pipe up a mixture of high-pitched 'pinks' and sonorous croaks. A riverbank could be in that direction, I thought, and as I walked some distance towards the sound a deep, rhythmic booming filtered through from the forest beyond. For some reason the camp generator's deep tones seemed to carry well through the trees. Soon I would be back at my temporary forest home.

A flag to wave? The toco toucan's beak is more than a tool for fruit-picking. In a crown full of toucans, the beak helps species to spot their own kind, and pick up a mate. With few canopy animals large enough to eat them, toucans can afford to be loud – in colour.

Animals need to communicate with each other for a variety of reasons. Firstly a male might wish to attract a mate. Having done so, he might wish to let other males know, to keep them away. If a good food supply is located it might be worth broadcasting the find to enable friends to feed, or alternatively, protecting it and keeping others at bay may be more important. It may be necessary to keep a group together so that none gets lost.

To hunt prey, it's best not to be heard or seen, and the same is true if you don't wish to be eaten. If your body is likely to make a predator throw up by cunningly being filled with poisons, you might as well let everyone know about it, so they will learn that you're not worth having. On the other hand, disguising yourself as a wolf in sheep's clothing might prove an easier way to steal up on a meal.

To perceive these and many other messages, animals have at their disposal eyes which can see visual signals, such as colour or movement, auditory organs to hear sounds, and olfactory devices to smell odours. Colour and smell have been heavily exploited by many species to convey a variety of messages. A toucan's beak is a flag to wave at others of its kind, perhaps to rally them to a feeding tree or, as many of the species look superficially similar, as an aid to recognizing a mate. Many West African forest-living monkeys, particularly the red-tailed guenons, employ a form of colourful semaphore on their faces and limbs, which are potent signals to help

distinguish one variety from another. Though the voices, bodies, and arboreal existence vary little throughout the group, the colour and patterns of their facial fur are remarkably different – some have blue spectacles with a red nose and white cheeks, others have the same but a white nose, or perhaps a V-shaped white moustache and orange cheeks. Combined with contrasting streaks of black-and-white fur, the position of the head and tail and the posture of the animals as they move about the forest, convey both who they are and often what they are doing.

Interestingly, their colour patterns seem also to be connected to where they live in the forest, so that the smaller species, which utilize the thinnest branches where they might overbalance should they try to convey messages with eye-catching postures, concentrate their visual signals in their faces, which can easily be turned in any direction as a flag. The monkey's niche in the canopy also dictates the way in which it uses its signals. The brightly contrasting coat of the Diana monkey is easily displayed as it ranges widely over the topmost branches in search of fruit and leaves. It is very alert and will flee at the slightest sign of danger. The sombre greys of the de Brazza's monkey act as camouflage in the swampy understorey where it lives, but this too has a bright face dominated by a magnificent white beard. They search diligently for a wide variety of food in a much smaller area of forest than their canopy-living relative, and learn to know it intimately, marking favourite trunks and branches with aromatic scents from modified sweat glands on their chest. Should danger threaten, they will freeze for hours at a time and hide their distinctive beard behind a branch or cupped hand to avoid detection.

Quite why parrots and lorikeets should display such brilliant colours as they fly across the canopy remains something of a mys-

The green anolis's dewlap provides a quick 'flash' to signal mates and rivals, before being hidden beneath the lizard's bobbing chin. Bright colours are a good way of staying in touch over short distances in the forest.

tery. Perhaps without too many predators to chase them they can afford to be spectacular without fear of endangering themselves, but it can work directly to their advantage in a crown full of flowers, amongst which Australian nectar-feeding lorikeets blend safely and almost disappear. As with toucans and guenons, their plumage is also a breeding aid to sexual identification. Amphibians and insects, too, produce a blaze of bright colours either as camouflage or advertisement. Insects disguise themselves as bird droppings or perhaps a water droplet; and their uncanny ability to mimic the colours, form and even activity of creatures quite different from themselves is equally remarkable. Smell, too, is a potent signal and many primates in addition to de Brazza's monkeys use it to mark their home ranges on branches and twigs. Sexually alluring pheromones floated on the wind by female moths can draw males from several kilometres away, but few animals in the forest are equipped with sufficiently sensitive noses to use perfumes for conveying messages over long distances in the forest. With colours only usable over a limited range, many animals turned to another, and possibly the only effective way of keeping in touch over long distances – sound.

Across the rainforest canopies of the world there are monkeys and apes that have extraordinarily loud voices. One voice is so loud and so unlike a monkey it is easy to believe its call is that of a leopard. But no leopards live in the forest where these monkeys occur, though a very similar creature, the jaguar, does live there. When the first explorers from Europe arrived on the shores of Central America and moved inland into its jungles, they were on occasions terrified by a deep howling roar within the columns of trees. The resonating sound would first come from one direction, then spring up somewhere else, and then again from another position, so that they believed themselves to be surrounded by terrifying beasts. In fact the noise came from a primate whose name takes after its powerful voice: the howler monkey.

Howler monkeys can be found in undisturbed rainforest all the way from Mexico south to the northern border of Argentina: they are the most widespread primate in the forests of the New World. There are six species in their genus, *Allouata*, and all are covered in thick fur that ranges from a deep reddish orange through shades of brown to black. They are not the largest monkeys in the Americas but males can weigh as much as a small child, with females weighing about a third of that. It is the males that have the loudest call.

On an early visit to the Darien jungles of Panama I too was taken in by the howlers' call. Strolling through the forest, my mind was overloaded with all the sensations the tropics offer. Weaned on early accounts of jungles I trod carefully, expecting with every tentative footstep a death-dealing fer-de-lance to strike with hideous fangs, or gigantic stinging wasps to zoom out at me. I know now that snakes are a rare sight in most forests, and only once have I been stung by a fierce hornet, and that through my own stupidity,

Scents from the protruding hair pencils of the male common crow butterfly induce females to copulate. Many female butterflies, like their human counterparts, waft potent perfumes to attract passing males, but theirs may be effective for two kilometres, above the forest.

though I must admit it was remarkably painful. Nonetheless, I was proceeding with caution, not quite knowing what to expect when suddenly a deafening roar directly overhead made me jump almost out of my skin. I knew about howler monkeys but nothing I had read prepared me for the sheer volume of that call close at hand. Like those early explorers, for a moment I feared the worst. I was in good company. Even the determined John Oppenheimer, who made the first study of capuchin monkeys in Panama, ran terrified from the forest on his first day, scared rigid by the extraordinary noise he had heard. A minute's rationalization, however, assured me that jaguars do not ordinarily live high in the trees, so the impressive growling calls must belong to howler monkeys.

Howlers live in mixed sex groups of some eight to twenty animals, with usually about three times as many females as males. They prefer mature forests of tall trees and rarely venture down to the ground. High in the crowns, they move at a fairly sedate pace, picking leaves which they pop into their mouth by hand, sometimes supplementing their diet with fruit. They have a long prehensile tail and will often hang from this alone to reach some morsel that would otherwise elude them. When a male calls he juts his head forward, pouting pink lips in sharp contrast with the dark face, his throat swelling. Inside this is an enlarged larynx containing a hyoid bone with a hole in it, over which air is passed to make the call, rather like blowing across the top of a bottle to make a sound.

Howlers usually call in the early mornings before moving off to feed, and can be heard over a kilometre away. But who are they trying to impress? Darwin argued that the males with the loudest voices were the most successful at attracting females. Later it was believed the calls announced the defence of territories. After following groups through the forest in Panama for three months at a stretch, the primatologist David Chivers discovered that these monkeys kept no permanent territories but roamed the forest in large overlapping home ranges. So what was all the shouting about if not to safeguard a food supply? The value in keeping groups apart lies in prevention of conflict because when they meet, bedlam breaks out as males try to prove their dominance and their right to be there. Chasing off other male howlers when they come too close for comfort is much more exhausting than sitting still and shouting at them from a distance – so, howlers howl. By roaring in the early morning and occasionally during the day each group learns of the others' positions. Thus they avoid each other on their daily round, and as a result reserve the particular patch of forest they are in for their own exclusive use. By so doing, howler troops make the best use of the resources the forest canopy has to offer, and have become highly successful.

In the rainforest canopy of West Africa there are other noisy monkeys, including roaring black-and-white colobus monkeys, which sound rather similar to howlers and the colourful guenons, but there is one monkey that calls louder than most and has a

The South American black howler monkey has a call as loud as a roaring leopard. Elsewhere, other monkeys have similarly loud voices to serve notice that they occupy the forest roof. All of them use sound windows to project their voices further than the forest might otherwise let them.

particularly distinctive sound: the grey-cheeked mangabey. This species is found in wet evergreen forests from south-west Cameroon to eastern Uganda, where it lives on a mixed diet of fruit, seeds and leaves accompanied by insects and the occasional flower. Like the howlers, mangabeys range in groups of fifteen to twenty animals over large areas of forest, four hundred hectares or more, and use their loud call similarly to keep other groups at a safe distance. The calls are given spontaneously by a seated male who, with closed lips drawn into a pout, billows out his cheeks, jerks his body forward and produces a tremendous low-pitched resonant whoop. Tensed with the effort, he will pause for about five seconds with his eyes half-closed and shoulders quivering slightly. Then, raising his head towards the forest roof and jerking his shoulders violently up and down, he utters a loud 'gobble-gobble-gobble', rather like a deep-voiced turkey. The timing of the call and the number of 'gobbles' identifies each calling male, and therefore his group, to others within earshot. The call does not vary and is not made by young-sters yet to reach maturity. They, like young boys, must wait for their voices to break.

By playing back tape recordings of mangabeys' calls it is possible to see how any one group reacts. A group will only move towards the call of one monkey, usually the dominant male. Calls of other males within that group merely illicit answering calls but no other response. However, if 'whoop-gobbles' of stranger males are broadcast to them all the mangabeys will move away, excepting the dominant male who will answer loudly with his own call, and may rush as much as a kilometre through the forest to confront the supposed rival. No doubt he would be somewhat confused if he came upon the tape recorder.

Other powerful callers exist in the canopy of other parts of the world. In the south-western tip of India, two small areas of moist evergreen forest still remain to echo to the call of the male lion-tailed macaque. Another loud-calling monkey, the nilgiri langur, lives alongside it and both have very similar calls, but they divide the forest's offerings between them, the macaque feeding on fruit, the langur mainly on leaves. There are sixteen species of macaque in Asia, ranging from northern India to the Far East, but only the lion-tailed macaque has such a loud voice, designed for long-distance communication in the forest. It is a magnificent monkey with a thick mane of deep orange fur and a long tail, tipped like that of lion, but it is now one of the world's rarest primates. Only eight hundred of them are thought to exist in the wild, one population in the Silent Valley and the other in the Ashambu Hills, both localities part of the Western Ghats mountain range and both severely threatened by the sacrifice of the forest to developmental interests. Soon the Silent Valley may live up to its name.

Moving further east to the forests of South East Asia, there are many leaf-eating langurs which call loudly to each other as they forage through the canopy. The dusky langur has a loud, honking

Largest of the gibbons, the siamangs have a spectacular call. An inflatable throat sac enables them to bark, scream and boom at each other's families in the hope that one group will not tread on the other's ecological toes.

call as comical as its clown-like face adorned with white eye-rings and muzzle. The silvered langur of Sumatra, Java and Borneo has a call with similar qualities, whilst banded langurs, found from Malaysia across to Borneo, prefer to chatter. There is so much competition for calling times that they must apportion the day between them; banded langurs call before dawn or after dusk; dusky langurs at dawn, followed by gibbons and finally the siamangs, calling two to three hours after dawn.

The gibbons are perhaps the most tuneful of all mammals. There are nine species in the Far Eastern forests and each has its own distinctive song. In the far north, in Southern China, Laos and Vietnam east of the Mekong, the concolor gibbons exploit a higher frequency range than any of the others, giving their calls a twittering, whistling quality. In the north-west, in Assam, Bangladesh and Burma, the duetting calls of the hoolock gibbon dominate the forest in the early morning hours. In south-east Thailand and western Kampuchea the great call of the female pileated gibbon has short introductory whoops followed by a rich series of bubbling notes occasionally interrupted by the male's own whoops, or coda. These three species live in the more seasonal monsoon forests. Males and females look quite different; the former black, often with distinctive white eyebrows or cheeks, the females buff or golden brown or even grey with a black cap in the pileated species. Lar gibbons have

spread from the Malay Peninsula across to north Sumatra and even into northern Thailand and beyond; the female's call rises to a powerful scream and gradually fades to soft 'whoo-whoos'. The silvery grey Javan or moloch gibbon has a call similar to the lar's; competition for living space with humans in Java has made it the rarest gibbon in the world. Only on the Mentawai Islands to the west of Sumatra is the long rising and falling call of the Kloss gibbon heard; it is the only species in which the sexes do not engage in singing duets, but call quite separately.

The largest species, the siamang, lives in Sumatra. The calls of these enormous black gibbons are among the most complex and impressive of any creature in the forest. Beneath their chin is a large inflatable throat sac which allows them to make high-pitched barks, chatters and screams, interspersed with low-pitched resonating 'booms' which carry through the trees for up to two kilometres. Listening to their calls close by can be a devastating experience. As with all gibbons, whilst the male opens the bidding, it is the females who call the tune. The introductory booms of the male cause the female to launch into a series of barks and booms, at the climax of which the male gives an ear-splitting scream. The female follows with a shorter series of barks and booms and just when it seems to be all over, the male delivers an even louder and longer scream. The finale has both animals barking and chattering furiously as they swing vigorously around and shake branches, adding a visual element to their already remarkable display.

The local people of central Borneo were aware of the existence of two species of gibbon there long before they became known to science, just over ten years ago. One had a wailing 'great call', the other a strange call that rose in volume and ended in a prolonged bubbling sound. Folklore told that the difference arose during a battle between the different species to see who could hold their breath longest under water. One of the species is the agile gibbon, which spread from Sumatra across to south-western Borneo between the Kapuas and Barito rivers at a time when the sea level between the islands was much lower, millions of years ago. Both species call as they breathe in and out, giving their calls a 'whoo-haa' sound. But the Bornean or Müller's gibbon was there first, and has a call which to me is as delightful as bubbling laughter or the sound of a rippling stream. No doubt that is why the people of the Bornean forest say that it emerged from the waters victorious after the battle with its neighbour.

If the loud location calls of many monkeys convey relatively little information other than 'I am here' and possibly 'I'm looking for a mate', primates living in monogamous pairs in small families of parents and three or four offspring who wish to divide up the canopy efficiently with other groups, obviously require a more complicated call. The haunting sounds of the indri in Madagascar fulfil such a need, as do those of the tiny marmosets and titi monkeys in South America. The high-pitched calls of springing

tarsiers are often mistaken for birds in Asia, but no sound in the forest is more beautiful and evocative than the duet of a male and female gibbon. Both call differently and often at separate times of the day, and as all the nine species in South East Asia have their own distinct calls it is easy to learn which gibbon inhabits a particular piece of forest merely by using your ears. Usually the songs consist of 'whoops' or 'whoo-haa' calls by the male, who is later joined by the female. A co-ordinating sequence follows with the male and female whooping together, and then the female goes into her magnificent 'great call', followed by the male's coda of answering whoops. Unlike howler monkeys or the 'whoop-gobbling' mangabey, gibbons defend fixed home ranges of about twenty to fifty hectares from other gibbons, in order to protect their resources. They largely depend on selected fruit trees for food which may be hard to come by in times of seasonal scarcity, so it pays them to stay in one place where food sources and the routes to them are known, and to repel intruders. In this the male's spacing calls are similar to those of other foraging primates and enable gibbons to reserve an area of forest for their families. Territorial disputes between males do happen every few days, but these help to reinforce boundaries, which once known are rarely crossed.

Though the calls of different species vary both in sound and therefore possibly in meaning, it seems likely that the initial calling of the males indicates ownership of a territory, serving to divide up resources with minimum conflict; but why should the female bother to call and why is her call so different? It must have another purpose. Gibbons live for twenty to thirty years and choose a mate for life. When single, young males call often, both to define a new territory for themselves and to secure a mate. Once they have found one their calling rate lowers, perhaps indicating that they have now chosen a family way of life. When a pair first choose a life together they must learn to sing in harmony. By making tape recordings of the calls and analysing them with an audio-spectrograph – a visual print-out – it is possible to see that gibbon pairs do improve their duets as they get older, possibly indicating a more stable bond to other listening gibbons.

Young males, after seven to eight years, when they become adolescent, are gradually encouraged to leave the family group through increasingly acrimonious altercations with their fathers. Once on their own, their calls serve to attract single sexually mature females who might also have left home. Having chosen her mate, a female is loath to lose him so it pays her to broadcast to other females that he is not available. Any adult female gibbon already in a stable family unit could lose her calling spouse to a more attractive rival, so her 'great call' serves notice that hers is a strong pair bond and unlikely to be broken. Her daughters must learn to 'great call' too, and will sing along with their mother. At first their duet is poorly co-ordinated but with time the daughters improve. After some years they too must leave the family and try to begin one of

their own. Having learned to 'great call' from their mothers they will soon find a lone male to duet with, and let others know that they are no longer single.

In the undisturbed forests of northern Sumatra and most of lowland Borneo male orang-utans will occasionally announce their presence. Their 'long call' may last for four minutes or more. It begins as a series of grumbles, and then builds to powerful bellowing, which gradually subsides to more grumbles, finishing with an occasional sigh. The huge sac of skin beneath a mature male orang-utan's chin provides a resonating chamber to improve the distance over which the call can be heard to at least two kilometres. The orang-utan rarely calls more than once a day and may go for a month without calling at all. Orangs are solitary animals and it seems likely that the purpose of the long call is again to let mature males, which possibly recognize each others' voices, know where they are in relation to each other. It has been suggested that the huge crescents of fat on either side of a mature male orang's head could act as parabolic reflectors, focusing sound towards their ears in the same way as cupping hands over our ears does. Should the system break down and two males confront each other, the more dominant will give chase, sometimes descending from the trees to pursue the other along the ground. After successfully seeing off the trespasser the victor may bellow loudly. Confrontations are not common, occurring perhaps once a year. On one occasion, a male was observed to spy another sitting motionless in a tree not far away. The sitting male, on seeing the first, began a call but then thought better of it and never finished. The first advanced rapidly, shaking branches in a belligerent display of bravado. The sitting male refused to move. When the displaying male got within twenty metres, however, he seemed to lose his nerve, climbed down to the ground and ran away through the forest.

Another function of the long call, or perhaps a by-product, may be to attract sexually receptive females. When these meetings occur, the male's dealings with the opposite sex can be quite surprising. On rare occasions when copulation has been observed, males call with gusto either before or during the act. They will mate face to face, as humans do, but high in the trees, or indulge in more adventurous positions whilst hanging from branches. The most successful arrangement seems to be with the male lying on his back in the branches straddled by an energetic female; most pregnancies seem to result from this posture. Less co-operative females may be chased through the canopy amid much screaming, and even be pursued on the ground. If overtaken there, perhaps frustrated younger males may attack and forcibly copulate with them in what can only be described as rape, though surprisingly few pregnancies have been observed to result from these dramatic circumstances. This ground-level behaviour may account for the occasional reports of orang-utans raping female humans. In one published account, an unfortunate woman woke up from sleeping under a tree in the

afternoon to find herself being assaulted by 'a fat monkey'. No doubt with their immense strength, a gripping 'hand' on each limb, and a capacity for this kind of attack in their normal behavioural repertoire, such assaults are relatively easy for orang-utans. Certainly the sexual prowess of young male orang-utans is well known amongst local peoples, both in legend and reality. In a few areas there are stories of them being introduced into tribal long-house parties to indulge in some bizarre activities, so much so that there was for a time a fear that venereal disease might enter the wild population.

Some males seem unsuccessful at attracting female orang-utans and may never mate at all, but whether it is frustration which leads them to rape humans or whether it is simply a case of mistaken identity remains a mystery. Conversely, a calling male can attract a female orang, possibly adolescent, with whom he will not mate despite the young female wishing him to. Having failed to elicit his attentions from a neighbouring tree, the female may approach the male and hang in front of his face with legs apart, only to endure his supreme indifference. When this fails she may touch, groom, or even mouth his genitalia. Apart from the occasional grunt or grumble, the male often takes no notice at all, perhaps realizing that the female is not ready to become pregnant.

At the Orang-utan Research and Conservation Project in central Indonesian Borneo, Birute Galdikas has been studying orang-utans for many years. We owe much to her detailed observations and those of the many co-workers who have visited the reserve and trailed around the forest watching these apes.

In just this particular area, large male orang-utans seem to have developed an extraordinary method of long-distance communication which enhances the value of their calls. They push over dead trees. All over the forest there are rotten trees or 'snags' which have lost their branches and whose roots no longer grip the soil tightly. When they topple they make a terrific reverberating boom. Orang-utans of Tanjung Puting, where the research project is, know this and particularly on windless days will push and heave at these old trees from the ground to bring them down. One male is especially good at toppling trees and will even climb the rotten trunks and sway his huge furry orange body back and forth to uproot the tree. Then, as the tree begins to fall and it seems certain that the orang will plunge to his death, he reaches for a passing branch and pulls himself to safety, leaving the trunk to crash to the ground. The crashing sound of the tree hitting the forest floor carries much further than their calls and such 'snag crashing' by the orangs is followed by their long call; but they never seem to push over trees after they have called. Perhaps the crash serves to warn other males that a call is coming, rather like an after-dinner speaker tapping the table in the hope that someone will stop and listen. Perhaps the crash itself serves notice that its perpetrator is someone to be reckoned with.

The forest is a noisy place in which to be heard. Millions of insects buzz, scrape and stridulate, a host of different calls which swamp the forest in an almost constant hiss of confusing background noise. In the early mornings, when most primates like to call, frogs may be finishing off their night-time croaking and birds begin a dawn chorus that threatens to drown out everything else. In addition the forest is full of trunks, branches and leaves which scatter sound in all directions, causing it to attenuate and fade away far faster than it would on the open plains. The ground soaks up sound, too, so it's worth climbing up into the canopy to make a loud call, or even scale an emergent tree to throw your voice out over the forest. Many loud callers do this, both birds and monkeys, but scientists studying the calls produced by forest-living primates were intrigued to discover that nearly all the loud whoops, gobbles, roars or bellows fell within a narrow low-frequency band from 125 Hertz to 500 Hertz. The human ear can detect sounds which vary in frequency from 20 Hertz to 20,000 Hertz and other primates may do better than that, so why were the calls restricted to a small part of the audible range of most of the listeners?

Researchers from the University of Missouri carried speakers, tape recorders, microphones and amplifiers into the rainforest of western Kenya at Kakamega to find out how sound travelled through the trees. They placed speakers amongst the trees and microphones at varying distances and directions from them, and then broadcast pure tonal sounds at a variety of frequency ranges. High frequencies were quickly attenuated in the forest but those around 200 Hertz travelled much further than they expected. It seemed that there was a 'sound window' in the forest for noises on this frequency and it is just this frequency, or those near to it, that monkeys and apes use for long-range communication. Many primates include loud barks, screams, and alarm calls in their vocal repertoire but most of these are above the 1000 Hertz frequency range and travel, at best, a few hundred metres through the forest. But if they maintain the volume of the call and lower its pitch to 200 Hertz, the 'sound window' effect enables the call to travel a thousand times as far. Similarly the deep sounds of a tribal drum or our camp's generator are equally penetrating. But there are other tricks that primates have learnt to use.

Early morning seems by far the most important period for primate calls, but as we have seen, there is a good deal of noisy competition from other early risers. So why not call later, when the forest is quieter?

Sound travels through air as a pressure wave, bouncing molecules of gas one into the other. When the wave reaches a monkey's eardrum the membrane vibrates, enabling the monkey to hear whatever sound it is. As gasses contract when cold, the molecules in cold air are closer together than in warm air, so it's easier for pressure waves to knock one into another. Sound therefore travels further through colder air. It's rather like playing snooker: if several

A Waorani Indian thumps the buttress roots of a large tree. The low frequency boom it produces allows forest people to communicate with each other as effectively as a tribal drum.

balls on the table are gathered together and touch each other, the impact of another ball hitting them has a much greater effect than if the balls were already scattered. At dawn the sun's rays quickly warm up the air close to the canopy, whilst the air beneath the trees remains relatively cool. By calling before it gets too hot, primates can throw their voices further and even bounce their calls between the warm and cool air layers, as the sound waves tend to be drawn into the relatively cooler air within the canopy and not upwards and out of earshot into the sun-warmed air above. Why then do orang-utans and siamangs prefer to avoid the morning rush and let others know where they are later in the day, when their calls may not travel so far? Both these species have evolved resonating sacs beneath their chins and can thereby generate louder calls than the others, no doubt compensating for their less efficient calling hour.

Gibbons produce the most musical songs of any terrestrial mammal. In some ways they resemble a few of the larger fruit-eating birds, particularly hornbills; they inhabit the upper parts of the forest canopy, eat fruit, create long-lasting pair bonds, and occupy territories which they sing to protect. Some would also say that with their immense speed of movement they almost seem to fly, too. After the primates, birds must rank as the most powerful songsters in the forest. For birds living near the forest floor, keeping in touch with others of their species in the dense undergrowth presents major problems. They too use the low frequency 'sound window' effect for long-distance calls. In the Amazonian forests the booming curasow and the resonating trumpeters throw their calls over long distances; argus pheasants are renowned for their calls in Asia; and in New Guinea the huge flightless cassowaries have a deep booming call coupled with cackling and croaking. These enormous birds are rather like emus and are closely related to them.

They stand almost as tall as a man, with colourful blue and red heads topped with a horny helmet. They are ferocious and can run at speed through the forest on powerful legs that can rip open a human belly with one swipe. Whilst walking deep in the forests of Sulawesi I was once surprised to hear a cockerel crowing, but this was no farmyard bird – there were no farms nearby and its call was a little different. Then, of course, I remembered that a cockerel's piercing crow is not designed to rouse farmers from their beds but to penetrate the thick vegetation of tropical forests. All our domestic chickens are descended from four species of oriental jungle fowl, but it still sounds remarkably incongruous to be walking in the jungle and hear wild chickens crowing amongst the trees.

As the different layers in the forest have different accoustical properties, birds must use different kinds of sounds to make best use of the part of the forest in which they like to live. There is a curious haunting quality to many of the bird songs in the understorey. This is because the birds there tend to sing with pure-toned whistles but they lack the tuneful melody of European blackbirds or American robins. Birds such as small spiderhunters cannot match the dis-

tances covered by larger, booming birds as their voice box, the syrinx, is too small. Since there is a danger that their small voice will not be noticed amongst all the other background noises in the forest, they must use a song that stands out from the crowd. One way to do this would be to produce a highly complicated twitter, mixed with a few high-frequency chirrups. But if all small birds were doing this, the scattering effects of leaves and the noisy buzzing insects who first occupied the air waves in an evolutionary sense, would soon make a mess of it all, and any bird trying to listen to another's song would find itself very confused.

Many birds inhabiting the middle and lower layers of the forest therefore use simple repetitive songs which often approximate to the sounds of our own human vowels. Try slowly saying A-E-I-O-U but varying the tone with each one, perhaps in a rising scale, and you will do quite well as a rainforest bird. Altering the volume of the call is a poor way for coding messages as the changing nature of the forest would mean that the call would sometimes come through loudly and at other times softly. So a particular species tends to call with the same amount of volume each time it sings, but codes its message in a different way. If the volume is kept the same and the call is long followed by silence, then short followed by silence, and so on, birds can add meaning to their message rather like a repeated morse code. Altering tone adds further information. By repeating the same simple tune at roughly the same volume, it is much easier to recognize an individual call amongst a background of interfering noise, and this is just what the birds in the lower part of the forest have evolved to do.

Rising up the tree trunks and into the crowns themselves, the calls begin to change to higher frequencies as the forest becomes a little more open and they travel better. Above the canopy itself a large proportion of the smaller birds use complicated high frequencies to convey their message in much the same way as do those of open areas. The syrinx sits astride the junction where the bird's windpipe divides to enter its lungs, quite unlike that of primates, where the larynx is near the top of the windpipe. Birds have one great advantage over primate songsters and that is that they can vibrate both sides of their syrinx at once, but in different ways, so that they can sing two quite distinct songs at the same time. Thus an early morning spent up in the forest canopy is a delight of colourful twittering and chirruping birds capable of setting up territories, attracting mates or just maintaining contact with complex high-frequency songs.

Some of the larger birds of the canopy have the best of both worlds. The magnificent three-wattled bellbird of Central America is a good example, seasonally producing one of the most characteristic bird sounds in those forests. It has a snow-white head and shoulders, but is otherwise rust-brown and has three wattles dangling like dark worms from the base of its beak. On a high tree branch, it opens its mouth wide and with apparently little effort

In the jungles of New Guinea and Australia's Cape York, you may be fortunate enough to hear the hideous screams and high-pitched whistles of the palm cockatoo. Coupled with a one-step, two-step along the branch, crest erect and head bobbing, it is enough to send a rush of blood to the head, which is exactly what it does. In response, palm cockatoos blush with anticipation.

makes a noise like a powerful blow from a blacksmith's hammer hitting metal in his forge. Hence they, and others like them that make a similar noise, are known as anvil birds. The brilliantly coloured parrots and macaws with raucous guttural voices are some of the noisiest creatures of the forest canopy. A toucan's frog-like calls are surprisingly penetrating, though less obvious than the macaw's.

In African and Asian forests, hornbills are the toucan's fruit-eating counterpart. They also have huge coloured bills but those of most hornbills are topped with a lightweight hollow casque. In the West African male black-casqued hornbill, this is enormous and acts as a resonating chamber, helping to throw the bird's call half a

kilometre over the canopy with a sound like a braying donkey. One of the birds which shares Asia's forests with the gibbons is the helmeted hornbill whose red casque of ivory is much prized for ornamental carvings and has led to it becoming increasingly rare. In Borneo it is locally known as the 'chop-down-your-mother-in-law-bird', a name I couldn't understand until I heard its extraordinary call. It spends a lot of time working up to it, sitting high in the branches. The call begins with deep, rather embarrassed sounding 'choorks' interspersed with long pauses. After what seem like interminable minutes, the call rapidly speeds up to a series of repeated 'chor-corks', ending as the huge bird throws its enormous bill upwards and utters something like hysterical laughter. The local account for this spectacular call is that it is made by a husband who is fed up with his mother-in-law. He goes to her house, which is built on stilts as is the custom in that part of the world, and sets about it with an axe. Each initial 'choork' is the sound of the axeman's blows, and as he chops faster and faster and the house begins to fall, his laughter fills the forest.

In the warmer parts of the globe insects often make the most noticeable noises, and tropical forests are no exception. There are beetles that buzz, moths that hiss and caterpillars that scrape but the loudest and most remarkable are the cicadas and bush crickets, or katydids. They divide up the day between them, with katydids calling at night and cicadas filling the daylight hours with their jarring calls. Cicadas live for a very long time. Their nymphs lead subterranean lives beneath the forest floor, sucking juices from plant roots and requiring anything up to fifteen years to mature. They will then crawl out from under the leaves, climb plant stems and, hidden beneath a leaf, split open: the adult emerges to fly up into the forest. The adults have, to me, a rather disconcerting quality among insects of appearing to be intelligent, scuttling around behind a tree trunk on being approached, only to peep out at you from the other side. The adults live but a few weeks and during that time the males must attract a mate, so they sing for all they are worth.

On each side of their abdomen is a small convex plate in the cuticle, thin and highly elastic. This is the 'tymbal' and when a small muscle on the inside pulls it inwards, it buckles and makes a crack, and when it bounces back, it makes another, like a child's clicker toy. So for each muscle contraction it gets two clicks and by varying the muscle's contracting speed it can send a message. The more clicks per second there are, the more detailed the message can be; as there are fifteen hundred known species of cicada, the need for a specific song to attract the right mate is all-important. In fact cicadas have evolved to click faster and faster as they compete for call-signs. By measuring their buzz rates it's possible to discover that some cicadas can click more than a thousand times a second, which would mean contracting their muscles far faster than is physiologically possible – so how do they do it? The 'tymbal' of fast

After anything up to fifteen years maturing beneath the soil, a cicada climbs up to a twig, emerging to adulthood as the noisiest insect in the forest.

clickers has a characteristic pattern of tiny ribs on it, each of which buckles in turn, so producing a much larger series of clicks for every muscle pull. With their sensitive listening organs, cicadas can distinguish each other's call and so lure the right kind of mate. But, alas for the cicada, there are so many of them at it that this alone simply isn't enough. They have to divide the day up into shifts.

I could time my day by the 'six o'clock cicada' which roused me from my Borneo bed, and when I heard something like a miniature chain saw start up I knew that supper would not be far away. To improve the distance over which their calls can be heard, male cicadas will gather together in groups of the same species to chorus in a tree crown. Females attracted by the din, fly to the tree and land in its branches, where they will signal to the males by flicking their wings. A prospective suitor sidles up and in some species a staring match then begins, with the insects standing face to face and utterly motionless. This may go on for several hours before they move to the final act.

I think nightfall in the forest is one of its most enchanting times. The colours of the sky above the canopy delight my eyes and the smell of evening fragrances from nocturnally opening flowers tantalize me as well as the bats and moths, no doubt, that seek their nectar in the dark. But most enthralling of all is the night-time orchestra of frogs and toads. Not all forests are equally musical, and there is none better than that near Mount Mulu in Borneo. These are rich forests indeed, boasting numerous species of amphibian songsters. Again different species call at different times the better to be heard, but as the evening progresses, more and more join the chorus, so that shortly after dark the variety and sheer volume of calls are hard to believe. This is no music to send you off to sleep. In the space of about an hour the amphibian orchestra changes its tune, so that between dusk and darkness a great range of piping calls, yelps and croaks assaults the ear before a more regular theme settles down to last the night. Many of the smaller frogs, with throat sacs filled to bursting like miniature balloons, can make tiny calls as piercing as any calculator's bleeping alarm: a large, modern supermarket checkout, with its dozen or so beeping electronic cash registers, is very reminiscent of a collection of calling tropical frogs.

Spending a night in the forest canopy soon reveals that many of these callers are in fact in the tree crowns. Many tropical tree frogs produce separate components of their calls to repel males and attract females. The male coqui frog from the rainforests of Puerto Rico begins his evening's singing by marching to his usual calling spot and setting up a territory with a repeated 'ko' note. If answering males are too close together, they will come to blows amongst the branches until one gives way. After about an hour of this, he will begin to add a 'kee' component to his song, so that a 'ko-kee' note begins to fill the forest. This second part is designed to attract a mate. Females of the species will not move towards males making only the 'ko' note as they know they are otherwise occupied. When

they hear the 'kee' they know they are in with a chance, and advance towards him. But amongst the trees there may be many different species in the frog chorus all calling at once and varying their songs similarly, so picking out a partner could be a little confusing. The female coqui frog solves the problem by being remarkably deaf: her ears are highly specialized, and though she can hear calls of a wider range, they are most sensitively tuned to her species' own love song and those of no other.

Communication by means of sound remains the privilege of animals, but it is not only they that need to convey their breeding condition, to mate, and to provide for their offspring. Trees, too, must compete to breed, but they have no voice at all with which to lure the opposite sex, nor can they walk about to find one. Unable to move, they indulge in sex by proxy, broadcasting their needs over long distances to attract messengers that help them reproduce, and scatter their seed. High above ground, within the secret world of the canopy, until quite recently the sex lives of the giant rainforest trees remained tantalizingly beyond our knowledge. To lure and encourage the loyalty of their helpers we could guess they offered a multitude of sweet morsels, and filled the canopy with tempting colours and fragrances. Yet who they mean to attract and whether their desires are met remains one of the world's most intriguing biological mysteries for mankind, and one which is intimately connected to the survival of the great forests themselves.

In the Costa Rican forest, a male dink frog appears ready to burst with the effort of calling up a mate; but part of his message is to keep other males away.

6 | The Flowering of the Forest

High above ground and out of sight from anyone walking on the rainforest floor, giant trees conduct their sex lives concealed within the privacy of the canopy. The forest understorey is, by comparison, a gloomy place of almost unrelieved green. A few flowers do grow here on small trees and shrubs, and a few others grow out directly from the bark of certain trees. Where they do occur they provide startling brightness, perhaps brilliant red like the starburst clusters of *Brownearosa-de-Monte* flowers, or the orange and yellow of *Heliconia*'s spiky, cockatoo-crest bract. Some, appropriately coloured, look like a human pout and are known affectionately as 'hot lips' flowers. Walking through rainforest in various parts of the world I could find such flowers at arm's reach, and gently part their bright petals with my hand to see what was inside. And of course it is comparatively easy to watch and see what bees and birds come to visit them here at ground level.

By comparison, almost nothing is known about the flowers the majority of giant trees hold up to the sun, and still less about who their visitors might be. The reason for this is not surprising. Walking through the understorey the only indications I had that a crown high above might be in bloom were fallen flowers around me, and even then it was surprisingly difficult to be sure which tree the flowers came from, if in fact they were tree flowers: they may have fallen from a vine sprawling through the branches. Occasionally I found white flowers, still strongly scented, others of lavender blue or perhaps bright yellow, their little spiky stamens now lying useless, the pollen gone. From the base of some, where the petals joined, I could squeeze sweet nectar, a pleasant taste after the salty sweat produced by my own exertions.

Climbing uphill in rainforest is hard work but is often rewarded with a view out over the canopy due to a tree fall or perhaps a landslide. Most times the sights displayed are not valleys and hillsides swathed in pale flowers, as it might be in many temperate forests, but great upwellings of colour from individual flowering trees and vines, isolated fountains of deep reds, purples or yellows rising above the canopy on the huge emergents.

The flowering cycles of these giant trees have always been something of a puzzle. In lowland rainforests where the temperature fluctuates little either side of very warm and rain falls throughout the year, most trees seem to flower without any obvious pattern, perhaps missing several years, then flowering, then not flowering for years more. Unusual seasonal changes, such as a dry spell, may

A view from a hillside or a flight in a plane generally offers the only chance of seeing rainforest trees in flower. How such trees conduct their sex lives remains a mystery, the key to which is crucial to the forests' preservation.

act as a trigger, but the flowering of some trees in these forests seems to be controlled by very strange phenomena. It is claimed that one tree in South East Asia only flowers after being bathed in ozone from electrical discharges when lightning strikes a tree nearby. It flowers within hours of the event, sets fruit, and then will not flower again until another severe storm sends more lightning bolts close by. *Tachigalia* trees in Central America count the years with some kind of internal clock, flowering all together just once, and then dying en masse for no apparent reason once they have fruited. The bamboo forests of Indo-China do the same, to the detriment of pandas depending on them for food. However, in the rainforests of Malaysia and Indonesia, every five or six years an extraordinary synchronized event occurs. Over huge areas of the forest and at some unknown signal, thousands upon thousands of trees of many different species inexplicably burst into flower, all at the same time.

The vast scale of this flowering is unique to these forests, sometimes covering hundreds of square kilometres. It involves one genus of tree which dominates the environment there, the dipterocarps. Some of the tallest trees and the finest hardwoods in the rainforests of the Far East are dipterocarps, so named after their twin-winged seeds which spin their way to the ground. They represent a pinnacle of arboreal evolution: many tower seventy metres high or more, spreading majestic crowns above their lesser neighbours. Such excellent timber is of great use to mankind, and with little regard to future supplies these valuable trees, like the *Shorea*, are being felled apace; most will have vanished from the earth by the end of this century. To discover how such trees reproduce and how the forest is sustained is therefore of vital importance if we are to continue to enjoy beautifully grained veneers on our furniture, strong hardwood timbers for our window frames, plywoods for our shop fittings and lasting joinery in our buildings of tomorrow, to say

To get a close look at a tree's flowers remains the goal of many an arboreal naturalist. Many flowers, like these of the cannonball tree, are high above ground and virtually impossible to get at. The design of flowers lends a clue to the identification of their pollinators, and to how the trees pass their genes around.

nothing of enjoying the forests themselves. But, as we shall see, the complexity of the mechanisms involved between plant and pollinator require patient enquiry to unravel, demanding the one ingredient neither the scientists nor the rainforests have on their side – time.

What advantage do all these dipterocarps gain by flowering together? They don't in fact flower quite simultaneously but in a staggered sequence, so that as the blooms of one species begin to fade, another comes into flower and so on over a period of three to four months, filling the forest with heavy scent. The scientists at the Forestry Research Institute at Kepong in Malaysia were intrigued to know the cause and in the 1970s they set about trying to explore the trees' sex lives. At first it was believed the mass flowering was linked to wind pollination: by all flowering together the trees ensured that there would be plenty of pollen in the air to be carried from one flower to another for successful fertilization. The real story turned out to be very different.

As mass flowering occurred only at intervals of several years, the scientists had to keep a regular watch on the forest roof with binoculars to be ready for it when it came. An unusually dry spell in January 1976 alerted them, and when the first flowers appeared in February they were well prepared. It was obviously important to study the flowers while they were on the trees and not wait till they had fallen, for by then pollination would have taken place. And the only way to find out who the trees were spreading their flowers for was to get up into the canopy. Bolting ladders to the tree trunks would only give access to the centre of a tree, whereas the flowers were on the outer fringes of the crowns. A new method of access had to be found.

With the help of Dr Peter Ashton from the University of Aberdeen in Scotland, an extraordinary bosun's chair system was deployed. First, a tree climber scaled a tree and placed a block and tackle on one of the sturdier branches. A rope was then reeved through the block and brought down to the ground where it was attached to the middle of a large extendable aluminium boom resembling a ship's spar. On one end another block and tackle was attached and to this the bosun's chair, in which an observer could sit, was fixed. By heaving on a jack, the boom could be hauled up into the canopy and could be swung round by a rope attached to the end opposite the bosun's chair. Into this precarious contraption an intrepid scientist climbed and gradually rose into the canopy, strapped into the swaying chairlift. Suspended beneath the boom like a counterweight in some gigantic balance, the airborne human veered towards the flowers on the fringe of nearby crowns and at last could get a close look at what was going on.

Most trees bloomed for only fifteen to twenty days, depending on the species, and anything up to four million flowers were put forth per tree. Some opened 650,000 flowers in one day, collectively producing litres and litres of nectar. However, using the bosun's

chair arrangement safely during the day was somewhat confounded by one unexpected fact: the flowers seemed to open only at night. Each morning countless blooms had fallen to the ground, an exotic floor covering, at least for humans. But there was still a heady fragrance in the air. Surely it could not have been offered merely to the wind? It must have been there to attract some other kind of pollinator, perhaps an insect. Using binoculars next day, they could see numerous bees and small flies cruising over the tree crowns but they ceased to be active at sunset, when the flowers were just opening. Swaying about high in the trees on the end of a pole in daylight was bad enough, but at night it tested the most enthusiastic of volunteers. Nevertheless, ascend they did and what they found in the flowers was very surprising. They were full of thrips.

Thrips are minute insects barely two millimetres long; superficially they resemble a microscopic earwig, without pincers but sporting tiny feathery wings. Most of us will have little interest in them other than as garden pests of onions or roses, but in South East Asia, the forest could not survive without them. After many nights in the canopy the scientists began to piece the story together.

When the flowers opened, adult thrips flying about the trees were attracted by their scent, flew into them and crawled into the crevices between the petals. Some of the larger thrips such as *Megalurothrips*, which is still not very large, even engaged in battles and chased off other thrips that tried to enter their flower. Inside the flowers the thrips began to feed on soft petal tissue and pollen that had fallen from the stamens onto a special meshwork of anthers where the thrips crawled. The pollen grains were covered in oil droplets which made them sticky and some stuck to the thrips. Here at last was the answer to how the trees were pollinated: when the thrips flew out, they would carry pollen to another tree and so act as the pollinating agent. But the problem was – they didn't leave the flowers.

Each morning the flowers rained to the forest floor with their small cargo of two or three thrips, and there the minute insects remained until evening. Thrips find the smell of dipterocarp flowers irresistible and only in the evening, when the next crop of flowers opened, were they lured back by the strong scent floating down from the canopy. On their tiny wings millions and millions of thrips slowly spiralled up in search of open flowers. Most landed on the protruding stigma of a new bloom and there preened themselves of any pollen grains. Some of these grains would lodge on the stigma, so fertilizing the flower.

However, if the thrips merely flew back to the tree from which they had fallen, the tree would simply be pollinating itself and the purpose of mass flowering would be defeated. Fortunately, the tiny thrips are so small that even light wind currents are too much for them, and like plankton in an aerial ocean they are wafted over the tree crowns and so disperse the pollen grains to neighbouring trees.

Other questions remained to be answered. For the thrips to be of

use to the trees as pollinators they would have to reproduce explosively to keep pace with the rate of new flower production. By breeding the little thrips in laboratory conditions, it was discovered they complete their life cycle from egg to adult in just eight days, so that a few hundred thrips laying eggs in the flowers would produce millions more within a month. It transpired that some flowers would never open, acting solely as enclosed thrip-breeding sites. The sequential flowering of the dipterocarp trees gives the thrip population plenty of time to catch up and enables many species of tree to make use of the same abundant pollinator over a relatively short span. But what happens to the thrips when the mass flowering is over? Six years is a long time to wait until the next floral dance. Millions and millions of them will die, but there seem to be a sufficient number of suitable trees where they can feed and breed to maintain a residual population until the next mass flowering, and thrip numbers can once again go through the roof.

Incredibly, all the trees synchronize the production of their seeds as well, so that those which are last in the sequential queue for pollination set seed much faster than those at the head of it, enabling them all to drop their seeds together and swamp any would-be predators that may wish to eat them or the young seedlings that would later develop. As there is little wind in the lower forest to disperse their falling winged seeds, and because there are so many of them, the distribution of dipterocarps tends to be in clumps and not in scattered individuals, as with many other rainforest trees.

For most other trees requiring efficient fertilization, relying on pollen-laden thrips wafting through the tree crowns is a method fraught with uncertainty. The wind may blow the wrong way, or the insects may be more attracted to another tree, or the nearest available sexual partner may be hundreds of metres or even as much as a kilometre away, separated by numerous other trees of totally different species. Because of the distance a pollinator would have to travel between flowering crowns, it was believed for a long time that most species of rainforest tree did simply rely on insects to transfer pollen amongst the flowers within their own crown: in this way they had the benefit of certain fertilization even if they lacked the mixing of genetic information that pollen from different individual trees would bestow.

However, once experiments were begun on trees in the canopy, it was found that surprisingly few trees would produce fruit if fertilized with their own pollen: they did require cross-fertilization. Some had even evolved separate male and female trees, each producing male-only flowers with pollen, or female flowers waiting to receive it. Such trees are called 'dioecious' after the Greek word meaning two houses. Clearly those in the female-only house could not fertilize themselves as they produced no pollen, so they must rely on some agent to bring it to them.

To ensure that precious genes are delivered into the desired flowers of widely separated trees requires a more devoted pollen

messenger than a feebly flying thrip. But to exploit an animal pollinator, a plant must overcome several problems. First it must entice the carrier into its flowers, then it must ensure that it picks up pollen, and finally it must encourage the carrier to visit the flowers of another plant of the same species.

If I were a flower, what would I do to attract an insect? When I take a walk through the forest, the dank and sometimes musty smell of the understorey is occasionally brightened with a sweet odour. Like me, insects are attracted by fragrant perfumes, and like me they may search the greenery to find the source of the smell. It is hard to spot an individual plant in the tangle of vines and bushes, but fortunately I have colour vision and I can quickly spy a brightly coloured flower. So can birds and insects, so flowers employ colour to enable their pollinators to home in on them. As I walk up to the flower and thrust my nose into it to sniff its scent, pollen sticks to my skin and goes up my nostrils. I pull away and sneeze. If I walk on to another shrub of the same species and do the same thing, I would be acting as a pretty efficient animal dispersal agent; but of course the flowers were not designed for my nose and I failed to get any tangible reward. To do that I would have to pick the flower and suck a little of its nectar, but in doing so I would destroy it.

There is only one purpose behind the flower's attractions: the collection and transfer of pollen. Birds and insects need more than aesthetic pleasure to make their visit worthwhile. So for them the flower's reward is readily accessible. It can take several forms. Nectar is really just sugary water, easy for a plant to produce, so it is the most common reward. Often the nectar has body-building proteins added to supplement the diet of those species which largely depend upon it for food, such as hummingbirds. Pollen, too, can be rewarding as it is highly nutritious; alternatively, a flower can make its petals tasty.

Were I to try to enter a flower it would quickly be broken apart. So, flowers must design themselves to suit their customers, with mechanisms to ensure that their precious dust is spread on the right messenger to carry it to others of their kind. Thus a small trumpet may befit a bee or hummingbird, but stout petals with hooks may be needed to help a perching bird or bat.

Picking my way along an animal trail through the shrubs on the forest floor, I might come across a bright splash of floral colour here and there. Many of these are not single flowers but bunches of them massed together in what is called an inflorescence; they make a bigger show in the poorly lit understorey and so are easier to see. They may also be rich in nectar. Watching one of these, I might see a bean-sized bee come buzzing in and scramble about the petals from flower to flower, and then disappear through the forest, weaving through the tree trunks with great singleness of purpose. As there are so few clumps of flowers here these bees, and many other pollinators in the forest basement, memorize the location of inflorescences and fly on a daily round, visiting each one. Because

Brownea flowers lend brightness to the largely flowerless understorey. Few trees in the canopy produce flowers such as these: their colour attracts hummingbirds which their stamens then dust with pollen.

this behaviour resembles a hunter's trapping round, such pollinators are known as 'trapliners'.

High in the canopy, too, the most obvious pollinators seem to be bees who are attracted to flowers in various shades of yellow or blue; the most powerful of these may trapline between tree crowns rather than inflorescences. Pollen is also used as a food by insects and many plants provide it abundantly as a bribe to bees or beetles. Some flowers offer fatty oils to bees which have special furry hind legs to collect it; other flowers ooze waxes and resins which insects find useful in nest building, particularly in the wet tropics.

Hummingbirds, such as the hermits which flit about in the lower strata of Central American rainforests, also adopt a traplining technique and learn the route they must follow between the flowers, sometimes covering long distances in the process. In the tropics, birds may be almost as important as insects in pollination, perhaps assisting fifty per cent of plants. As birds generally fly in the daytime, most flowers carrying nectar for them open during the day and not at night. Birds can see very well but have a poor sense of smell, so brightly coloured flowers are a better advertisement for them as well as bees, and few bird-pollinated flowers have strong scents.

Watching hummingbirds at work is a delightful pastime. Once in Panama, I had the good fortune to spend some time observing the flowers of *Brownearosa-de-Monte*, each with its own long spiky stamen on which the pollen sits. Crouched in the bushes beside the

<Brownea> tree I sat down to wait and watch. Hummingbird eye pigments respond well to red and so guide the birds to the flowers which contrast strongly with the predominantly green background. After some minutes a long-tailed hermit, emerald green with a white tip to its tail, announced itself with a buzz of wings, and flashed brilliantly into view, materializing briefly in front of the *Brownea* flowers to insert its curved beak deep inside a number of them, gathering their copious nectar. While the bird drank, the flower dusted its head and breast feathers with plenty of pollen from its long stamens. Then the hummingbird vanished as quickly as it had come to visit other flowers elsewhere, but now laden with the *Brownea*'s pollen. On another occasion I was wearing a red sweatshirt with a large Operation Drake logo on the front. Suddenly I was surprised by a weaving hermit hummingbird which zoomed in to take a look. Hovering at arm's length, it closely inspected my face and chest and then darted in to take a look at the logo. Realising its mistake, it flashed away into the forest, no doubt a little puzzled.

Since hummers do not perch, 'their' flowers provide no landing platform as do many bee-pollinated flowers. But other birds are not as adept at flying as hummingbirds and the flowers they use are equipped with tough petals, or else flower close to useful twigs for the birds to perch on.

In temperate lands flowering seasons are short and birds which relied on flowers as a food source would go hungry for most of the

The furry tongue of a rainbow lorikeet helps it to lap nectar from flowers in Australia's rainforests.

year; but in the tropics nectar is available all year round and bird pollination has developed best there. There are eight families of birds which specialize in nectar-gathering and all are generally localized in quite different parts of the world, suggesting that nectar-feeding has evolved independently in different groups of animals. Most of them have either a U-shaped tongue to suck up nectar by capillary action, or tongues tipped with brush-like projections to hold the liquid they lick so deeply from the flowers.

There are three hundred species of hummingbirds in the Neotropics alone. The sunbirds of Africa and Asia are their Old World equivalents, possessing long thin beaks, often curved to fit their respective flowers. Sunbirds rarely hover but they do rival hummingbirds for brilliance and flying ability as they flash between flowers high on a tree crown. There are few purely nectar-feeding birds in the Far East but further south, in the northern rainforests of Australia, a wealth of honeycreepers and nectar-feeding lorikeets are to be found. These small, brush-tongued parrots are perhaps the most spectacularly coloured birds in the world. They pick their way through the branches, chewing petals off flowers and nipping buds off, too, to get at the rich store inside. Their furry tongue-tip is also used to pack pollen into a neat ball for swallowing, and through these they obtain much of their protein; indeed the purple-crowned lorikeet feeds on little else.

The large fast-flying bees traplining in the canopy mostly lead solitary lives. They tend to be opportunists, seeking pollen or nectar where they can; but there is intense competition for resources, so some of them defend their patch, like the male *Centris* bees in Costa Rica. Other solitary bees which dare to intrude are aggressively repelled and may be forced to visit different trees. Some bee species, however, team up together in mixed groups of anything between fifteen and three hundred, and patrol the canopy like a bunch of thugs. The heavy mob persuade the solitary bees to move by head-butting them with frightening force. I have even received the same treatment myself from an extremely irritated solitary carpenter bee.

From the tree's point of view, all this fighting over flowers makes perfect sense, as it increases the chances of bees having to buzz off to other trees, thereby improving the possibility of some of the tree's pollen being carried to another of its own species elsewhere. It is even conceivable that trees may have evolved to encourage all comers in the canopy with their massive colourful crowns with just this purpose in mind. By restricting the nectar they provide, the resulting scramble for it ensures that some bee species will get fed up and try the trees somewhere else, rather like the way humans behave at the January sales.

Alas for man, he is not good at scrambling around the fringes of tree crowns. Since the earliest days of tropical science those who have wished to investigate the most intimate aspects of the sex life of high rainforest trees have been doomed to frustration and ignorance, peering through the obscuring foliage at bees, birds and bats

forty metres above. Hanging precariously from an aluminium pole could only provide access to a few trees, and walkways had other limitations. To be able to gain access to every part of the forest roof in three dimensions is the arboreal naturalist's dream. What is needed is some method of floating around the edges of tree crowns and over the top as well. In Costa Rica's forests in Central America, an American biologist has invented a way of doing just that.

In 1978 Don Perry was studying the pollination biology of canopy trees in the Costa Rican rainforest near the Organization of Tropical Studies' Research Station at La Selva. From a platform thirty metres up, he noticed two huge almendro trees towering over the forest nearby. These trees have such strong wood that it can resist nails hammered into it, so he reasoned that they might be strong enough to support a tensioned rope web, strung out across the canopy, from which he could suspend himself like a spider with access to the crowns in between. In 1979, with engineer John Williams, he set about building it.

Using a crossbow they fired ropes over the branches of the almendro trees, climbed the ropes and attached pulley blocks in the crown of each tree. Through these three hundred and fifty metres of strong sailboat rope was run, creating a continuous, tensioned triangle of rope, with an almendro at two angles and a platform in a monkey pot tree at the apex. By pulling from the platform, the rope could be moved round clockwise or anti-clockwise through the pulleys and around the triangle. Then they ran a second rope from the monkey pot tree across to the baseline rope on the far side of the triangle between the two other trees. By pulling this baseline rope round to the left or right, the new internal rope could be swept across the canopy. Sitting in a harness attached to this central rope by a rolling wheel, Don Perry hoped to coast out to any part of the canopy within the triangle. The whole web was tensioned like a bowstring. How much would it sag with his weight? Would the branches be strong enough to take the strain as he launched out over the forest roof? There was only one way to find out.

Poised on the edge of the platform, he clipped his harness to the roller and prepared to commit his life to the canopy. A safety rope was tied on so that he could be hauled back should danger threaten at any point, but if the web broke between the supporting trees as he hung beneath it there would be no chance of pulling him back in time. There would be a loud report as the ropes snapped, and he would fall. There was a chance that he would not be injured too badly if he landed in a tree crown, perhaps a leg broken or ribs fractured against the heavy branches. If he slipped down through the crown, however, he would plummet to the forest floor and never climb again. He sat down in the harness, letting the central rope take his weight and, nodding to his partner, swung out over the abyss. The wheel made a slight rumbling noise as it rolled out along the rope, which sagged into a shallow V as he coasted into the centre of the triangle. There he stopped and twisted gently round. His feet

Don Perry dices with death on his rope web above the Costa Rican forest. From here he can scoop messenger insects out of the air or peer into a flowering tree crown, gaining a view of Nature unseen by humankind before.

had almost touched the tops of some of the trees he had passed over on the slow roll out. The gentle buzzing sounds of the forest roof surrounded him, interspersed with the occasional bird call. Bees flew past almost at arm's reach over patches of flowers spread beneath. He was enveloped in the scent-rich air floating on a light breeze. It worked.

Carrying a net on a long pole he could scoop insects out of the air or hang close by a flowering branch and peer into its blooms. Epiphytes on numerous tree limbs were at arm's length, and fruits normally only accessible to an agile spider monkey or chestnut-mandibled toucan were there for the plucking. And more than that, by using a vertical climbing rope and jumars he could inch-worm his way downwards too, perhaps into a tree crown or below it to the forest floor, and back again, so having remarkable access to a volume of forest almost half the size of a football pitch and thirty metres deep. Such a circus trapeze act is not for the faint-hearted and depends, as do all canopy access techniques, on a good head for heights and scrupulous adherence to safety standards to ensure that a fatal fall does not occur. At last, with a way of getting close to the crowns of several trees, a start could be made in unravelling who their pollinators might be.

Around May in Costa Rica the almendro comes into bloom, producing well over half a million flowers in its crown during its two-month flowering period, with twenty thousand open on any one day. This is the wet season, when the numbers of bees in the canopy are at a seasonal low. Rather than flowering all together, when there would not be enough bees to cope, the almendro trees flower one after the other, with a little overlap, so increasing the chances of the few bees available transferring pollen from one tree to another during the flowering period.

Opening around sunrise, the pinkish-lavender flowers release a strong scent, rather like that of sweet peas, which fills the canopy for a wide distance around. Nectar is produced for only two hours after the flowers open and numerous bees scramble in the rush to get it, but only the larger bees seem to release the mechanism for dusting their bellies with almendro pollen. Perry discovered that many bees carried pollen from different plant species but usually in different positions on their bodies. As the bees foraged over the canopy trees, the pollen they were carrying would be placed on correspondingly positioned female receptive parts of the flowers they were visiting, so fertilizing them. By placing the pollen on different parts of the body, and matching the position of female receptive stigmas to receive it, each tree ensures that it receives only its own pollen. Sweeping his net through the crowns of the almendro trees, he found *Epicharis metatarsalis*, a large, powerfully flying bee that ranged widely over the crowns of many trees. This bee alone carried six different kinds of pollen, each more or less placed on a different part of its body. Perry also found, by artificial fertilization, that almendro trees cannot be fertilized by their own pollen. Because

each tree supplies only a limited amount of nectar, the almendro encourages bees to shop around, so it can rely on receiving visits from pollen-bearing bees that have found insufficient nectar at other almendro trees.

Spectacularly advertising their goods in the floral shop window is a fine way for trees to attract their pollinators, but they may also attract less welcome visitors. There are nectar and pollen robbers who plunder the rewards but serve no purpose as pollen carriers, either because they do not come into contact with the pollen at all, merely raiding the nectar supply through an alternative route to the one the tree intended, or because they forage solely in one tree crown, refusing to move. By shaping their flowers specifically to suit the best pollinators, many plants can exclude these unwanted takers, but there are often specialists who, finding the front door barred, manage to get in round the back.

In the tropics almost all the pollen robbers are female, highly social, stingless bees in the genus *Trigona*: hardly any solitary bees are known to be robbers apart from the carpenter bee. Many of these robbers have chewing mouthparts designed for mining resin from woody plants but their jaws are also ideal for tearing soft flowers apart. Nectar robbers usually attack bird-pollinated flowers as they bear larger quantities of the sweet energy. Many bees also dine on protein-rich pollen as a body-building food, and when first I

Trigonid bees raiding a passion flower. Their object is robbery of a plant's nectar and pollen supplies – rarely do they fertilize it. To protect their flowers from these raiders, many plants employ ant guards, armour-plate their petals, or lure the robbers away with gifts.

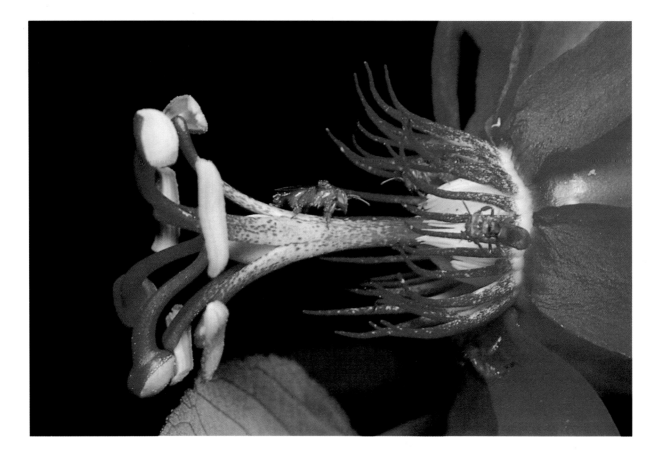

climbed into the forest roof I had the opportunity to study a tree which turned out to have an intriguing way of coping with pollen robbers. It gave them all a gift.

When lightweight walkways were first strung through the rain-forest canopy in Panama on Operation Drake we were delighted to discover that a number of trees within arm's reach were covered in drooping inflorescences of the bright yellow *Swartzia panamensis* flowers. Volunteers, including myself, were directed by botanists to watch them from the walkway. Armed with a pair of binoculars, a stopwatch and a notepad, I spent many enjoyable hours recording who the flowers' visitors might be and what they would do once they decided to pay a call. There were many distractions during a morning spent on the walkway. As the trees moved in answer to the winds, the walkway also moved. Large blue *Morpho* butterflies would flash brilliantly amongst the leaves. Some macaws might settle, out of sight, in a nearby tree for a squabbling match, or a bird wave would noisily chatter its way through the tree crowns. Concentrating on the flowers proved more exhausting than expected, as large numbers of small bees visited them busily; all had to be noted carefully, and their behaviour watched closely to see what they were doing. But apart from bouts of cramp and the occasional inquisitive mosquito, time would pass very pleasantly.

Though scented and coloured to attract insects, the *Swartzia*'s buttercup-sized flowers provided pollen and not nectar as their main reward. Strangely, there appeared to be two bunches of it to each flower. Near the top of the flower was a bunch of untidy, tangled stamens covered in rather poor quality pollen, which was probably infertile. In the lower part was another small line of stamens, sticking out like tiny fingers tipped with what appeared to be healthy pollen, and here the female part of the flower or stigma was concealed, waiting to receive a delivery of fertile pollen from another *Swartzia* tree. Shortly after dawn, numerous small bees arrived, thirteen different species in all, some tiny and black, others iridescent green, some with yellow-coloured bottoms and another bee, much larger than the rest, with a huge amber behind. Whilst most of the bees seemed to move systematically from one flower to another and rarely left the tree crown on which they were foraging, the 'huge' bee, as we called it – in fact a species of *Eulaema* – homed in from some distance away, weaving between the tree crowns like a miniature helicopter to land with devastating effect on any other smaller bees already gathering pollen on its chosen flower.

Each of the thirteen species appeared to have a distinct behaviour on landing. Most aimed for the haphazard collection of stamens in the upper section of the flower, and only a few landed on the lower section with the waiting stigma. Only these, therefore, could be potential pollinators, as it was only here that they could be powdered with the potentially fertile pollen grains. But most of these bees were *Trigona nigerima*, a well known pollen robber that sallied forth from tree-top nests and rarely ventured far once it had found a

good food source such as a *Swartzia* tree. So they could be ruled out. Only the enormous *Eulaema* seemed a likely candidate. As it embraced the flowers, gathering food from the top bunch of stamens, the lower spiky section brushed its abdomen, which fitted perfectly against the fertile pollen grains. By providing a 'gift' of abundant low-grade pollen, *Swartzia* was able to draw off potential 'robbers' too small to act as pollinators, and the fertile pollen grains were thus left largely intact for the occasional visits by the bee most likely to carry its genes to another tree in the area, the powerful *Eulaema*.

Since insects are the most numerous animals in the rainforest, it is not surprising that most plants there should have chosen them as pollinators; in the wettest Costa Rican forests, ninety per cent of trees are insect-pollinated. Some trees produce white foul-smelling flowers rich in pollen to attract beetles which enjoy eating it. Red or orange flowers with long tubes may be designed to attract butterflies, as they see these colours as well as birds and have a long proboscis to probe for the nectar denied to other, less well equipped insects. These flowers may have a small landing stage, since butterflies prefer to alight whilst feeding, but those flowers destined to attract hawkmoths have none, as these insects usually hover like hummingbirds in front of the flowers and probe them with their extra long proboscis. In Madagascar's rainforests the orchid *Angraecum sesquipedale* has a tube-shaped flower twenty-five or thirty centimetres deep, and is exclusively pollinated by the hawkmoth *Xanthopan morgani praedicta*. By evolving an ever-longer proboscis to match the lengthening flower, the hawkmoth reserves for itself an exclusive food supply, making it increasingly dependent and therefore, from the plant's point of view, a more reliable pollinator.

As hawkmoths fly at night 'their' flowers only open then and, having no need of bright colours which could not be seen, are usually white. As if to compensate for the lack of visual clues, they produce a thick, sickly smelling perfume which, to an ill-equipped human nose, fills only the air round about the tree but will draw hawkmoths from far and wide.

As darkness falls and the twittering songs and whistles of birdlife die down, bats appear on silent wings, fluttering over the tree crowns. Many of them will seek fruit or tiny insects but a number feast on nectar and pollen, and some even dine on the flowers themselves. Bat pollination is essentially a tropical phenomenon. In forests from West Africa to northern Australia some flying foxes obtain almost all their protein from pollen and eat little else, other than nectar. The Macroglossids are part of this group and, as their name implies, they have very long tongues, sometimes tipped with papillae, with which to reach into the flowers. The flying foxes never reached as far as the Americas, so there the smaller Microchiroptera, which are insectivorous in the forests outside that area, evolved into fruit-eaters as well as pollen- and nectar-feeders.

Most bat-pollinated plants are found high in the canopy. Here trees, lianas and occasionally epiphytes hang large inflorescences on long pendulous stems, set well clear of the surrounding foliage so as to give the bats plenty of flying room. In many bat-pollinated trees, the flowers are clustered on branch-tips so that the bats may land on nearby twigs. Such trees often seem to produce their flowers when they have no leaves, perhaps to give the bats a better view and less restricted surroundings in which to fly.

Because bat flowers open at night they too tend to be drab in colour but issue an odour rather like sour milk or slightly sweaty feet. Bats are attracted to this – many smell rather like that themselves. The flowers receive them in a number of guises. There are those that resemble a trumpet with a large open mouth which engulfs the bat's head as it reaches inside in search of nectar. In the shrub *Oroxylum* there is a tipping mechanism which, triggered by the arrival of a bat of the correct weight, in this case *Eonycteris*, tips the trumpet forward, delivering nectar. Smaller bats are too light to tip the flower and larger bats cannot get their noses into it, so the flower singles out its own pollinator. Other bat flowers look like shaving brushes; in fact they are tightly bunched masses of stamens, rich in pollen. Finally, there are those which consist of numerous small flowers packed together into a ball-like inflorescence or capitulum. In these there is a division of labour amongst the flowers, some producing nectar, others designed to dust the bat with pollen on its nocturnal visit.

Parkia trees are found in tropical rainforests all over the world – thirty species have so far been discovered – and nearly all of them produce capitulums, held outside the tree crown on a long woody stem; in some species they stick up above the crown, in others they hang below it. Each capitulum has a fringe of long stringy stamens; in flower the tree looks just as if it has a collection of elongated tennis balls wearing furry hats sticking out of it.

Helen Hopkins and her husband Michael, researchers from the University of Oxford, knew that bats were active in *Parkia* pollination but were faced with a major problem. They couldn't see the bats and didn't know which species was involved. Some trees grew to over forty metres and at night, when the bats were out doing a little fertilizing, it was impossible to spot them. So they resorted to a useful piece of modern science, an image intensifier or nightscope, to reveal all. These devices magnify the light available from stars and the moon to such an extent that tree tops and bats can be perfectly visible in total darkness.

The Hopkinses managed to observe bats visiting the flowers of eleven tropical American species of *Parkia*. To get specimens of the flowers themselves, they used the single rope technique, with harness and jumars. Once in the crowns it was possible, though with difficulty, to snip off the strange inflorences with a long pruner pole and return with them to the ground where they could be taken apart to see how they were made. Capturing the bats that visited them

was just as difficult. Using a longbow, they fired lines over the tree limbs and hauled fine mesh nets up into the canopy braced with rods at either end to keep them taut. Into these bats would fly, and identifications could be made once they had been lowered to the ground: almost all were a variety of leaf-nosed bat. More importantly, it was possible to see what pollen they were carrying and therefore get an insight into which trees they had been visiting before this one.

Though each tree was slightly different, the capitulums on most trees consisted of a fringe of long infertile stamens at the top, a collection of flowers beneath which produced copious amounts of nectar, and below them, a larger section of tiny fertile red flowers — up to two thousand of them — with plenty of pollen. Watching the bats revealed that as they came in to land they did a 180-degree flip to land face downwards clutching at the fringe with their hind legs: the woody stem would have given the bats no purchase for their claws. The fringe may also act as an umbrella to prevent the nectar inside the flowers from being diluted during tropical downpours.

Once on the fringe the bats leaned over to lick nectar from the flowers concealed below it, leaning so far that their head and neck became thoroughly coated in yellow pollen from the fertile flowers in the lowest section of the ball. After a few seconds of frantic licking the bats dropped away and flew to another capitulum. In large *Parkia* trees several hundred bats may flock into the same tree, embarking on an orgy of nectar and pollen gluttony, but in others only a few flowers are produced and the bats visit in smaller numbers. Other nocturnal visitors try to enjoy the flowers too: kinkajous and possums climb through the tree tops and balance precariously to make a grab for them, but by placing them outside its crown, the tree ensures that most are inaccessible to mammals that cannot fly, and reserves its flowers for the bats.

There remains one puzzle. Why do the bats spend just a few seconds only at each capitulum, when they could fill themselves by staying longer? One very good reason is that some animals visiting the flowers are not looking for nectar. On one occasion the Hopkinses saw a tree boa move to the tips of branches near to one ball of flowers. Several times it tried unsuccessfully to grab a bat as it came in to land. Other bats mobbed the snake furiously. It moved to a new flower stalk and there it waited. The first bat to come within reach was snatched from the air and with piteous squeaks was dragged back into the tree and strangled. Even possums have been known to capture and kill bats, and no doubt many other tree-living mammals would gratefully eat them, given half a chance. So perhaps the bats prefer not to linger over their food, lest they become a meal themselves.

Bats are not the only mammals to utilize flowers in the canopy. Many monkeys and other non-flying mammals have a taste for nectar too, and even though they are less likely to move long distances, some plants appear to be adapted to using them as their

pollinators. One such plant is the robust canopy liana, *Combretum fruticosum*, which sprawls through riverine tree tops in seasonally flooded forests in South America. The flowers appear yellow-green at first and then change through bright yellow to a deep red as they mature, sticking up like tiny cups in horizontal sprays, secreting large amounts of nectar into their base. When dawn breaks spider monkeys, capuchins or squirrel monkeys may appear and work their way along the flower spikes, eagerly lapping the nectar out of the cups; saddle-back tamarins may also spend most of their feeding time licking the sweet fluids from the flowers. In all cases their muzzles and facial fur become covered in bright pink or orange pollen which they may later transfer to another vine when they set off across the tree crowns in search of more nectar. Though many birds such as parrots, caciques, hummingbirds and oropendolas may feed amongst the vines at the same time as the monkeys, they do not collect pollen on their beaks or feathers, so it seems the flowers are not designed for them.

As *Combretum* flowers become scarce at the end of August, the tree *Quararibea cordata* bursts into a profusion of yellow flowers. These too are like little cups full of nectar and grow directly from stiff horizontal branches, easy of access to a primate during the day or perhaps a passing potto or possum by night. All end up with faces covered in yellow pollen. These floral nectar sources help the animals of the canopy survive when fruit may be seasonally scarce but the importance of non-flying mammals as pollinators has been largely overlooked, due partly to the difficulty of observing them in the obscuring tree crowns and the fact that many of them are nocturnal. Anyone patient enough to spend a night in a flowering *Quararibea* crown is likely to make some fascinating discoveries.

In all cases the animals which visit these flowers are amply rewarded for their services with nectar or pollen, or in some cases with a juicy petal or two. But there is another strategy a few plants employ which saves them the effort of producing any reward at all; this is the art of deception. In Costa Rica there is a tree called *Plumeria* which appears to be pollinated by hawkmoths. Its flowers are very similar to other hawkmoth flowers in that they open at night, are a pale reflective colour, tube-like at the base and produce a strong scent. In April and June the crown of the tree is covered in a mass of these white flowers — and not one of them produces any nectar. The hawkmoths are duped into thinking that they do and by the time they realize they have been fooled it is too late, and they already have a small load of pollen which they may deposit at another deceitful *Plumeria* tree.

Getting access to the tree crowns to study the delights of pollination is not merely for the entertainment of adventurous and somewhat eccentric naturalists. It is a vital component in gaining an understanding of how these forests work, without which we can have little hope of saving them and the millions of species they harbour for the benefit of future generations. That such magnificent

As dark falls, sugar gliders take to the air on cloaks of skin. Lapping nectar at flowers designed to receive them, they collect pollen on their noses, then glide on through the forest to deliver it elsewhere. Without their assistance, some trees would cease to exist.

trees should be dependent on perhaps just a few bees or even tiny thrips for their very existence demonstrates both the complexity and the vulnerability of the forest. Should a particular tree be selectively logged out, then a bee dependent upon its nectar supply at a crucial time of the year when little other food is available may go with it. Other trees may also be reliant on that particular bee as pollinator and if it no longer exists to carry pollen between their crowns, they too are denied a vital link in their reproductive cycle, and may begin to vanish from the forest.

The unforeseen knock-on effects can be considerable. In the past, tropical brazil nut farmers wondered why their trees' multi-million-dollar crop began to fail, until it was shown that the carpenter bees responsible for pollinating the brazil nut trees had vanished along with the forest that used to surround the plantations. Establishing how far bees need to fly on their foraging flights helps to determine optimum sizes for protected areas: some species are believed to cover anything up to ten kilometres in their daily search for the right kind of tree to provide them with the resources they need. Bats too can be vital pollinators of crops important to man. Durian fruits are the oysters of the plant world, either revered as a gastronomic delicacy or reviled as the most revolting thing on earth. Their consumption has been described as eating the most delicious fruit in the world through an old pair of smelly socks.

Nevertheless they are in great demand and international trade in them runs to hundreds of thousands of dollars. It comes as no surprise to find that the durian crop of Malayasia has been steadily falling, along with the gradual disappearance of the pollinator of the tree's flowers, the flying fox bats. Human population pressure on the bats' roosting sites has resulted in a drastic fall in numbers, which is now being reflected in a declining durian crop and falling revenues.

The ultimate aim of attracting pollinators is for the trees, and the plants which reside in their branches, to reproduce themselves. Later they will set seed and then must, as with pollinators, compete for creatures to disperse their seeds to growing sites elsewhere in the forest. Whilst some, like the dipterocarps, may use the indifferent wind, others seduce animals to eat their fruits in the hopes that some of the seeds they contain will survive the gauntlet of crushing teeth and grinding gizzards to germinate away from the parent tree. The appearance of all these seeds in the canopy, often encased in a tasty coating, results in a continuing feast of enormous proportions, stretching from the tip of northern Australia across the jungles of the world all the way to the Amazon. But if you thought that fruit was the only food on the canopy table, you would be very wrong.

With great upwellings of colour, flowering crowns signal to their pollinators that a reward is in store. Few trees use the wind to float their pollen to other trees but often rely on powerfully flying insects, bats or birds.

A red howler monkey will not find all the leaves in the canopy to its taste: many are poisonous, hard to digest and provide little energy. However, some monkeys do specialize in eating highly toxic leaves, aided by bacteria which neutralize the poisons and help to release the leaves' sugars. With a bellyful of slowly decomposing leaves, they are in effect mobile compost heaps.

7 | Feasting in the Tree Crowns

On the tropical island of Mauritius in the Indian Ocean there was recently concern about the fate of the beautiful *Calvaria* trees: no young trees could be found and seeds from the existing ageing specimens refused to germinate. *Calvaria* seemed in danger of disappearing from the island as surely as the dodo had done three hundred years before.

The islanders were determined that another piece of their national heritage should not vanish and called in a botanist to investigate. He found that the germination process of the *Calvaria*, like that of many plants, required the seeds to pass through an animal, but no animal lived on the island that was capable of eating their large, tough capsules. As many creatures had become extinct on Mauritius since human beings arrived, perhaps the one responsible for eating the *Calvaria* seeds no longer existed. Some of the trees were about three hundred years old, few were younger: could it be that the dodo itself had originally been responsible for eating the seeds, so triggering their germination? Alas, none of these extraordinary flightless birds, looking rather like oversized turkeys, would ever wander through the forests of Mauritius again. But perhaps turkeys themselves, with their strong gizzards, could produce the same effect, the botanist suggested. Turkeys were duly force-fed with the seeds and, miraculously, for the first time in centuries, they germinated. The *Calvaria* was saved from the very edge of extinction.

This remarkable story illustrates how closely some trees depend on animals to distribute their seeds and survive. Similarly, the seeds of *Panda oleosa* will only germinate once they have passed through an elephant, and get off to a good start by utilizing the elephant's dung as a food supply. It may well be that many of the larger seeds which drop to the forest floor in Central America were once destined to be picked up by mastodons, huge elephant-like creatures which once roamed the forests there. Should a plant's dispersal agent disappear, as was the case with *Calvaria*, the plant is left stranded. But though the mastodons and many other larger mammals which once lived in the American continent mysteriously became extinct, the plants there which depended on them survived by hedging their bets on a suite of other dispersers, rather than relying on just one. Should one disperser animal then be removed, others may take its place and in the vastness of evolutionary time the plant will attune itself to meet their requirements more closely, and in so doing satisfy its own.

Having gone to all the trouble of getting themselves pollinated, the next problem trees must overcome is to provide their offspring, in the form of seeds, with enough food to start as seedlings. They must also make sure the seeds are carried away from themselves and do not grow up too close for comfort where they might provide adverse competition.

The giant trees which reach up to the canopy, and the myriad plants that colonize their branches, suffer from the fact that they are either rooted in the ground or firmly fixed somewhere else high above it. This means that they cannot scatter their seeds where they choose, nor can they run away from any creature that wishes to eat them. However, as we have seen, having its seed eaten is not always a disadvantage to the plant; in fact many positively encourage the idea by providing tasty morsels which we ourselves enjoy eating. We call them fruits. But wrapping seeds in this way to encourage the dispersal of encapsulated offspring can also be asking for trouble, as many of the would-be takers have a habit of eating all the good bits and leaving the kernel, the seed, behind. Plants therefore face a dilemma of how to be eaten and how not to be eaten and in the tropics, where animals and plants appear to have evolved to get along well together rather than merely survive the elements, as in harsher environments, they have come up with an entertaining array of solutions. The simplest one is not to use animals at all.

Wind is the simplest and 'cheapest' way for a plant to disperse its seeds to new growing sites. All it has to do is provide the seed with a parachute or a pair of wings and let the breeze do the rest. 'She loves me, she loves me not, she loves me ...' When picking a fluffy dandelion seedhead and blowing its little parachutes out into the air, we are dispersing seeds on the wind. Wandering through the forest understorey I could find few plants with such fluffy seeds, as there is so little wind to carry them. But in an open area in Costa Rica, in the shade of a large balsa tree, I was surprised one day to find the ground beneath it littered with what looked like rabbits' feet. They were in fact the fluffy seedpods of the balsa tree, pale buff in colour and as soft as a rabbit's fur. Attached to the fine hairs were small seeds which could get blown about in the wind. Since these trees are fast-growing pioneers, colonizing open and sometimes windy gaps in the forest, this method of blanket dispersal with numerous seeds serves them well. Kapok, which used to be so valuable as stuffing in mattresses and warm jackets, is in fact designed by the silk-cotton tree to transport its small seeds across the canopy. Floating on such silken threads is only viable if the seeds are small: to increase the size of the seeds they can disperse on the wind, some trees provide them with wings. One, two or even five wing-like outgrowths may protrude from such seeds, which are released one by one from a pod high in the canopy or drop directly from the branches to spin down towards the ground. Dipterocarps, as we have seen, disperse their seeds in this way, but even so they do not generally travel far, as the clumped formation of these trees

In the canopy of a Central American forest a spider monkey drinks from a balsa flower. Forest primates are surrounded by rich pickings: fruit, leaves and insects, a feast of gigantic proportions.

demonstrates. Only in storms can their seeds be carried high above the canopy; then they may be deposited several miles away from the parent tree.

It is only up in the canopy that sufficient wind filters through the tree crowns to make such a method of dispersal worthwhile, so it is mainly tall trees and epiphytes that use it. Many epiphytic seeds, such as those of orchids, are dust-like and easily borne in the wind. But as the seeds are so tiny, they carry little food for a germinating seedling and must quickly form an association with fungi where they fall, to help them gather nutrients from the immediate environment. Without the correct fungal network they will quickly die among the branches. That is why orchids are so difficult to grow from seed at home.

So, wind dispersal has certain flaws: if there isn't very much wind, the seeds do not go very far; because they need to be light it is not possible to provide seedlings with a large nutritious seed to sustain them in the early stages of growth.

On my walks through the forest, despite brushing through grabbing vegetation and sharp-thorned vines, my clothes were not covered in clinging burdock burrs and hooked goose grass seeds, not because these kinds of plants cannot grow there but because inside primary forests there are few large grazing animals, for which the hooks are designed, to disperse them. However, though the density of big animals in the understorey is low, the canopy

abounds in primates and large birds, which do make excellent dispersal agents, carrying fruits away in their mouths or stomachs. Consequently, trees have gone to enormous lengths to advertise their wares and seek such passing custom, and in tropical rainforests these associations between trees and their dispersal agents have become quite remarkably complex.

Without the cold winters which freeze our temperate world, there are no seasons in the rainforest in which last orders are called, so the canopy feast goes on throughout the year. Far from being a disorderly affair with numerous species scrambling to be first in the queue, trees, vines and epiphytes portion out their offerings to a selection of diners by advertising their offerings in a similar way to flowers with sweet smells, bright colours, and seductive flavours. As there is strong competition for trade, plants provide a bright and tasty range of goods, many of which now find their way onto tropical market stalls and, increasingly, onto our own tables. Most of these tropical fruits are exaggerated versions of those originally preferred by primates foraging in the canopy and were evolved by plants simply to make their seeds more attractive to potential dispersers.

Since most agents, such as monkeys and birds, scatter seeds in a somewhat random manner, either by dropping them, being sick or defecating, there is little hope of having the seeds placed exactly where the plant would like them, on a perfect growing site. Only mistletoes have managed to arrange this. Once in Brunei I was surprised to see a small bird running up and down a telephone line, apparently wiping its bottom on the wire. I was a little confused as to why it should do this until I discovered it to be a flowerpecker, a bird which particularly enjoys eating mistletoe berries. Succulent mistletoe fruits may be, but they contain a laxative which induces the birds to eject them soon after eating. Many of the seeds would fall to the ground, and therefore fail, were it not for the fact that they are covered in a thick sticky coating that causes them to adhere to the bird's bottom and its surrounding feathers. To rid themselves of the troublesome seeds the birds squat down on a twig and skitter rapidly backwards and forwards, rubbing themselves along it. This seemingly rather uncomfortable behaviour leaves many of the seeds sticking to the branch instead, and soon they will germinate. Whilst some plants do germinate on telephone wires, flowerpeckers usually deposit mistletoes in more suitable places.

The canopy table offers three basic types of fruit, each designed to tempt different groups of dispersers. There are those which aim to attract opportunistic feeders that sample a little bit of everything: these are often small, grape-sized, highly coloured fruits filled with many small seeds. The fruit flesh is composed mainly of carbohydrates and is not very nutritious; tomatoes and figs are good examples. The animals which eat this type of fruit rely on additional items, such as insects or leaves, to supplement their requirements. This makes them less dependable from the tree's point of view, but

A pair of double-eyed fig parrots enjoying a meal of figs. From small beginnings as an epiphyte, the fig tree grows to become a prolific and vital food supply to numerous forest animals. The tiny size of its seeds ensures that few are crushed in beaks and jaws, so most will survive consumption to be deposited in a tree crown.

by producing plenty of small seeds per fruit there is a good chance that some will remain undamaged and will fall in the right place once they have passed through the animal's body.

An alternative strategy on the part of the plant is to provide a complete diet for its disperser. To cater for all their needs requires a much larger fruit, rich in fats and proteins, on which the disperser can afford to depend. Animals which rely on these tend to be large themselves, and have a huge gape to swallow the fruits whole. The cultivated avocados we eat are an example of this type. The seed inside is too large and indigestible for us, so we throw it away; animal dispersers may swallow them and regurgitate them later, some distance from the parent tree. By designing its fruit to suit the disperser, the tree gets a more personal service and can therefore afford to 'spend' more on the resources it provides for each seed. The germinating seedling thus has a good source of food to rely on until it becomes established and can survive on its own. This is a useful plan, for many seedlings may have to survive a considerable length of time in the dim understorey, waiting for a falling tree to make a gap in the canopy and provide them with sufficient light to begin making food of their own.

In between these two extremes are those trees which produce medium-sized seeds and instead of covering them with a thick juicy fruit, wrap them in a thin but bright covering called an aril. This

Like chocolates in the tree crowns, fruits are covered in colourful wrappings to attract animals to eat them. A poisonous protective coating prevents damage before they ripen.

covering is nutritious, as its bright colour advertises, but is less of a drain on the plant's resources to produce than a large fruit would be. To prevent the aril from being robbed before the seed inside is ripe, the colourful package is hidden beneath a tough, often poisonous, husk. Only when the seed is ripe does this husk open, exposing the aril. This is often bright red or orange, colours easily seen by birds. Birds are early risers, so the new crop of arils are revealed at dawn and hungry flocks raid the trees, tossing away the seed which is too tough to eat. Most seeds will therefore fall beneath the parent tree, but some birds carry the fruit away before eating the aril and may drop the seed in a good place for it to germinate.

Getting a close look at this arboreal banquet is almost impossible from the ground, though much has been learned by crick-in-the-neck practitioners staring skyward through the obscuring leaves with a powerful pair of binoculars. Others, more adventurous, have built towers or constructed platforms high in the tree tops, and from these lofty positions looked down upon the canopy to play 'I spy' in the hopes of glimpsing what the frugivores are up to and how they divide the spoils between themselves. The variety of species and their beautiful colours create a bewildering display of feather and fur, and watching them by day or night, hidden in the tree tops, can be an entertaining business. There is one tree in particular which is more rewarding than all the rest both as a source of food and interest: the strangling fig.

Watching a fig tree banquet is one of the most remarkable experiences in the canopy. Hundreds of animals may descend upon a fruiting fig crown during a day. In Thailand four giant hornbills, six wreathed hornbills, ten pied hornbills, twenty-five mountain imperial pigeons, one hundred and fifty lesser thick-billed green pigeons, a family of white-handed gibbons, twenty-five each of Humes' barbet, green-eared barbet and little barbet, fifteen yellow-headed green leafbirds, twenty-five fairy bluebirds, thirty-five hill mynas, five species of bulbuls, plus sunbirds and white-eyes too small to see, and a flock of hanging parrots were all counted gorging in one single giant fig tree. How I would like to have climbed up into its crown and hidden myself amongst the leaves to watch the multitude that had gathered to feed. The figs cater for all comers. The hornbills hop over the branches on their strong feet, picking the fruits whole and tossing them into the back of their throats. The smaller birds, too diminutive to eat the fruit whole, would peck chunks out of them. The beautiful fruit pigeons, resplendent in bright plumage, are of little use to the fig as they destroy its seeds in their gizzards. Siamangs are very discerning, testing each fruit to find the ripe ones rather than stripping them off wholesale, leaving those that are too firm until another day. A male little barbet will also select a couple of ripe figs and then move on, next day he may return to the same branch and select a few more that have now ripened. I might be lucky enough to see him carry a fruit as a present to an elegant little female in a neighbouring tree. There, with wings fluttering, he

would prance up to her, hoping she will accept his offering. If she did he would return for several more, each time approaching her with quivering anticipation. More often than not the female barbet will fly off, leaving her courtier to swallow his gift and his pride.

As night falls around me in the tree, the day shift retires and nocturnal feasters creep into the crowns. A slow loris with ponderous, measured pace may pick its way through the branches to sample a fruit or two. A flying lemur may glide in and shamble up from the trunk below. Flying foxes sweep in from their daytime roosts and clamber about on their hooked wings and feet, biting into the fruits with their dog-like muzzles and licking their lips with long pink tongues. Horny ridges on the roof of their mouths act as juice strainers; by squeezing squashy fruit against them with their tongues they extract the fluids and can spit out indigestible fibre and pips. A small-toothed palm civet climbs through the canopy, using its sharp retractable claws to sample soft fruit which it crushes between flattened molars. A large, shaggy cat-like creature with tufted ears and a long bushy tail might also be seen picking its way through the darkness along a canopy routeway and into the crown. It is a binturong, unique among the civets in having a prehensile tail with which it hangs from branches, pulling fruit towards its mouth with its front paws. All through the night the feast would continue. Siamangs, which often have favourite fig trees in which they like to sleep, are forced to spend the night elsewhere when these come into fruit, as they find the nocturnal traffic too disturbing. As the sky begins to lighten, the bats will fly back to their roosts, and the fruit-eating civets will disappear, leaving the fig tree to welcome the first hornbills once more.

Fig trees occur in all the great rainforests of the world, though most are to be found in South East Asia. The strangler begins its life in the canopy, as a small epiphyte, germinating from a sticky seed deposited by a passing bird or perhaps a bat. The seeds must germinate in compost, in the crotch of a branch or in an epiphyte garden. But unlike other epiphytes, the strangler grows prodigious aerial roots which seek the soil far below. Once their roots creep beneath the leaves of the forest floor and begin to tap the supply of food and water there, the fig grows apace and the tree upon which it germinated is doomed.

Its roots spread around the massive trunk and where they meet they fuse, encasing the tree in a living coffin. Meanwhile, high above, the fig's leaves track the sun like miniature solar panels, drinking in its energy, and as they spread they will shade out the host tree's crown and it will begin to die, starved at its top and its base. But the fig continues to grow, now standing on thick roots of its own in the soil. Eventually the original host tree's trunk will rot away inside, leaving the fig to stand as a massive, hollow canopy tree. In parts of Central America, strangling figs are known by the name of *Matapalo* which means 'tree killer', but their deadly touch provides great benefit to the animals of the forest. Hundreds of

A living coffin. The roots of this strangling fig have encased its host tree, in whose branches it first rooted as an epiphyte, so that the trunk has all but rotted away.

creatures make their home in its hollow trunk. Geckos, frogs and anolis lizards all reside in their own cavities, and paper wasps and stingless bees also live there. Ants will seed their colonies in old bees' nests and army ants will explore nooks and crannies for prey to seize – beetles, cockroaches or bugs.

The fruits of these extraordinary epiphytes are produced in abundance at various times of the year. Some larger strangling figs which have already dominated their host trees may fruit as many as three times in a year; others may do so just once. By being out of phase with each other, different trees and different species of fig provide food the year round when other sources of food may be in short supply. They produce squashy, juicy fruits full of small seeds which are easily eaten by many creatures, but the seeds do not remain inside them for long. It is no surprise that syrup of figs cases constipation: fig trees planned it that way. From the fig tree's point of view, the effect of fig fruit on the bowels encourages its seeds to be dispersed widely in all directions. This makes good sense for a plant that exists as such an opportunist colonizer.

Jamaican fruit-eating bats can often be seen carrying figs through the Neotropical forests they inhabit. Many will deposit seeds at roosts or in branches as they fly over the forest, ensuring a wide spread of fig trees.

The most productive figs are nearly always in the largest timber trees, often the ones most sought after by loggers. Timber companies which selectively remove such large trees, rather than clear-felling the whole forest, argue that their activities do little to alter the numbers of fruiting fig trees: any tree entwined in a strangler's deathly grasp is of little use to them, so it is ignored. But not all figs strangle their hosts. Many send pillar roots into the ground beside the trunk, leaving it unencumbered and a worthwhile prize for the chainsaw's hungry blade. Because of this association between figs and commercial timber trees, even low-intensity selective logging has been shown to reduce their numbers in the forest by about forty-two per cent. In these forests the prospects for the animals which depend on them look decidedly thin.

One of the interesting discoveries from the ultra-violet light traps we suspended from walkways high in the forest canopy during Operation Drake was the capture of an enormous number of aga-onid fig wasps, far more in the canopy than in any other part of the forest. These tiny insects, less than a few millimetres long, have a remarkable association with fig trees. Unlike those of other trees in the forest canopy, the fig tree's flowers never open to the world: they are concealed inside tightly closed fruits and the only pollinating agent capable of entering the fruits are these minute wasps. The way in which they do so and the tasks they perform inside are another remarkable example of co-evolution in the forest.

In the canopies of Panama, Papua New Guinea and Sulawesi, as well as in Brunei and Zaire where these UV light traps have since been placed, vast numbers of female fig wasps have been found but never any males. To lay her eggs the female fig wasp searches for a fig tree whose fruits are not yet ripe. The fig may float attractive scents on the wind to help her find them: it may be a giant strangler which has already taken over its host, or it could still be a small epiphyte growing amongst the branches. There are over nine hundred species of fig in the tropical world and each species relies on its own variety of wasp to transfer pollen. On selecting a suitable fruit, which may range in size from a small bottletop to a large one, the female wasp enters it through a tiny pore in the surface which is so tight a fit that her wings and often her antennae, too, will be torn off as she wriggles through. Some scientists suggest the tight squeeze may serve to wipe her clean of infective microbes and fungal spores which could contaminate the sterile nesting chamber. What is not removed is the vital pollen she carries in tiny recessed pockets in her thorax, collected from the fig tree where she was born.

Inside the darkened chamber the wasp finds numerous female flowers opened for her arrival. To these she transfers the pollen from her carrying pockets, so fertilizing them, but her intention is to probe deeply into the flowers with a long ovipositor. Inside the ovaries beneath the flowers she lays an egg; this stimulates a gall-like formation in which her larva will grow and feed on the developing seed. With other female wasps that may have entered with her,

she will deposit eggs in many of the ovaries: almost half the fig's seeds will be destroyed by their larvae but that is the price the fig must pay for its pollinator's services. However, there is a second type of flower which grows ovaries too deep for the wasp's ovipositor to reach and these, as they will also have been pollinated, develop viable seeds.

Their egg-laying complete, the female wasps die. Protected from attack inside the fruit, the developing young wasps somehow prevent the fruit from ripening, so that no passing monkey or bird is tempted to consume it and bring about their doom. But they are not entirely safe. Another small wasp, closely related to the larvae within, may alight on the surface of the fruit. She has a huge whip-like ovipositor many times her own body length. Encumbered with this, she cannot enter the fig fruit nor does she need to. Placing the tip of her ovipositor on the surface of the fig, she drills into it. How she locates the wasp larvae growing beneath at present remains a mystery, but she does. Next to them a lethal egg is laid and on hatching the grub either consumes the fig wasp larva or causes it to starve to death by voraciously eating the food on which it depends.

Fortunately many of the fig wasps survive such predations and after about a month, wingless males first emerge within the darkened chamber. The tip of their abdomen is long and through holes they cut they fertilize the new females still trapped within the plant's ovaries. Before they die the males must perform one more task. They tunnel through the wall of the fruit to the surface, and air floods in from outside. This somehow stimulates the interior of the fruit to bloom with hundreds of tiny male flowers, laden with pollen. The winged female wasps now emerge and gather pollen into their pockets before streaming from the tunnels the males have made, to disperse over the forest in search of fruits in which to commence their curious cycle over again. Behind them the fruits of the fig tree now change colour to purple or deep red, indicating that they are ripe and for the taking. Those seeds remaining, which survive the passage through the animal or bird that eats them, have the chance of growing into new fig trees.

Of all the fruit-eating birds in the canopy the hornbills must be the most spectacular and amusing. Their very appearance, dominated by such a large beak and often topped with a horny casque, coupled with large eyes fringed with chorus-girl eyelashes, gives them a rather ridiculous air. Yet they are efficient at gathering the canopy's harvest and will also snatch eggs, nestlings, or lizards and insects where they find them. Their serrated beaks are strong enough to shear through wire, but with only a stub for a tongue they must toss fruit upwards and let it fall into their throats. They are adept catchers and in captivity can be taught to catch a ball and toss it back. One pet young black hornbill enjoyed teasing a family dog by offering it a morsel of meat which the dog would beg for. Sitting on the back of a chair, the bird would sometimes swallow the meat

and at other times drop the titbit into the dog's mouth. But occasionally, much to the annoyance of the dog, it would carefully put the meat into the waiting canine's open mouth and then snatch it out before the frustrated animal could swallow it.

Some eighteen species of hornbill inhabit the forests of South East Asia and its island archipelagos and many more are to be found towards the forests of West Africa. They are gregarious and live in family groups of a mated pair plus a few offspring. Their nesting habits are remarkable. Despite their huge size, even the giant hornbills nest inside treeholes high in the forest. Having found a suitable hole they use their strong bill to widen the entrance sufficiently for the female to enter. When she is ready to lay she clambers inside and the entrance is sealed up by the male, assisted by the female. Using moist mud, possibly from the base of epiphytes, mixed with faeces and saliva, plus a few wood shavings from the inside they close the entrance until only a thin slit, just large enough for the hornbill's bill, remains. The female will remain imprisoned for several months but at least she is safe: any marauding snakes or monkeys in search of easy pickings are met by a rapier-like thrust from her beak, and would have a hard time reaching in through the narrow entrance slit.

Little is known about what goes on inside these arboreal nests, but the female probably loses most of her feathers, which may make useful nesting material. She lays two to four eggs, depending on the species, and about a month later they hatch. The nest would quickly become uninhabitable were it not for the fact that hornbills have extraordinarily strong cloaca muscles which enable them to squirt their faeces through the nest entrance with the accuracy of a tobacco-chewer aiming at a spittoon. It is not only the adult males who bring food to the incarcerated female and youngsters; other members of the hornbill community, perhaps closely related to the family, also seem to help. Once the nestlings are fledged, the entrance hole is pecked open, and the young hornbills are freed to make their first flight and begin a life cruising over the canopy.

An unusual frugivore which specializes in swallowing large nutritious canopy fruits is the oilbird of the American tropics. With a hooked beak surrounded by long bristles, it resembles an enormous nightjar or whip-poor-will. It feeds at night, particularly on the fruits of palms and laurels, snatching them from the branches as it flutters in front of them on long agile wings. Once, no doubt, it also existed on a diet of insects but whilst there was great competition from other birds in the day, during the hours of darkness there were only bats to contend with in the air, so it evolved to feed then and later specialized in fruit. With a bellyful of fruits the oilbird flies to caves where it rears its young, finding them in the darkness by emitting audible clicks, echo-locating its way around in a way similar to that used by bats. The young are raised on a diet of fruit from the day they hatch and in a little over two months weigh half as much again as the adults. They are rich in fats and are often sought

by Indians for their oil, hence their name. Thousands and thousands of regurgitated seeds litter the cave floor and cannot survive there should they germinate, but many others will be dropped in the forest once the oilbird's chicks have flown the nest.

The wild nutmeg is a tall emergent tree in mature forests in Central America. Between April and September, on Barro Colorado Island in Panama, it produces seeds enclosed in a bright protein-rich red aril which are fed upon by a discerning collection of birds. Of the seventy-eight fruit-eating birds found on the island, only seven eat the wild nutmeg's fruits. Of these, keel-billed toucans, sporting massive green, yellow and orange beaks and brilliant yellow chests, remove far fewer fruits than the larger Swainson's toucans which are the tree's most valued seed disperser. Though spider monkeys and capuchins also climb into the trees to feed, they drop so many fruits whilst eating them that few seeds are removed any distance from the tree. The masked tityra, a small cotinga splashed with a brilliant white breast that takes its name from eye patches and a beak as bright red as the nutmeg fruits, does systematically remove the arils, but as it rarely moves from the tree it too is a very poor disperser from the tree's point of view. However, the tityra does act as errand boy for another, smaller tree also found in Central American forests.

Casearia corymbosa provides a vital food supply for some twenty species of bird, including parrots, toucans and flycatchers, at certain times of the year when little other fruit is available. Providing food at a time of scarcity ensures maximum attention from the birds. Thus all the birds which feed on *Casearia* are highly vulnerable to extinction should the trees for any reason disappear, perhaps at the hand of man. Yet surprisingly only one of them is effective as a dispersal agent. Whilst most birds drop the seeds beneath the parent tree whilst sitting in it, only the masked tityra gobbles down seeds and then flies off to another tree crown perhaps a few hundred metres away to process the arils and later regurgitate the seeds. But why does it bother to move at all?

The reason is that all the activity in the *Casearia* crowns attracts others who are in search of a different kind of meal. Hawks patrol the canopy, too, and as soon as one is spotted overhead parrots and flycatchers give the alarm and the smaller birds in the crown dive for cover. The toucans, who are too large for most small hawks, can afford to remain aloof from all the pandemonium and the flycatchers are camouflaged and so are perhaps less concerned about moving. But the brilliant white tityras stand out like beacons and could easily fall prey, so they pick a bellyful of fruit quickly and then retire to a safer place. So the hawks are, in a way, doing the trees a service.

Casearia's other diners may be just as vital as dispersers to other trees at different times of the year. The pioneer tree *Cercropia glazioui* from south-east Brazil portions out its seeds between several species of fruit bat at night and three species of tanager by day. All these search for fruit, the seeds of which pass through them and

are dispersed widely in the forest; but seventy-eight per cent of those which pass through bats germinate, as against thirty-two per cent for the tanagers. The importance of one visitor over another feeding at a fruiting tree has received little attention. In fact, compared with the process of pollination biology, the way in which seeds are dispersed from tropical trees has barely been studied at all, and in most cases who actually disperses most trees' seeds is unknown.

Sulawesi is an octopus-shaped island in the middle of Indonesia, one of over thirteen thousand islands in that country and certainly one of its most unusual in terms of wildlife. Sulawesi has remained isolated for thousands of years from most of the surrounding islands, in particular Borneo to the west and Papua New Guinea to the east, and so has evolved a treasury of wildlife all its own. Excluding bats, over ninety per cent of its mammals are endemic. There is a dwarf buffalo, just a hundred centimetres tall; a grotesque hairless pig which grows huge curving tusks over its nose; a black monkey once thought to be an ape; and an extraordinary civet cat found nowhere else in the world. When I visited the island to co-ordinate scientific efforts to create a new nature reserve on the east coast, I was amazed to discover a place of such undisturbed natural beauty; the research team had chosen an idyllic site for a large camp of thatched huts on short stilts.

One member of the team was intrigued to discover that the forest there contained large numbers of ebony seedlings scattered about but few large ebony trees to produce them. Over half the ebony seeds on the ground bore tiny punctures where they had been bitten, but the pattern of teeth marks did not fit any of the mammals caught in the traps on the ground; so who was responsible for the bite marks? The answer lay thirty metres up in the canopy. An aerial walkway had been built between adjacent tree crowns and mist nets suspended there to sample bats. One night a bat was caught carrying an unusual load: in its mouth was an ebony seed. Matching the jaw gapes of various captured bats to the puncture marks in the seeds showed that *Rousettus celebensis*, a fruit bat endemic to Sulawesi, was responsible for most of them. Despite the seed being almost one third of its own weight, the bat was capable of flying with it easily and was probably a vital link in the reproductive cycle of the ebony trees.

Some trees, like the monkey pot tree, produce complicated seed structures specially designed for bats, since clearly a winged dispersal agent is better than a crawling rodent or possum. The tree's coconut-sized seed pod is shaped like an overturned bowl with a small entrance hole at the bottom. These pots hang down from the ends of branches, perilously out of reach for most arboreal mammals and birds; as the entrance is beneath the pot they cannot reach the seeds even if they do get there. The tree derives its popular name from the monkeys that do try to get at the seeds and, having pushed their hand inside the pot to grasp one, cannot remove their bunched fist. Local people will tell you it is possible to catch monkeys in this

Varied lorikeets are an attractive sight in the crowns of Australian rainforest trees. Many birds like these eat enormous amounts of pollen as part of their diet.

Tube-nosed bats inhabit the forests of South East Asia. Their diet of squashy fruit could give them breathing problems, so it may be that their tubes evolved to prevent their nostrils filling with pulp. Many such bats were commonly caught in the mist nets slung from our aerial walkways.

way, so determined are they not to let go of their morsel once they have it that they will not free themselves by letting go. Bats flying to the monkey pot are provided with a convenient lip on which to grasp the heavy bark of the pod with their hind legs, allowing their mouths to reach inside. The seed itself is tough and indigestible in order to resist being destroyed by animals before it has a chance to germinate once it falls to the ground. Ordinarily the bats would have no interest in eating it and would not act as dispersers were it not for the fact that the monkey pot tree provides each seed with a fleshy tip which is highly nutritious. This the bats do like, but the tree has cunningly evolved to place the juicy tips at the far end, deep inside the monkey pot. As the bats cannot feed from their foothold they must pull a seed out of its slot and, with their mouths full, fly to another perch to turn the seed round and consume the tip. Then they drop the seed, but by that time it may have been carried some distance away from the parent tree, and the tree will have achieved its aim.

There are, however, still further difficulties for trees to overcome. A tree may offer its crown full of fruit to a selected suite of feeding animals, including birds, monkeys and bats in order to achieve seed dispersal, but other visitors may be attracted who are uninterested in the colourful, tasty fruit and go for the seeds themselves, destroying their chances of producing new trees. Parrots are seed predators

breaking into a seed pod and cutting into seeds with their sharp and powerful beaks; so are monkeys, tapirs, pigs and peccaries that crush seeds between their molars, and pigeons that grind them down in their gizzards. Insects, too, are powerful seed predators, particularly beetles and weevils, which bore into seed pods either as they hang in the trees or once they have fallen to the ground. They may either eat the seeds themselves or lay eggs in them so that the hatching larvae can dine on them. So even if the tree has been successful in persuading some animal to carry off its seed, once it falls to the ground it must still run the gauntlet of a variety of creatures.

The seed pods of the tree *Hymanea* are rock-hard to resist such predatory onslaughts, but even so one small weevil manages to drill its way through a good many of them and lay large numbers of eggs on the seeds before the pods fall. However, on emerging from the seed the hatched weevil finds itself trapped inside the pod's tough walls, and there it must remain unless or until a further round of seed predation takes place. Foraging agoutis, searching for food, find the seed pods lying amongst the brown leaves of the forest floor. These large rodents have very sharp teeth and set them to work on the *Hymanea* pods. Once it breaks through, the agouti begins removing the seeds to eat them, at which point the little weevil makes its escape. But it doesn't move far: as soon as it is out of the pod it plays dead amongst the leaves, lest it too is seen and becomes an agouti snack. Only when the agouti moves away will the weevil go about its business. For the *Hymanea*, the agouti is a blessing in disguise since without it, its seeds might never be released from their hard coffin. By flooding the market with large amounts of seeds all at one time, the tree out-supplies demand and as the agoutis cannot consume everything they find, they bury caches of seeds, meaning to return to them later. But a perfect memory is not an agouti's strong point, and some seeds will escape their attentions to germinate into new *Hymanea* trees.

In this way the forest canopy is intimately connected to the ground: a tree may go to great efforts to attract an insect or bird to pollinate it, and then rely on some other beast to eat the fruits it puts on display in order to disperse its seeds. Most seeds can only sprout on the forest floor, subject to a host of other pressures from sunlight, moisture, predators or microbes that cause them to rot before they can germinate. But some can end up in very strange dispersal agents indeed.

In the wet season vast areas of Amazonia are flooded by the rising waters of the Amazon and its tributaries. Many trees and vines time the ripening of their fruits for this season, letting them fall into these waters to provide unlikely food for fish, migrating in with the floodwaters. Some fish have flattened molars to crush the seeds, but in many others they are unharmed, and dispersed upstream as the migrating fish move on and the seeds eventually pass through. It is a surprising thought that overfishing may result in certain tree species

vanishing from the flooded forests. Exploding pods of *Eperua rubiginosa* scatter seeds into the water, perhaps attracting fish by the sound. Local fishermen certainly believe this and imitate the explosions to attract fish for the catch, even using brazil nuts to hook tambaqui fish. Some fish appear able to eat seeds toxic to other animals, so much so that their flesh may become tainted at this season, another fact well known to fisherfolk. Could it be that these fish have evolved resistance to such seeds in order to protect themselves from predators?

Most trees are only too happy to have their ripened fruit eaten by animals, but when it comes to their leaves, that is a very different matter. Standing on a tree platform and gazing out across the canopy, fruits are hard to see but leaves are everywhere. Why is it that there are no herds of grazing animals in the canopy, harvesting this bounteous resource? Part of the reason is that digesting leaves is a slow business, requiring help from bacteria to break down tough plant cells before they will release their nutrients. To survive, a large volume of leafy material needs to be eaten then chewed over in a large stomach, preferably inside a large animal. Being big and heavy is, as we have seen, not conducive to swinging through the tree crowns. Monkeys which do depend on leaves tend to have fat, bloated bellies and must spend much of their day quietly digesting. They are in effect walking compost heaps.

Flying with a bellyful of decomposing leaves is not easy either, so few canopy birds subsist on them. Trees also have little to fear from reptiles, but once in Panama I was amazed to see an iguana scrambling about the branches thirty metres above ground. In the Neotropics iguanas appear to have invaded a vacant niche in the canopy, and climb up into it daily in search of leaves and the sunshine of the tree tops, which warms them after the comparative night-time cool of the forest floor and also speeds leaf digestion. To escape predators they will rush through the branches and hurl themselves into space, perhaps to land in a river far below with a huge splash. In the South East Asian forests, monitor lizards also scale trees, more often in search of fruit.

But there is another reason why there are few leaf-eating vertebrates in the canopy. Behind their uniform disguise of all-pervading green, many of the canopy's leaves are full of extremely toxic poisons. These were not created so much to ward off marauding primates or the odd iguana, as to protect their energy-trapping leaf material from millions upon millions of slicing insect jaws. They do so with a wide range of chemicals called phenolics, ranging from caffein, morphine, terpene and tannin to sticky latex, which gums up a voracious caterpillar's mandibles, forcing it to eat elsewhere. For a long time these secondary compounds, as they are called, were thought to have no particular biological function or to be waste secretions. Many of them have now become valued products for human use as precursors of drugs, from the pill to anti-cancer compounds. For example, tannin is used to cure leather and pro-

vides the bitterness in coffee; many of us prefer to reduce this bitter taste by binding the tannin to the protein molecules in cream. To us, the tannin is a minor irritant but to a leaf-eating insect it can be highly toxic; thus one beast's drink is another beast's poison.

Provided the energy cost of producing these so-called secondary compounds is less than the energy loss incurred through leaf damage, it pays the tree to become poisonous. Not only leaves are protected in this way, but fruits too, and mammals have in some cases become remarkably resistant to them. An African doctor, annoyed that fruit bats persisted in eating passion fruits near his home, injected the fruits with a variety of poisons from arsenic to cyanide, with no apparent ill effects. Then he tried strychnine and still the bats ate the passion fruits with relish, despite consuming enough poison to kill thirty-five to forty human beings. The particular bat concerned, Wahlberg's epauletted fruit bat, lives around forests where juicy yellow strychnine-rich fruits occur and has developed a virtually complete resistance to their poisons.

Once, when I sat down at a tropical fruit stall, I was overcome by a longing for the delicious taste of fresh pineapple. After gorging myself on succulent slices, core and all, I noticed the tip of my tongue felt sore. When my fingers touched it, they came away covered in blood. If we sprinkle meat tenderizer onto a juicy steak, the active ingredient papain goes to work on the proteins and begins to break them down in a process rather like digestion. Papain is a chemical invented by plants and is particularly concentrated in the cores of fresh pineapples. I had effectively tenderized my tongue. The kind of poison it uses, its concentration, and where it is placed depend on the kind of animal the plant is trying to deter. I don't eat many leaves but if I were a leaf-eating monkey or insect wandering through the tree tops, I would have to learn very quickly which bits on the green menu I could eat, or starve.

As most of these plant poisons were originally aimed at insects, the effects of millions of these miniature herbivores chewing their way through tree crowns is another growth area of study for the arboreal naturalist. On the forest floor it is easy to find leaves shot through with holes bored by caterpillars or leaf-eating beetles, but the numbers at work and the effects they have on the survival of the tree are likely to be far more profound amongst the new leaf growth up in the canopy.

Meg Lowman, an Australian botanist, had a problem. Something was eating her leaves. Not being especially adventurous, she preferred to keep her feet firmly on the ground whilst studying the way in which trees produced leaves in the tropical rainforests of North Queensland. She was mainly concerned with how leaves 'flush' and all appear at once in select groups amongst the branches; how long they remain on the branches; and how many a tree needs to produce in order to trap sufficient energy from the sun. But as fast as the leaves appeared something took great bites out of them and Meg began to despair. It soon became clear that she should be studying

the insects, not the leaves, and thus the fascinating world of insect-plant relationships opened up to her.

Meg reluctantly decided that the only way to work was to climb up into the tree tops and take a look. Climbing into an ornamental tree on the lawn at Sydney University under the expert guidance of some local cavers was hardly a comparable experience to scaling a giant rainforest tree. Undaunted, she obtained a licence for a sling-shot, a weapon for some reason considered by Australians to be almost more dangerous than a shotgun, and headed north. Once in Cape York, she fired fishline over a solid-looking branch and used this to haul climbing ropes over. Attaching jumars to these, she slowly moved up into the canopy. As she'd expected, it was not always a pleasant experience. At times the weather was cold, her hands felt numb on the ropes, rain smudged her notes and smeared her spectacles. Worse still were windy days, when the tree crowns swayed about violently and the ground seemed very far below. But she persevered and every month for three years climbed into the tree tops in her study area to enquire into leaf life histories.

The first problem was to mark the branches to ensure that she came back to the right ones. Black, brown or green tags had obvious camouflage problems, and young leaves often flushed red, so that colour was no good. Male bower birds, which inhabited the forest there, just loved blue and would remove tags of that colour to decorate their bowers and impress their lady loves; any blue pens dropped to the forest floor would go the same way. Meg settled on yellow. Tying tags to a branch thirty metres above ground whilst dangling on a climbing rope was no easy business. And then each leaf had to be tag-numbered as it appeared, with a waterproof felt-tip pen. Each month she would note which leaves had bites taken out of them, or grew galls or became infected with fungi; when they fell and when new ones appeared. Eventually she could

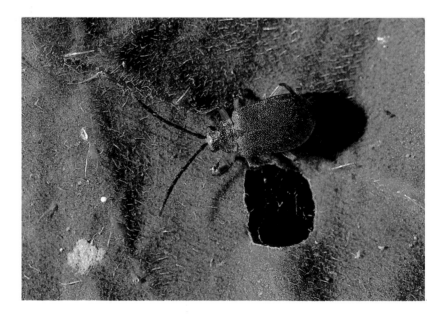

This small beetle, *Hoplostines viridipenis*, was found in the crown of a tree like a giant stinging nettle in the Queensland rainforests, munching undeterred on the leaves' poisonous, acid-filled spines.

predict almost everything that was likely to happen to a leaf in her part of the Australian rainforest canopy.

She found that insects prefer to eat shaded leaves rather than those in sun, because they are softer and chemically less toxic. They also prefer young leaves for the same reasons, so the greatest numbers of defoliators appeared in the spring and summer months. The stinging tree is a large emergent of the Australian sub-tropical rainforest rising to forty metres in open areas. Like an enormous stinging nettle, its leaves are covered in irritating hairs presumably designed to discourage animals from eating its leaves, yet Meg found that almost half the tree's canopy was missing, its leaves full of holes despite the poisonous hairs. Eventually she discovered that a tiny scarab beetle, *Hoplostines viridipenis*, was responsible; it specialized on the leaves and would even eat the spines as well, somehow neutralizing the defensive acids they contained. The beetle was a beautiful iridescent green, perfectly camouflaged with its host plant.

To assist in tracking down who the other defoliators were, Meg engaged the help of a Boston-based organization called Earthwatch, which provided teams of enthusiastic volunteers and financial support. They raised light traps up into the canopy at night to capture flying insect herbivores. One night, whilst gazing up into the tree tops for a good spot to raise the traps, some of the assistants were the unfortunate victims of a mass display of animal seed dispersal: some fifty brush turkeys that were roosting overhead, took fright and simultaneously defecated on their heads. Dedicated arboreal naturalists are not easily put off, however.

Climbing up a ladder into the canopy in Panama, I often admired the efforts of tiny leaf-cutting ants. In the mornings, I could see trails of these little brown creatures heading skywards with intense determination. Each step I took was worth a thousand of theirs, yet still they climbed, picking their way up the hillside of a vine or around the tangled jungle of an epiphyte. Five or six abreast, they would ascend all the way from their subterranean nest far below. It was as if I, and millions of others, had spewed out of the New York subway and each day had to negotiate the whole of Manhattan in each direction by climbing over the suburbs and then scaling a skyscraper on the way to work. Once in the tree crowns they set to work with butcher-like precision, carving out neat green crescents from the choicest new leaves of some trees, on others attacking only green fruit or old leaves, and from yet others removing flowers. How do they make their choices? These may change through the year and are probably related to the distributions of toxic chemicals positioned by different trees. Having sliced their choice free with powerful cutting jaws, they would march back along the branches towards the trunk, even taking a short cut along a walkway rope and down past my ladder all the way to the ground. They would also systematically remove our labels tied on leaves and carry these down to the ground. By evening the traffic would be predominantly

homeward-bound; there would be million upon million of these industrious marching columns throughout the forest, each worker carrying a canopy prize held rigidly over its back, flanked by powerfully jawed soldier ants.

Having to scramble over vine tendrils and deeply serrated bark carrying a piece of leaf proportionately equivalent in size to a small dining-room table would seem bad enough, but many of the ants appeared to be struggling along with another, smaller, ant hitching a free ride, clinging precariously to the top of the captured leaves. This behaviour seemed inexplicable. Streaming down the flanks of a tree's giant buttress roots, the column would at last find its own particular miniature motorway snaking across the forest floor, cleared of dead leaves and jungle debris, giving them a clear run for home. But just when the day's labour seems to be done, the columns would occasionally scatter, rapidly, in all directions, seeking cover under the decaying leaves, sometimes remaining there for hours, even abandoning their exhaustingly obtained loads, returning to the nest empty-handed. Equally inexplicable.

Parasitic wasps are the answer to both riddles. A certain species skilfully attacks worker ants by landing on their leaf trophies and thrusting its ovipositor in between their jaws, up into their heads where it lays an egg. The larva later hatches and feeds on the ant's brain, sending it mad and ending in death for the ant, but life for the larva, which will later emerge as an adult from the ant's body and seek more leaf-cutters. The sight or perhaps the sound of these wasps terrifies the ants, which cannot defend themselves with their mouths full. The wasps will fly circles round the soldier guards so if a worker cannot reach safe cover in time, how is it to be defended? It seems the little outrider carried on top of its leaf may be the answer. They appear to be riding shotgun and may attack the wasps as they come in for the kill, so with an ant occupying the landing zone, the parasitic wasp is forced to seek easier prey elsewhere.

Despite there being large numbers of leaf-cutting ants that I could see at work in the tree crowns, the canopy around the walkway was not stripped bare. The ants appear to conserve some part of the forest by selectively grazing the trees, rather than by using up the ones closest to their nest. These would be the least costly to exploit in the short term, but would result in the ants having to make longer and longer journeys in search of food. Even trees of the same species vary in palatability, often seasonally, so the ants cannot always eat the convenient trees they want. Their scouts may miss suitable species nearby and if they do find one, it may be defended by other aggressive ants which keep the rival colony at bay. This combination of factors helps the ants to sustain their resource and live in harmony with the forest. When the forest is removed and replaced with a monoculture, such as a citrus plantation, their system breaks down, and the ants, faced with unpalatable grass on the ground, attack the trees, destroying whole plantations and in the end, by incurring the wrath of man, destroy themselves.

Leaf-cutting ants get to work on more than leaves: they removed flowers as well as identification labels we had painstakingly tied to branches in the canopy. Outside the Neotropics, where such ants are found, other insects destroy enormous amounts of leaf material. To protect themselves, trees harden their leaves and fill them with poisons.

In the Pananamian forest canopy, leaf-cutting ants seemed to account for about eighty per cent of all leaf damage. They can defoliate a whole tree crown in a day. They were equally good at grabbing samples of leaves taken to the makeshift lab-hut on the banks of the Aila river. They were delighted: someone was bringing juicy canopy leaves down to the ground, saving them a laborious climb. Insects destroy about the same total amount of leaf material in Panama as in New Guinea on the other side of the world. This was a surprising discovery, as the animals responsible in each place are quite different: there are no leaf-cutting ants in Papua; caterpillars seem to be the culprits there.

Amongst the primates of the forest canopy it is the colobus monkeys that have evolved the most remarkable resistance to toxins in leaves and fruits. Black-and-white colobus can consume poisonous seeds by the dozen, two of which would kill a goat; leaves which cause human beings to vomit vigorously are eaten with relish. Their remarkable resistance allows them to exploit food unpalatable to other monkeys in the forest, giving them a competitive edge over their neighbours.

In the Miocene era, the fruit-eating apes flourished as flowering plants evolved apace; monkeys lurked in the evolutionary background, gradually gaining leaf-eating abilities as can be seen from their differing dentition designed to cope with tough, poisonous leaves. Then the monkeys became able to eat unpalatable, unripe fruit, too, before the apes had a chance to consume them, and this may have been responsible for many earlier species of apes disappearing from the Earth. The colobus monkeys continued to eat leaves but some of these were too well protected chemically even for the monkeys. Another problem was that the sugars in fruit fouled up their sacculated stomach fermenting system, rather like a cow's rumen, in the same way that it causes acidosis in cattle, so some monkeys became specialized seed predators, like the satanic black colobus of the Camerouns or the maroon leaf monkey in Borneo. In the jungles of South America, the uakaris and sakis also evolved into seed predators, using special protruding incisors to crack nuts and eat the nutritious kernel inside.

Leaf-eating monkeys would be as stranded without their microbes as leaf-eating cutter ants would be without their garden fungi. The monkeys need microbe enzymes to break down plant cellulose and extract proteins and sugars from them, and have evolved to grow microbes in certain parts of their stomach. Howler monkeys belong to a group known as hind gut fermenters: they house their plant-attacking bacteria in enlarged sections of the caecum and colon to do their digestive work. But with only a relatively short bit of gut left over, there is not much of it to absorb the goodness before the plant material makes its exit. Colobus monkeys have hit on a better method by evolving a sacculated stomach. Leaves making their departure from branches down a monkey's throat are met upfront with a powerful broth of digestive microbes to detoxify

poisons, leaving plenty of time and space for absorption further down the line. This adaptation has made colobus monkeys the most successful of leaf-eating primates in the world.

At certain times over the forest canopy of Central America an amazing sight can be witnessed. The day is hot and humid, the rainy season is in full swing. Large numbers of beautiful, highly coloured butterflies, resembling swallowtails, begin to emerge from the tree crowns and gather together in clouds to float off on tumbling wings, far across the forest. They are not butterflies at all but day-flying moths called *Urania*, though with green-and-black iridescent pigments, flecked with white and pinks, they are just as beautiful. The moths rely on a vine called *Omphalea* on which their larvae feed, but as the vine is found all over the canopy why should they suddenly up sticks and 'migrate' to another part of the forest where the vines look no different from the ones they left? It seems that *Omphalea* gradually becomes resistant to *Urania* caterpillar-onslaughts by increasingly investing itself with poisons. To begin with, the caterpillars can munch the leaves with impunity but the damage stimulates the leaves to protect themselves, and gradually there are fewer and fewer unaffected vines where the *Urania* moths can lay their eggs. At this point they must move in search of fresh vines, and it may be this which triggers such a mass exodus.

One cannot but admire the natural testing ground which has evolved a plant like *Omphalea* or like *Melinea* which, on sensing a caterpillar's jaws biting through its leaves, also quickly puts poisons into its veins and flows them through the injured leaf. Whilst most caterpillars are deterred, there is one that knows what the plant is up to, and clips through the leafy veins at their base, cutting off the poison supply and so enjoying its meal untainted.

If all these stories appear to have neat answers we are deceiving ourselves. How do we explain a tiny mosquito that, on spotting an ant scurrying home along a trunk, flies in and alights before it. With a vibration of its wings it inexplicably encourages the ant to squeeze out a droplet of honey dew between its jaws into which the mosquito places its long proboscis and sucks its fill. For the mosquito the benefit is obvious, but what is in it for the ant?

The study of such interactions of plants and how they orchestrate their seconday compounds into a complex array of defences is but in its infancy. Most tropical plants have yet to be screened and most that have been are those near to the ground. Countless natural pesticides wait to be discovered along with an equally remarkable range of pharmaceuticals which plants have kindly tested for us over millions of years. Already some fifty per cent of the drugs we use are developed from natural derivatives. Cancer is one of the most feared diseases still on the increase, yet cures have been discovered by screening rainforest plants. As these forests diminish their storehouse of products of benefit to us is going with them. But there is hope that at last we are waking to the knowledge that medical benefits they contain are an apothecary's dream.

A three-toed sloth asleep in a *Cercropia* tree. Hanging beneath the branch may conceal it from predators walking above, but cannot protect it from its most dangerous enemy.

8 | Killers in the Canopy

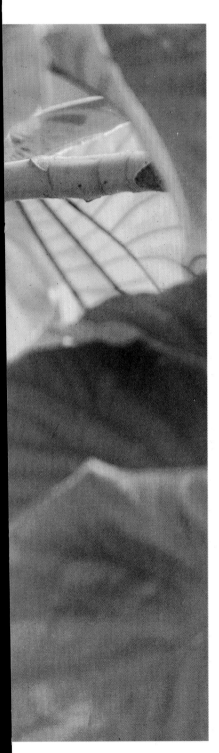

Death for a sloth comes on silent wings.

The day may begin with cold drops of dew dripping from the sloth's coarse fur, stained a perfect shade of green by algal lodgers to render it invisible amongst the leafy crowns. At least almost invisible. Hanging beneath its chosen night branch, the sloth pulls its head out from between its front legs and peers around its high-rise home with a slow, measured gaze, as if it had all the time in the world. Unable to shiver away the cool of the night it must move to brighter places, out from beneath the concealing leaves, in search of sunshine to warm its slow-moving muscles.

'No time to lose' is a phrase without meaning when applied to sloths. Up into the open crown of a *Cercropia* tree the three-toed sloth climbs with glacial slowness. Without epiphytes to negotiate on these ant protected branches, the journey is a relatively easy one and at last a gap flooded with sunlight is reached where it can hang, perhaps from its back legs alone, stretching in the glow of the morning's sun. It may be that sloths also use these sun patches to display the bright blaze of orange fur on their backs, possibly as a signal to other sloths nearby. But another creature too, can see it from afar. The sloth settles beneath a comfortable branch, time, perhaps, for a gentle snooze in the sun. Then the killer comes.

Had the sloth been awake and alert, as alert as a sloth can be, it would have made no difference. They have forsaken the ability to run and once their disguise has been discovered by a hunting animal they are helpless but for the fact that, suspended beneath the branches, they are hard for most predators to reach and take hold of. But not for the huge bird, itself concealed within an emergent crown, head crest of feathers erect. Leaping from the tree it makes its approach on enormous, powerful wings. Stooping low over the tree crowns, it fixes the sloth with dark, amber eyes.

Travelling now at some fifty kilometres per hour it dives, not over the tree crowns but down into them, weaving with incredible speed between the largest branches to the more open area beneath. Its wing feathers tearing through the moist warm air, it rushes through the gloom unseen, upwards, and at the sloth. Holding out giant talons poised to grip and tear, it twists itself sideways almost upside down, offering its claws, outstretched, towards the unsuspecting sloth. With stunning force they plunge into its flesh, and break its sleepy grip. And then it is gone, leaving only an empty branch quivering in the sun and a few green leaves spinning and floating down towards the ground.

Harpy eagles are the largest and most powerful in the world.

They inhabit tropical forests from southern Mexico to northern Argentina and because they nest only in the highest trees in these inaccessible environments, little is known about how many there are, what they live on and how they will fare as the forest in which they live disappears. The female harpy is larger than the male, as with most raptors – she weighs about nine kilos and is just under a metre long from head to tail – but the male does most of the hunting, and is equipped with enormous yellow talons, about the size of a man's hand, tipped with long, black, razor sharp claws. Their grip is fearsome, enough to crush fragile ribs or drive the claws inwards like a gin-trap.

As their wings, each about as long as a man's arm, are broad and barred with dark colours, the harpy uses them to fly with rapid wing-beats followed by a glide, not soaring over the forest as do many other birds of prey, but flying from tree to tree in short bursts, then waiting upon a branch, listening intently for the sound of a distant monkey troop or watching for a movement within the trees. The dark feathers on its folded wings camouflage it from above, and from the ground the white of its breast blends with the sky, and its head crest with the branches, making the bird almost impossible to see either by a human observer searching the crowns with binoculars or by an animal on which it may wish to prey. In the canopy of these forests, the harpy eagle is the predator large mammals fear most.

The rainforest canopies of West Africa and the Philippines as well as those of South America are also dominated by powerful eagles. The African crowned eagle is fractionally the smallest, though still a magnificent bird by any standards. Like the harpy, it has broad black wings to provide speed and manoeuvrability within the forest, though this bird will also soar above the tree crowns to search for prey. Diving into the tree tops, it can snatch a fleeing monkey and lift it high above the forest to carry back to its large nest to feed its single, white, fluffy young. These nests are used season after season over many years; when the nest is empty, the eagles will drop to the ground within the forest to eat their prey there.

In the dwindling forests of the Philippines, the enormous monkey-eating eagle can still be seen flying over the forest in just a few places; forest clearance and specimen hunting have put paid to most of them. They are very similar to the harpy, a little smaller but with a more impressive feathered crest. Their name is a misnomer as they prey largely on flying lemurs, watching for them in high trees with intent, ferocious, gaze. As the lemur glides between trees on its membranous cloak, the eagle drops; when the lemur lands exposed upon a tree trunk, the eagle swoops to snatch it. They have even been known to fly into villages and attack pigs and dogs.

Getting close to these eagles within the forest is almost an impossibility: occasional glimpses across a valley are all that most have the good fortune to see. Harpy eagles tend to nest in the tallest trees, often using silk cotton trees. These large emergents are evidently

ideal, being easy for returning parents to locate and generally having a T-branched crown suitable for nest construction. It is one of the few rainforest trees to drop all its leaves at once and at this time of year the nests can be spotted more easily from the ground. In a few places local Indians know of nest sites, and these provide the best opportunity of getting a closer look. From the ground there is still little to see other than a huge pile of twigs and branches, so a daunting climb is the only way to have a chance of seeing how the birds raise their young.

The first detailed observations of harpy eagles in the wild were made in 1960 by James Fowler and James Crome in the north-western section of the Kanaku mountain range in what was then British Guiana, now Guyana. Eighteen years later when Neil Rettig, an American naturalist and film-maker, decided to attempt to photograph harpy eagles rearing young, the same nest site was still in use. To get close enough he needed to climb into the actual nest tree – a silk cotton tree sixty metres tall – before the birds had laid their eggs. With sharp-spiked boots and a long leather belt that could be wrapped around the trunk attached to the harness in which he sat, Rettig clambered up. At the top there were new dangers. The female harpy eagle didn't like intruders.

She'd already made her views clear to Rettig's assistant, who had helped construct a hide a short distance from the nest, swooping towards the trespassers, talons outstretched. Fortunately on most occasions she had been dissuaded from pressing her attack home by much arm-waving and shouting, and had veered away at the last minute. However, sometimes she did strike, lunging into the middle of the platform builder's back, fortunately with her talons closed. Yet once the two men were hidden behind the blinds, the eagles took no notice of them. Humans were not entirely unknown to them: local Indians said the eagles would call, with an eerie wailing 'weeeeeeee' sound, as they flew over village clearings.

The nest Rettig filmed was very large indeed, composed mainly of large twigs and bleaching bones from past victims. As the mated pair worked to prepare it, the male would launch himself at the crowns of nearby trees and appeared to attack the branches with extraordinary ferocity. Flapping on top of them or even hanging beneath, he tore at the branches with his beak until a piece came free, then flew back to the nest, where it was added by the female to the growing structure. The bowl of the nest was lined with green leaves, some of which were used to cover the eggs once they were laid, perhaps to protect them from the fierce heat of the sun.

Whilst the female was sitting the male perched in the crown nearby, but more often than not was out in the canopy, hunting; he would bring prey to the nest for her about once a week. Just under two months after the first egg was laid a downy white chick hatched. The second egg was then ignored and soon disappeared beneath the debris of the nest. Should a second chick hatch it is often pecked to death by the first. With these birds of prey existing in such

PREVIOUS PAGE
A female harpy eagle returning to build up her nest with a sprig snatched from a nearby tree; such nests may be used from year to year. Only found in the forests of Central and South America, they are the most powerful eagles in the world, and will snatch sloths and monkeys from tree crowns with great skill.

small numbers in the forest this may appear wasteful but it seems that one chick is more than enough for the parent birds to raise, and one well-fed youngster stands a better chance of survival than two poorly fed ones. Once the eaglet had hatched, the female became more aggressive towards the male, calling loudly and quickly taking any prey he brought, mantling both prey and young. Only when the male had flown off would she begin to feed the chick.

Apart from an agouti and a red brocket deer, all the animals the harpy hunted were arboreal, mostly sloths, with capuchin monkeys being the next most common prey. Possums, tree porcupines, and kinkajous, as well as howler monkeys and even ant-eaters were all brought to the nest and each consumed over a period of days. About four and a half months after hatching, the young harpy eagle left the nest and perched on branches in the nest tree; in another month it would fly but it would remain dependent upon the parents for food for some months after that. Eventually, it would be forced to hunt on its own and search the canopy for a new territory.

Anyone searching the forest roof for a harpy eagle in the American tropics will almost certainly do so in vain. They are extremely rare and with the destruction of tropical forests proceeding apace, are likely to become rarer still, even endangered. All forest-loving birds of prey are of course hard to spot in such a tangled environment, a fact especially true of the enormous eagle owl which takes over from the daytime eagles and patrols the canopy by night, using high trees to listen for nocturnally moving prey with its extremely sensitive ears. On broad wings, sound-proofed with soft downy feathers, it flies between the tree crowns in search of kinkajous or possums. Other large owls, such as Fraser's eagle owl and the Akun eagle owl, inhabit West Africa's forests and the Philippines are home to yet another species. Mottled owls may snatch bats as they feed in a fruiting tree, whilst other species prey on small mammals and insects.

There are eighteen genera of exclusively forest-living raptors; almost nothing is known about fourteen of them. These elusive birds of prey include the hook-billed kite, believed to feed on arboreal snails; the double-toothed kite, a relative of the cuckoo falcon, three honey buzzards; two snake-eating eagles; various hawks; some large eagles already mentioned, as well as falcons and tiny falconets, the smallest of all birds of prey. These last breed in old woodpecker holes high on tree trunks and hunt insects over the tree crowns by day. Lastly, there is the extraordinary laughing falcon, whose call resembles maniacal human laughter; it attacks snakes which it plucks from the branches.

The raptors which seek prey within the canopy are faced with much greater difficulty than those that hunt above it. Exceptional skills are required to chase a small bird through a tangle of branches and vines, so most are equipped with short, broad wings and a long tail to give power and agility. Tiny hawks memorize the territorial perches or feeding stations of hummingbirds and lie in wait for

them. Double-toothed kites follow monkeys around, hoping to capture insects disturbed as the monkey troop feeds. The crane hawk has a double-jointed foot which enables it to reach more effectively into holes in tree trunks. Perhaps the most interesting hunting technique of all is that practised by the *Micrastur* forest falcons.

These small birds of prey drop down from the upper parts of the canopy to the bushes in the shrub layer and immediately expose their position by uttering a high-pitched 'eek-eek-eek' about every twenty seconds, an odd thing to do for a bird which supposedly depends upon surprise to secure its prey. Soon a mob of excited birds gathers round the falcon, giving equally high-pitched alarm calls. They like to know the position of their attacker rather than be ambushed out of the blue. After a few minutes of this the little falcon suddenly stops calling and jumps to the ground, hopping through the undergrowth to begin calling from a new location, wings poised to fly. The mobbing birds cannot now see where it is and nervously look this way and that, trying to find it. A small tanager may fly to a new branch for a better view, so giving its own position away, and like lightning the falcon leaps from the forest floor and seizes it. Mirandolle's forest falcon develops this deception and because its voice, like a ventriloquist's, is hard to place, it confuses the mobbing birds and so secures a meal.

There are other sources of food on the forest floor sought by much larger meat-eating birds which live outside the forest's twilight zone and patrol the vast expanse of the canopy on enormous outstretched wings. These are the vultures, and the species which prefer to live in rainforests are unlike those found anywhere else in the world. One of them, the greater yellow-headed vulture, is rarely found outside rainforests; in the Old World there are no such exclusive forest-living vultures. Turkey vultures belong to the Cathartid group and have their centres of distribution in the Neotropical forests of Central and South America. Though they appear similar in plumage and their soaring mode of flight, they are quite unrelated to the larger vulture species familiar over the grasslands, savannahs and semi-deserts of Africa and Asia, and are actually more closely related to storks. Theirs is a classic example of convergent evolution, where natural selection in widely separated groups of animals has come up with the same kind of creature as a perfect design for a particular mode of life, in this case scavenging.

A rainforest might seem a strange place for vultures to make their living, a hard environment in which to locate any creature that may have died. One might also be led to believe that there would be little carrion to find in the forest roof, as fewer large animals live there than on open grasslands. Surprisingly, calculations have shown that in rainforests, as there are few scavenging mammals to compete with vultures for food, the amount of carrion available to them may be as much as that left to vultures on the Serengeti plains.

The sight of a turkey vulture circling near their nest tree infuriates

A crested serpent eagle clutching a lizard in its talons. These birds range all the way from India to Indonesia. They are adept at catching reptiles and small birds, but the baits of smaller rainforest birds of prey are hardly known at all.

harpy eagles. Sitting on the nest, the female eyes the vulture as it approaches, her head bobbing as she fixes it in her deathly stare. Then she launches herself from the nest and gives chase, quickly overtaking the startled vulture, and though she could easily strike it, the mere sight of such an awesome creature swooping past is enough: the vulture will quickly fly off to less hazardous parts of the forest.

Apart from recalcitrant harpy eagles, a turkey vulture cruising the canopy in search of a rotting meal is faced with other difficulties. A dead monkey or sloth does not conveniently give its position away by moving. Though it may die in the branches, its body almost invariably falls to the forest floor to decompose, and cannot be seen there either. Many of the larger forest animals, such as pigs or tapirs, a valuable source of food when they die, already live on the forest floor and are as invisible in death as in life to the vulture flying high above. In most birds two lobes near the front of the brain are associated with their ability to smell. Usually these lobes are small and consequently many birds, including most vultures, are unable to perceive the scents we enjoy. But the turkey vulture's olfactory chambers are enormously enlarged and it appears to have an uncanny sense of smell. Unlike other vultures, it does not soar in search of prey but prefers to float around immediately above the tree crowns, using updraughts on the windward side of emergent

trees both to keep aloft and detect putrid odours wafting up through the forest.

In the sweltering atmosphere of the forest understorey, it takes just a day for an animal carcass to begin smelling strongly. For the vulture it is a race against time: it cannot locate the carrion until it begins to smell, yet if it is too late the carcass may have been consumed by other creatures. Bacteria quickly set to work and soon rot the flesh to such an extent that it will be inedible. Contrary to popular belief, vultures will not eat carrion that is heavily putrefied, though their tastes are somewhat less discerning than our own. The reason for this is that the bacteria release toxins as they multiply in the flesh. It may be that they have evolved to do so, to render the meat unpalatable as quickly as possible, so securing it for themselves. Amazingly, the vultures locate most carcasses within a matter of hours and in one experiment using chicken carcasses, they found ninety-five per cent of them within three days, even though some had been hidden under leaves.

In open savannahs vultures heading towards and squabbling over a kill can be seen for miles around. Having sniffed out a suitable meal, the rainforest vulture lands in the canopy above it and slowly hops down to ground level to feed, removing almost all the flesh and some bones as well once it gets there. Other turkey vultures that have seen its descent may join in the feast but there is no disorderly

Spectacular king vultures soar over the forest, watching for turkey vultures to lead them to carrion: king vultures cannot smell out carcasses beneath the forest but their stronger bills help turkey vultures open up tough skin, so that all can enjoy the feast.

display of gluttony like that so often seen on the African plains. Turkey vultures appear to eat their meal with a certain sense of decorum and take their time. Surprisingly, mammals such as possums, which may also be partial to a bit of dead flesh, rarely find carrion before the vultures do. Unable to cover such a large search area as the vultures, few forest-living mammals can rely on scavenging for a major part of their diet. But there is another competitor, much larger than itself, which the turkey vulture must give way to — the magnificent king vulture. These huge birds are found in undisturbed forest in much smaller numbers than the turkey vultures. They have enormous white wings, spanning over a metre, black on their trailing edges like the tail feathers. Their great bill, the most powerful of any American vulture, is bright orange and is attached to a head adorned with spectacular black-and-orange folds of skin, finished off with piercing white eyes encircled in ochre. They, too, seek carrion in the forest but experiments have shown that they have a poor sense of smell. So how do they find it?

Unlike turkey vultures, the king vulture does soar high above the forest on rising air thermals, and from this vantage point it can get a good view of what the smaller vultures are up to below. As soon as turkey vultures home in on a tree crown, the king vulture will spot them and move in as well. On the ground, turkey vultures are no match for the larger bird, which will force them away from the carcass. But with their more powerful bills king vultures can tear open the tough skins of large animals which the smaller vultures cannot manage, and so they do benefit once the king has had its fill.

The canopy is in fact filled with skilful predators ranging in size from the powerful harpy eagles to tiny insects. There are wasps that specialize in killing spiders; praying mantids which, disguised as flowers, clutch insects fool enough to visit them. Numerous spiders cast webs across flyways to capture insects buzzing between tree crowns, some bearing zig-zag lines of white silk, perhaps to tension the webs or disguise the spider's shape lurking at the centre. These bands may also make the webs visible to birds, so that they do not accidentally destroy them. The enormous orb-weaving spiders wait to snare small flies, beetles and butterflies or moths that may blunder into their sticky traps. These spiders do not throw silk over their prey from a distance but must grapple with them, using their black legs, as long as fingers, and must bite, delivering lethal poison. Some insects are well defended and squirt back with noxious chemicals, startling the spider and managing to escape. Occasionally a hummingbird will dart in and seize the spider's prey before it has time to immobilize it. Orb weavers will gather into large colonies, each web attached to another; in New Guinea huge aggregations of colony-living species have been found, comprising many thousands of spiders, floating on great sheets of silk stretched between the trees.

The rich pickings amongst the leaves make ideal hunting grounds for chameleons, masters of camouflage which can change their hue at will to match their surroundings perfectly, or lighten their skin,

By night slow lorises steal up on insect prey with a measured pace. Fixing a grasshopper or caterpillar with a stare, it suddenly clutches its meal with its forepaws. Lorises are capable of staying perfectly still for hours at a time to avoid being eaten themselves.

so reflecting the intense heat of the sun. Each eye appears to have a life of its own, scanning the vegetation independently of the other for creeping insect prey. With breathtaking speed the chameleon's long sticky tongue shoots out and returns with a helpless fly. Golden pottos and slow lorises move with equal stealth, staring with saucer-shaped eyes in the hopes of finding a bright caterpillar too poisonous for others to eat. Pottos and lorises walk with a fluid, measured pace and seem totally oblivious of gravity as they crawl on gripping hands over branch tips, curling under them to proceed upside down, or moving sideways to reach across an almost impossible gap, hollowing out their backs as they pass under a twig, perhaps to avoid shaking leaves which might give their position away. Having sniffed out a foul-smelling beetle or caterpillar to

their taste, they creep forward until the prey is at their arm's length, then lunge, and grasp it. Holding a caterpillar's head in its teeth, the potto rubs it vigorously with both hands to remove any troublesome hairs before swallowing it, after which it wipes its lips clean on a branch.

Bush babies are agile nocturnal predators in West African forests, springing with astounding leaps from branch to branch, their large ears quivering and turning as they listen out for the soft rustlings of a scurrying beetle. In South America marmosets make nimble hunters; some find grasshoppers irresistible, spending much of their day searching just for them. Birds, too, as we have seen, glean the branches in waves of many hunters working together in noisy, colourful flocks, busily poking into nooks and crannies, under leaves and into epiphytes in search of the canopy's rich bounty of insects. Many of the larger primates will also supplement their diet with insects picked from the hanging gardens, or grubs prised from their hiding places beneath bark.

Of course birds and primates are not the only large predators in the rainforest. One Sunday morning, suspended amongst the trees in Sulawesi, I was looking forward to a lie-in. Much of the previous night had been spent attending traps hauled up into the forest roof as we lured insects to an untimely death in our pursuit of science. Now I could lie back in my hammock as the forest understorey very gradually lightened, and enjoy listening to the growing sounds of insects welcoming the dawn, mingled with the tip-tap of water droplets descending from the dew-laden canopy. Suddenly I was brought sharply awake by a violent snarling noise coming from beneath my hammock. There were sounds of a scuffle and then the snarls rushed to a new point some feet off.

Peering through my mosquito net I could just make out two civets engaged in fearsome dispute. They grappled at each other's throats and bowled each other over, scattering utensils and belongings, apparently oblivious of the fact that they were inside our camp. As the battle raged, they neared another hammock. The mosquito net was gingerly pulled back, revealing the stubbled face of our senior entomologist. 'B—— off!', he growled, showing little respect for the fascinating display of mammalian territoriality being played out before him. Entomologists, I find, appear uninterested in most things unless insects are involved. The two civets, startled by this hostile reception made off into the forest as fast as their legs could carry them.

This is the only time I have ever seen a wild civet in the jungle; though they certainly climb high into the canopy, I have never seen them there, neither have I had the good fortune to come across a live leopard or a jaguar. All I have seen was the skin of an illegally caught jaguar in Panama, pinned out to dry on a river bank and then left to rot. These animals are never common and in any case their cryptic coloration and nocturnal activities mean that to catch sight of them anywhere is a truly rare event; to observe them in the

canopy is even less likely. No large cats chase monkeys through the forest roof, though the clouded leopard of Borneo and other parts of South East Asia is much more arboreal than either leopard or jaguar and spends much time clambering about the branches. It will sleep in the tree tops too, lying in wait for a monkey or a large bird to pass by, which it then swats with large spoon-shaped paws. It will even hang upside down from branches, waiting to drop onto an unsuspecting pig or deer as it passes beneath.

Concealed within a tangle of vines amongst the branches a female African palm civet may give birth to two or three young. She will be one of several females in the dominant male's home range which may cover many kilometres along a network of memorized arboreal routeways. He is a good climber and forages around the branches chiefly in search of fruit from trees and vines, but he will also take frogs, lizards and the occasional insect. The civet's fur has a background of buff brown with wide bands of black, as though someone had decided to paint its coat with a broad, clumsy brush. Civets, along with genets and linsangs, belong to a family shared with mongooses called viverrids, found inhabiting the forests of West Africa and South East Asia. Of these the most skilful are the linsangs.

These sleek creatures, with their long, black banded tails, are among the rarest and least known of their genus as well as the most beautiful. They are rarely found outside tropical forests and probably hunt lizards and small mammals amongst the tree tops. The African linsang is believed to make daytime leaf-lined nests in the branches; emerging at dusk, it prowls along branches in search of young fledglings which it will pick out of a nest and devour, taking eggs if they have not yet hatched. In self-defence, many birds build their nests on branch-tips where the linsang cannot reach them. The two Asian species, the spotted and the banded linsang, make their nests under hollow logs or amongst tree roots on the ground but will climb into the trees to hunt, using their sharp, retractable claws. Genets look rather like the spotted linsangs, with the same almost fox-like faces topped with enormous ears, but their tails are more bushy; the West African forest genet is a particularly good climber.

Madagascar has its own extraordinary equivalent of the clouded leopard, the fossa, a large arboreal hunter closely resembling a dog-sized cat. It has a reddish-brown coat and a head equipped with large eyes and powerful jaws with which it captures lemurs as well as ground-living insect-eating mammals and birds. It is Madagascar's largest carnivore and is only found in undisturbed forest, most of which has already gone on the island and the rest of which is rapidly disappearing. Since large predators in these forests suffer most from the resulting diminished food supply, the fossa must now be considered highly vulnerable.

In all the major rainforests of the world there are various spotty felines ranging in size from that of a medium-sized dog to a household tabby. Many of them, such as ocelots and margays in the

Many small cats hunt in the canopy branches, patrolling arboreal highways in search of young birds and small mammals. Ocelots are larger than most canopy cats, and will also take animals on the ground.

American forests are excellent climbers and hunt mice, small birds and lizards amongst the branches; the marbled cat of South East Asia does the same. But since most of these numerous small species of nocturnally hunting cats are hard to follow, almost nothing is known about how important they are in the complex forest ecosystem. Almost the only way to pursue them is first to catch them in a baited trap and then, with the aid of a radio telemetry device attached as a collar, track the beast with an aerial and receiver once it has been released. Walking through the forest is difficult enough, without holding a large contraption like a television aerial as well, and as radio signals do not travel far through the trees, keeping in touch with such a prowling predator at night is, to say the least, frustrating. Outright hunting, with today's sophisticated weapons, is infinitely easier and since large numbers of people would secretly

love to wrap themselves up in an ocelot skin coat, the fur trade does very well out of them with nearly seventy-seven thousand skins being imported into Britain alone in 1975. Since then tougher international controls and changing public opinion has greatly reduced such trade though West Germany remains a major importer of cat skins. Needless to say, these animals cannot live wild without their forest habitat and unless things change our children's children may have to content themselves with knowing that they once existed, or observe them stuffed in natural history museums. Of course they may still be able to enjoy running their fingers through granny's old fur coat.

One day on a tree platform in a rainforest tree crown, I got to thinking about predators. It was a warm and sunny day when all seemed to be right with the world and I stepped towards the edge of the platform, reaching up to take hold of a small branch to steady myself. Just above my head a reasonably large, apparently dead, twig suddenly pulled itself on to the branch I was grasping and began to sidle down towards my fingers. I let go of the branch double quick; it sprang backwards, giving the poor snake an awful shock, and it turned round and went back the way it had come.

I have no idea what sort of snake it was and have no doubt either that it was as startled by the experience as I was. Human beings in rainforests get very concerned about snakes, and they are not helped by stories about explorers dropping inert within a few paces of being bitten by a fer-de-lance, or of their having been eaten alive by a truly enormous python. Some people are eaten by large snakes, of course. Not far north of an area in eastern Sulawesi where I once had to work, the body of an Indonesian farmer, still in his T-shirt and shorts, was cut from a bloated python. Sulawesi and its nearby islands are famous for harbouring the largest pythons in the world, some exceeding ten metres in length. Quite large pythons will drape themselves through the branches in search of monkeys to catch but more often they concern themselves with nesting birds, or an unsuspecting pig.

Coming across such splendid reptiles in the rainforest is a disappointingly rare event. One has to be content with occasional sightings of much smaller species, though sometimes even these can be a little too close for comfort. The camp cook in Sulawesi awoke one night, sensing some movement across his stomach. He put his hand down outside his sleeping bag and discovered he was sharing his bed with a moderately large snake. Being cold-blooded, the snake's preference for a warm place to lie up seems perfectly understandable, but quite what human beings should do in these circumstances is much more difficult. Another colleague of mine in Arizona, on waking to find himself staring into the eyes of a rattlesnake took time to consider his options. His arms were inside his sleeping bag. Any attempt to move them resulted in a furious rattle, so he elected to wait until the sun rose sufficiently for the snake to warm up and move on. Staying absolutely still for several hours in the dark is not

Snakes are ideally suited to canopy hunting. Neotropical emerald tree boas are well camouflaged and may be quick enough to seize unsuspecting birds.

Anolis lizards hope to escape predators by sleeping on branch tips whose movements give the predator away as they approach, but blunt-headed snakes have special spines which get them round the problem.

an easy option and it is unlikely that our cook gave it serious consideration: the volume of his yell and the speed with which he left his camp bed would have earned him a place in *The Guinness Book of Records*. Despite searches with a torch and a large parang we found no sign of the snake, which only goes to show that it was a master of camouflage as well as stealth.

Encounters with snakes are infrequent not because snakes are not there, but because we do not see them. Not being noticed is very important for a snake wanting to creep up and make a kill. No comprehensive studies have been made of snakes in the canopy, so what they do there must be a matter for conjecture, though with their excellent ability to move swiftly and silently around branches it is likely that they are one of the most effective of forest predators. Some of the most elegant species are vine snakes, often brilliant green and thin as a whiplash. With their pointed snouts they nose about the branches in search of nests of tasty fledglings, or perhaps a roosting adult fluffed up in a ball of feathers against the night-time cool. A number of crown-frequenting snakes, such as emerald tree boas, are also camouflaged green unlike their ground-living relatives, which prefer shades of brown.

Like us, small anolis lizards need to sleep at night and if they suffer from nightmares, they must be full of blunt-nosed snakes. To conceal themselves from predators the lizards doze along the mid-ribs of leaves, particularly V-shaped ones, such as those of palm fronds. If these are not available they will lie down lengthwise along a small twig, or choose a perch on a leaf at the end of a fragile branch, allowing their tail to curl over the end, mimicking a drip-tip. Any snake closing in for a kill will shake the branch or palm leaf, giving the lizard time to leap into the air and land somewhere less dangerous.

Last orders for a Brazilian *Tachimenys* tree snake.

The ability to slide over fragile branches calls for some special adaptations. The blunt-nosed snake has evolved back vertebrae which enable its body to reach up into space and remain vertically rigid whilst still being able to move horizontally from side to side.

The principle is similar to that of a bicycle chain lain on its side. Having sensed a sleeping anole, the snake manoeuvres to a position on a nearby branch and can reach across a surprisingly large gap to snatch the lizard. The same technique can be used to capture bats visiting a flower at night, or roosting under a leaf by day. Eyelash vipers are, by contrast, sometimes camouflaged yellow. They will wait near flowers visited by hummingbirds and strike as they come in to feed. It may even be that the hummingbirds are confused by the snake's yellow colour, and fly in to make a fatal inspection.

For human beings the canopy is a curious place to spend the night: we can barely imagine what it must be like to creep through the branches during the day, let alone in darkness. In Costa Rica I decided to spend a night up on one of our tree platforms, from which an aerial walkway had been built some twenty-five metres across to another tree. On the forest floor it was already dark and I chatted with some scientists in a small illuminated gas-lamp world amongst the 'pinking' sounds of frogs and motionless leafy silhouettes. Above, in the forest roof, the pale blues of twilight still embraced the trees, leaving some leaves dappled with orange from the setting sun. Grabbing harnesses and ropes, I put on a head lamp and stumbled off, following my pool of light towards the base of the platform tree. My clothes, already blotted with warm daytime sweat, soon felt cold and clammy against my skin.

I strapped myself into the climbing harness, tightened the buckles, clamped two jumars onto the climbing rope stretching up into near-darkness and began to inch my way up off the ground. All around there was only the effort of the tropical night, and humid air that hangs like a warm vapour, as I pulled myself upwards to the accompaniment of my straining breath, trickling sweat and the sound of whining cicadas. Pointing my head lamp downwards, I could still see the brown, leathery leaves on the forest floor between the exposed knuckles and fingers of the tree's huge roots. Further up I switched the lamp off to sample the void and listen. I could have been suspended in the ocean depths, floating in the rich forest air. Below was total darkness and on either side I could dimly make out large tree trunks. Above were ink-black branches just discernible against the dark blue night. Warm musty smells floated up from the forest floor and with them came the sounds of trilling and piping frogs, and further away, the clink of aluminium utensils being washed in a stream near the camp.

Switching the lamp back on, I shone it towards the tree trunk and noticed spindly harvestmen in black coats striped with yellow picking their way over the moist bark in search of tiny prey. The occasional large, solitary ant busily prowled around and a ceaseless traffic of termites disappeared up towards the branches or wound its way down the trunk towards the ground, too far for me to see. Many termites build their football-sized nests in the forest roof, foragingthrough its branches by night, clipping tiny pieces from lichens that grow on the bark amongst the epiphytes. They may also

supplement their diet of wood with nitrogen the lichens have trapped from the air. These small creatures, as well as ants, are, by virtue of their vast numbers, the staple diet of a few climbing hunters which can afford to specialize in them and eat little else, the anteaters and pangolins. As I climbed I hoped I might meet one.

Higher up the rope, I shone my lamp into the branches and noticed a large, rounded, hanging object looking as though wet mud had flowed all round it and then set in a series of ripples. In the darkness it reminded me of some kind of curious stalactite. In fact it was the nest of an *Azteca* ant colony, a favourite food of the tamandua. Perhaps I would be lucky enough to see one of these delightful furry anteaters of the New World, creeping along the branches with huge gripping claws and a groping prehensile tail, looking like some extraordinary long-nosed arboreal dog. The colonies may contain several million ants and the tamandua sniffs them out with its long nose. Though its eyesight is poor, it may be able to distinguish between different species of ant nest by the colony's odour. In one part of Panama, tamanduas only feed on a sixth of the one hundred and fifty ant species available to them, and on a third of the termites, but this may largely be due to the defences these tiny insects put up.

Tamanduas like to lick up ants by the thousand on their long sticky tongues, and to do so they lick under bark or rip open ant nests and probe inside. But some ants, such as army ants, are too aggressive for them and others have painful stings; leaf-cutters are just too spiny to go down well in the tamandua's toothless mouth, so they avoid them too. *Azteca* ants have no such defences but even so the tamandua does not have it all its own way. As it tears open the papery nest, thousands of ants pour out and over the anteater's body, biting with tiny jaws and releasing noxious chemicals. Soon the onslaught is too much for the anteater: after a few minutes it moves away for a furious scratch. In this way the colony is not completely destroyed and will soon recover from the intrusion.

Further up on my rope, I came across a termite nest. It was rounder than the *Azteca* nest, darker brown and harder, with a more spiky appearance. There were scratch-marks on it, perhaps where an anteater had tried to break in. Amongst the moving columns of termites, I could see some which appeared to have a little tube poking out of their foreheads. If I made a small hole in the nest, a number of these termites quickly crowded round and appeared to shoot something out of the tubes and onto my finger; it smelt a bit like pine oil and was rather sticky. These termites belong to a group called *Nausitermes* and are equipped with a deadly weapon. Their tube is in fact a chemical gun which fires a noxious mixture of liquids designed to immobilize attacking predatory ants. The sticky fluid gums up the ant's legs, enabling it to be disposed of quickly by the soldier termites. Surprisingly, the mixture works quite well on tamanduas too: when they gingerly nose their way into a nest they are met by a barrage of termite weapons. Meanwhile the worker

termites run for cover, deep within the nest and the poor tamandua quickly retires, wiping its nose on its foreleg or on a nearby branch.

I had now reached the base of the tree platform and could see the small square hole cut into it, through which I could pass. A few more heaves on the jumars and push-ups on the stirrups and I was through the hole and level with the surface of the platform. I stepped out of the stirrups, allowing the seat-harness to take my weight, and placed my feet on the platform's firm timbers, always a welcome feeling. My shirt was dripping with sweat from the exertion of the climb, or perhaps from the rather disorientating experience of ascending in the dark? Side-stepping the thought, I unclipped the jumars from the harness and attached my own safety line to the steel wire rope running across the platform: should I step over the edge, I would at least not fall very far into the blackness. How I would get back up again I preferred not to think about.

I was now perched in a little island of light, high above the forest floor on a gently swaying tree. The limits of this arboreal island stretched to the edge of the table-sized platform and to a few branches on which I could lean. With my lone spot lamp, I could see across to the tree crowns nearby. If I stood quietly I could hear frogs calling, but differently from those on the ground: they were up there with me, or rather I was up there with them. I wondered what they looked like. Scanning the branches, I could see nothing. Further away I could pick out a tree crowned with what appeared to be hundreds of white, twinkling 'fairy' lights, in fact the flashing signals of numerous fireflies. My gaze shifted to the tree limbs nearer the platform and I decided to have a look at their jumble of mosses and clinging epiphytic plants. Scrambling through the Lilliputian world of tiny roots and fields of moss, ants toiled beneath the brilliance of my lamp. Inside bromeliads, others moved amongst the leaves, picking through the mulch like some kind of high rise gardening consortium answering to an inaudible beck and call.

Ants such as these are the favoured food of another, smaller anteater. About the size of a squirrel and covered in fine fluffy fur, the silky anteater picks its way along small branches and vines using its prehensile tail and grasping, padded feet. Its front paws sport razor-sharp claws, which it rears up and displays like small curving sickles should a predator threaten. They are more often used to break open hollow twigs which are the home of *Crematogaster* ants. One *Crematogaster* colony may fill numerous branches within the crown of certain trees and some may overlap to include several crowns. Liana stems also provide refuge for these arboreal ants against many insect hunters, but the silky anteater can rip into them and using its long thin tongue will consume anything up to fourteen thousand ants in a day.

But there were no silky anteaters to be seen on my branches that night. Had I been lodging in a West African tree, or perhaps one in a South East Asian rainfoest, I might have seen an extraordinary armour-plated pangolin patrolling the branches, also in search of

ants. Pangolins are not found in the Neotropics where tamanduas and silky anteaters live; like them they also have prehensile tails, but instead of soft fur they are covered in a mesh of tough scales, giving them the appearance of an elongated artichoke equipped with a nose and a long, armoured tail. The scales are made of similar material to our nails and no doubt afford the pangolin extra protection against biting ants. Additionally, pangolins can curl up like a hedgehog, presenting a formidable exterior to any potential predator. Their eyes are protected by a thick membrane against any defensive chemicals the ants may spray into them: both ears and nose can be closed at will to thwart any attempt at entry. Pangolins hunt down ants by smelling out their colonies, tearing into them with powerful claws and licking them up with a long thin tongue coated by two enormous salivary glands. The tongue flicks in and out of a toothless mouth with a speed a viper would be proud of. Inside, the pangolin has a gizzard which, helped by a few stones swallowed for the purpose, grinds the ants up into a nutritious broth.

A bat fluttered, white as an albino, through my lamp's beam. I could hear clicking sounds as it echo-located its way around, but could not find it in the beam again. I sat down on the platform, pulled a candle out from the small rucksack I had brought with me, and lit it. Dripping some wax onto the timber floor I stuck the candle down, pulled out a bottle of beer, opened it and leant back against the tree trunk. The beer tasted good high in the trees. I switched off the headlamp and my world shrank to the glow around the candle. I continued to listen for the bat. A small white moth flew under the platform's wooden railings and danced crazily round the candlelight. I wondered at its confusion. Evolution had not equipped it to cope with strange lights in the forest roof. But some moths are well equipped to deal with bats.

By flying at night, moths avoid the attentions of insect-eating birds but then they must contend with bats. In the tropical night numerous bats course the canopy in search of insect meals to scoop out of the air with their wings or spoon into their tails, before transferring them to their mouths. Other species, such as the fast high-flying mastive bat, catch them directly with cavernous mouths whose flabby cheeks close over the wings of many a frantically fleeing moth. The tropical bats have developed their remarkable bio-sonar in uniquely admirable ways to hunt for insect prey.

Gleaning bats turn their sonar onto the surfaces of leaves to detect insects crawling there, and some may even specialize in the twilight hour to sense moths vibrating their wings as they warm up in preparation for an evening's flying. Others scan the night as they fly listening for the returning echo from insect wings and bodies. Even so, in the dark, to catch a darting moth a bat needs more than a notion of where the moth is — it needs the direction and speed in which it is flying. Bats seem to have solved this, too, in a number of quite different and astonishing ways.

Some bats shout at their prey, a series of high-frequency noises which to our ears sound like clicks, then see how long it takes for the echo to return. As the moth gets closer, the time taken for the returning echo will shorten, and by measuring the difference a bat can assess how fast the moth is moving. Traffic police radar traps use similar technology to measure the speed of motorists. By varying the frequency or speed at which they emit their signals, the bats probably 'see' a sound picture of their quarry in the same way that sound can reveal a clear image of a child inside a mother's womb. Bats which use this technique are known as frequency modulating, or FM, bats.

Most of us will have noticed how the sound of a car's horn changes in pitch as the vehicle rushes by. This change in tone, known as the Doppler shift, is caused by the number of sound waves reaching our ears increasing as the horn approaches and decreasing as it goes away. Hunting bats use this property of sound to attack moths as well as other insects. By making a constant high-frequency tone, a bat equivalent of the car horn, some bats can listen out for the change in pitch in the returning echo, caused by the Doppler shift, as the moth gets nearer. I would occasionally see Doppler bats hanging from a branch-tip in an open area between the trees, listening for insects with their enormous ears. By remaining stationary they save energy and it is easier to assess the sound waves. Having located their prey they then set off after it, and in the final stages of the approach change to FM sound to get an accurate sound picture before making a strike.

If all this sounds as though bats have got moths in the bag, think again, for the system has one very simple flaw. Many moths have ears. As I leaned on my tree trunk, straining to hear a bat's fading click, I could only hear the occasional hoot of some distant owl mixed in with the chirping frogs. But if I had ears as sensitive as some moths, no doubt the night would have sounded like a room full of screaming children.

The problem for a moth fluttering through the trees is to decide which of the many voices in the night to tune in to. Most moths seem able to hear bats only when they are within a few metres of them. This no doubt filters out some of the extraneous noise but this necessitates some drastic last-minute avoiding action. Tiger moths, which are unpalatable but whose warning colouration is invisible at night, produce a series of clicks of their own when predatory bats get close. This may be to jam the bat's radar or to let it know that this moth is not for eating. Jamming bat radar might seem a good way to avoid becoming an item on its menu, but some bugs seem to have found a simpler way of confusing these cunning little mammals.

The trees began to sway about in windy gusts and I could hear the sound of an approaching curtain of rain splatting onto the leaves some distance away. I had a few minutes before it would reach the tree platform. I pulled a lightweight plastic tarpaulin out of the

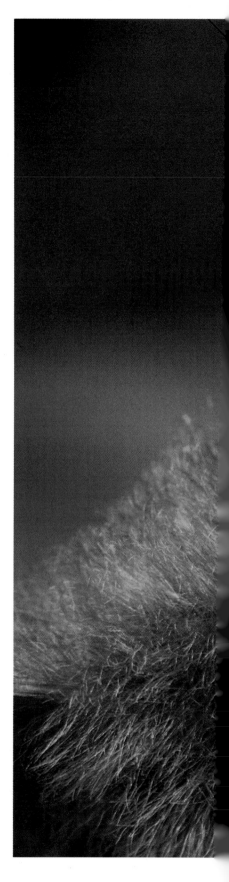

rucksack and began setting it up over my little island in the trees. The first droplets began to splash onto the makeshift roof as I tied off the last bits of cord and crawled underneath and into my sleeping bag. The candlelight flickered. I thought back to evenings years before in Sulawesi, where clouds of moths swarmed round a white sheet reflecting the glow of an ultra-violet lamp out into the darkness. The more it rained the more moths, beetles and bugs seemed to come. The effect of a water droplet the equivalent size of a bucket hitting an insect must be devastating, yet the insects seemed to welcome the rain and only when it really poured in torrents did the numbers in the air decline. It may be that the smallest insects are pushed aside by the air wave surrounding the drops and mathematically, the chance of a larger insect being hit are

PREVIOUS PAGE
Though it can see, the funnel-eared bat has little need of eyes: its sonar guides it through the night to scoop insects out of the air with its wings, then transferring them to its pointed teeth. Many bats which hunt in the canopy are barely known, as they are seldom trapped on the ground.

A host of smaller predators inhabit the canopy, some with surprisingly gourmet tastes: here a horned katydid devours a snail.

quite small. A string of light traps had been placed from the canopy to the ground in the forest nearby and we realized that on dry nights we caught fewer insects, in particular much lower numbers of sap-sucking bugs. On wet nights the numbers of insects increased, and we caught much greater numbers of bigger bugs, about five to six millimetres long, of a similar size in fact to rain droplets. It may be that these bugs only flew when it rained in order to avoid being eaten by bats. In rain it would be hard for bats to distinguish between a flying bug and a falling water droplet because bugs, like all living things, consist mostly of water and therefore have similar density and reflective qualities. So it is safer for the bugs to take to the air when they are screened by the rain, and to sit tight when it stops.

I pulled my sleeping bag up around my chin and listened to the frogs. Some bats can capture frogs at night by tracking their calls. Apart from frogs one of the noisiest creatures in the night-time rainforest are the katydids, so could bats catch them too? Jacqueline Bellwood, a researcher from the University of Florida working in Panama, found that the male katydids sit on leaves calling a tune to their mates, but surprisingly they call only in short bursts interspersed with long periods of silence. They do so with good reason. Foliage-gleaning bats flutter through the forest, eavesdropping on their love songs in the hopes of finding them. An over-zealous katydid would soon be snapped up, so the males keep it short and sweet to give themselves the best chance of survival whilst still attracting a mate. Only the biggest katydids, which may be as large as my hand, are too hefty for the bats, and can sing continuously.

All around me I could hear their serenades. Leaves in the branches nearby rustled with the movements of other creatures I could not see. After a while the gentle swaying of the tree rocked me to a contented sleep.

Fifteen million years ago our ape-like ancestors left the trees to begin a new life on the open plains, but some humans have not altogether lost the art of climbing. These young Waorani boys practise their skill in much the same way as our own children scramble about trees, but for them it is a vital aid in gathering food from the canopy.

9 | Tree People

It is extraordinary that so many children love the idea of living in a tree house. What is it that is so fascinating about the notion of living up high? As a child I loved climbing trees and like many others occasionally built platforms there from which I could gaze down in majesty on the rest of the world. Could it be that we still carry some strange link with our arboreal ancestry? Man's yearning for such a life was epitomized in the highly successful Tarzan movies, which still enjoy remarkable popularity. With Jane, Tarzan pursued a fantasy life of some style in a spacious tree house amidst a diverse population of creatures from almost every jungle on earth. In its heyday, Tree Tops safari lodge, built in a tree crown in Kenya, had a special charm few modern safari centres can match. But are there any human beings who actually live their lives and make their homes in the canopy of tropical trees? In the Manoquarie Hills of eastern New Guinea, there are.

Of all the tropical countries of the world, New Guinea must rank amongst the most extraordinary, a country which for me holds great mystery and enchantment. It sprawls on the map like a giant kangaroo leaping across the top of Australia. It is one of the largest islands in the world, populated by peoples similar in looks to Australia's aboriginals. Little has changed over much of the country since the first European, Jorge de Meneses, a Portuguese, landed on the northern coast in 1511. He called it 'Ilhas dos Papuas' after the Malay word meaning frizzy-haired. Thirty-seven years later the Spaniard, Ortiz Retes, sailing along the north coast in an attempt to reach Mexico, thought the people reminded him of those of the Guinea Coast in West Africa, so he named the land 'Nova Guinea'; hence Papua New Guinea.

An almost imaginary line now divides the western half of the island from the eastern, along borders once set by seafaring Malay sultans who ruled that part of the country before the Dutch adopted it as their own. Following the Second World War and independence from the Dutch, the new Indonesian nation received it on the bold stroke of a pen and a United Nations resolution. It is now known as West Irian or Irian Jaya. Amongst its knife-edged mountains and deep, forested valleys exist some of the most remote tribes of the world. Cut off from each other by the inhospitable terrain and the enclosing forest, they each developed cultures and, in many cases, languages of their own: New Guinea has spawned a quarter of all known tongues. It also harbours the world's rarest disease, the Kuru syndrome, a form of lingering madness leading to fits and

death, only contractable by eating the brains of another human.

In all the great tropical regions of the world there are people well versed in the art of living within the forest and subsisting on its abundant resources. One might think their presence must always be known, yet still new peoples are found every so often, living deep in the forest almost totally without contact with the world outside. The Tasaday tribe were not observed by Europeans until 1971; now they comprise a mere twenty-four people, living almost stone-age lives in the craggy southern tip of Mindanao in the Philippines. They had apparently only learned to prepare sago from the pith of palm trees a decade earlier, formerly foraging for frogs, fish, fruits, nuts and grubs. One of our Operation Drake patrols, exploring an uncharted section of the Strickland River in Papua New Guinea came across an isolated tribal group who called themselves the Pogaia. Once they had been coaxed out of the woodland where they had fled at the patrol's approach, they showed amazement at their pale skin – they had never seen the like of it before.

Everything had to be translated through a series of interpreters, from English to pidgin to Duna to a dialect which was close enough for the Pogaia to understand. It was a bit like a game of tribal Chinese whispers. In this way they gained their first knowledge of the New World outside the steep mountain ridges bordering their valley, beyond which they had only rarely ventured. There were but two metal implements in their village, highly prized axe heads traded from other tribes further downstream in the Bulago valley. How strange it is that just ten years before the Pogaia were discovered within the unexplored forests of our very own planet, man was stepping onto the moon.

In just one small area, in the Arfak mountains in the far east of Irian Jaya, the New Guinea tree people are to be found. It takes seven days of walking over some particularly steep and treacherous terrain to reach the area from the nearest small airstrip cut into the forest by evangelical Protestant missionaries. The mountains are steep and forest-covered, through which a slippery clay-covered path winds across ravines and narrow log bridges. The constant dampness mixed with sweat turns clothes to clammy rags and unexpected sink holes open in the limestone to reveal chasms hewn out by subterranean waterways beneath. Narrow suspension bridges made solely by vines sway unnervingly across raging torrents far below, whilst stones and roots cause unskilled walkers to trip and stumble, cutting skin on the sharp limestone outcrops. The only respite, a pause and a piece of cold roast taro root. Small wonder few people from the developed world have ventured there, even to this day.

Breaking out of the forest and into a clearing there are three small houses surrounding a very large tree. A long crude ladder of bamboo poles rises into the crown where a large tree house was built amongst the branches. Perched crazily twenty-five metres up, the house appears to be part of the tree itself with branches full of leaves

sprouting through the walls; there are a few others nearby. These are the homes of the Mava and Muscona. The tree houses are rectangular and made of logs with a roof made from woven palm thatch. There are no windows: the only light enters through the door and gaps between the branches. Cooking smoke filters through the roof into the air. A precarious-looking covered catwalk surrounds the whole structure. A few men and children watch self-consciously from the base of the tree.

After some simple introductions, and smiles, nervousness gives way to friendship and they will eagerly show you up the ladder. Inside the house is segregated – one side for the men, the other for the women – a corridor separates them. The house moves gently in the wind. The men's side has a large fire around which they sleep during the cold night. The space for sleeping is small and they must huddle together to avoid putting their feet in the fire. On a sturdy floor of logs, a few mats are strewn. Round the outside of the tree house the covered passage provides access to a series of precarious aerial lavatories which jut out over the ground below. Despite the rather delicate looking bamboo floor which leads to them, they can adequately support the weight of a large man, though the area below is to be avoided at all costs.

The Mava and Muscona are mainly hunter-gatherers, growing few crops save a little taro root, supplementing this with animals hunted in the forest with their bows and arrows. In the evenings they might offer a stew of wild rats or a roasted bat. Why do they build their homes in trees? One practical reason is that the terrain round about is very steep and there are few flat areas on which a large communal house could be built. But there may be another more compelling reason. Territorial disputes with neighbouring tribes often give rise to fearsome battles and their homes in the trees afford a magnificent view of approaching enemies and are more easily defensible than those on the ground. Also the terrain does make keeping in touch on foot very time-consuming. To reach another village by climbing down a steep-sided valley and up the other side may take many hours or even days. They have developed a sophisticated yodelling language which enables them to communicate over quite long distances, and the aerial houses help their message to carry much further than would be possible from the ground, just as the song of a gibbon does.

To many hunter-gathering people living in the world's remaining great rainforests, the canopy represents a valuable food source in the form of animals and fruits. Medicinal plants which grow beneath the canopy provide cures for diseases or contraceptive potions, whilst others can be prepared to yield deadly poisons with which to tip weapons. All of these things are to be found in the forest, yet to get them presents some difficulties. Tree people are not all skilled climbers, though many have learned remarkable ways of getting themselves into the canopy. Most climb by reaching round the trunk with their arms and bracing their feet against the bark,

PREVIOUS PAGE
A Mava tree house in eastern New Guinea. A ladder is the only way up to these aerial homes. Several families may live there, men and women occupying separate sides of the house. Inside they are relatively safe from attack by neighbouring tribes.

The spiny bark of the chonta tree makes it impossible to climb, so this Waorani boy has climbed a neighbouring tree to reach across to the valuable chonta fruit.

walking up step-wise, using alternate hands and feet. Chimpanzees use the same method but are rather better at it, having longer arms and greater strength. Depending upon the tribal tradition, the big toes, or alternatively the ankles, may be bound together with thin vines to provide a more secure purchase on the bark for their feet; yet only stout vines and small trees can be climbed in this way. But in one part of the world there is a group of people that surpasses all others in climbing ability, the pygmies of West Africa.

There are approximately one hundred and fifty thousand pygmies scattered through the equatorial forests of Cameroon, the Central African Republic, and northern Zaire, divided into at least eight different groups. The Mbuti, which inhabit the Ituri forest of Zaire, live in small bands of about thirty households, totalling fewer

than a hundred individuals. They are possibly the world's smallest people: fully grown men measure barely a metre and a half in height. Their families are diffuse and all members of the band regard each other with equal kinship. There are no outright leaders; all decisions are reached through group discussion. The women do most of the gathering of fruits and the few crops they grow, whilst the men do most of the hunting, and much of their time is spent making and repairing weapons.

Pygmies tend to have a special relationship with other tribes living nearby, less well versed in the art of forest living. In their eyes the pygmies have a special affinity with the forest and its spirits, and are often brought in to adjudicate in tribal disputes; they are also valued as guides and preside at important ceremonies, such as circumcision. In return for their knowledge the pygmies receive metal for axeheads and arrowtips, and cloth.

The men of the Central African Aka pygmies will skilfully shin up vines into the tree crowns to search for tree hyraxes, small mammals rather like guinea pigs. If they find one inside a hollow they will snatch it out, but they must be careful to avoid a savage bite. The Aka will even smoke hornbills out from their nests, as well as the occasional parrot. Efe pygmy hunters spend a great deal of time in trees, perhaps waiting for a forest duiker, a small shy antelope, to pass by. The trees are those with fruits that attract duikers when they feed in the early morning and late afternoon. Perched on a branch a few metres above the ground, the hunter waits until the duiker is beneath, then fires an arrow into it. Quickly jumping down, he gives chase, perhaps accompanied by a dog, and follows the animal until it falls.

The Efe also climb to gather fruits, which takes them much higher. One or two men usually climb up a vine or small tree simply using their hands and pressing the soles of their feet against the bark, but they may also shin up smaller trees by placing both hands above their heads on the trunk, grasping it with their legs and feet, and simply pulling themselves up, then taking a new hold with their feet. Either way it is a remarkable exhibition of strength and agility. Once in the crown they walk fearlessly around the branches, exhibiting a sense of balance that any tightrope walker would be proud of. As many as twenty climbers may be in the crown at once, gathering fruit and wandering around the tree limbs as happily as children out blackberry picking. As they step nimbly past each other, slapping backs and laughing, they seem totally unafraid of the fall that awaits them should they make one slip. Some fruits they pick and eat with relish above ground, but more often they shake the branches vigorously, letting the fruits tumble down to be collected by the women.

Faced with a tree too large to be grasped securely with his arms, the Efe climber will scale a smaller tree nearby and scramble across its branches into the other's crown. If there is too large a gap he will construct a bridge of vines between them. This can be a lengthy

process, but the Efe are determined people. They may even build several such bridges, from a small climbable tree into the crown of a medium-sized tree, and thence into the branches of the tree they wish to explore. The Efe are superb arboreal engineers and can tie their vines into many different knots, each with a special function. The most important reason the Efe and other pygmies climb, however, is not for fruit or a vantage point, it is to obtain honey. Such a harvest is a time for great celebration and gluttony, but before they can eat their honey, they have to find it.

The time to search for bee nests is towards the end of the rains, in June. At the approach of the two-month honey-collecting season a sense of anticipation grows amongst the pygmies. Groups of hunters may gather from different parts of the forest. It is a time for renewal of old friendships and the making of new ones, amid a strong festive spirit. As the rains end, the bees become more active, perhaps because there are more flowers in the forest at that time, and they fill their nests with honey to feed their growing grubs.

The Aka pygmies, like most others, seek both the nests of the stinging honey bee, the workers of which also exploit the flowers in our gardens, and those of the many non-stinging bees. The hunt begins with a night-long dance, then, before dawn, when the bees will still be in their nests within a hollow tree, the men go in search of them, walking quietly in groups of four or five, occasionally accompanied by children. Some nests they may already know of having found them in the course of searching for monkeys and squirrels, but if these have no honey yet they must seek others. As they walk through the slowly waking forest, every so often they stop and listen, straining for the sound of bees as they become active inside their trees. Around them birds are beginning to sing and the cicadas also scrape their morning call, so it is not easy to make out the bees' soft hum. To hear better, they tear off leaves from a liana with a red stem and rub them over their chest; this will bring them good luck.

To the seasoned hunter, there are other signs which give the nests away. Many bees die and fall to the foot of the tree but scavenging ants will soon carry off their bodies and dismember them in their own nests. The ants then cast out the inedible chitin which forms the bee's exoskeleton, and the pygmies look for this, piled in small middens outside the ants' entrance holes. Bee chitin shines in shafts of sunlight and to a pygmy's trained eye signals that a bee nest is at hand.

Once they have identified a nest tree, they scan the trunk for the hole from which bees may be seen buzzing in and out. A small tree can be felled with axes but the biggest trees take too long to bring down, so first they climb to inspect the nest and see if it has honey worth extracting. Bees often colonize the largest trees, giving themselves easy access to the tree crowns' flowers, but these massive trunks are often too wide for a pygmy's small arms to grip, and may even stand alone in a clearing. The pygmies are still not defeated.

Pygmies so enjoy the taste of honey that they will risk great danger to obtain it. Their skill at climbing trees is unequalled in the world.

They cut two lengths of vine, enough to go round the trunk and to spare. The first is slung about the tree and knotted with a loop, forming a stirrup into which the climber steps. The second vine is then looped round the trunk higher up and the climber steps into the second stirrup pulling himself up with his arms. Then he undoes the first loop and throws it round the trunk above his head, repeating the process all the way up the trunk. To an onlooker it is a terrifying procedure as the pygmy leans out over space, a tiny figure clinging to the tree, his life suspended on a vine of indeterminate strength. Despite the dangers and uncertainty, they very rarely fall but on occasions a breeze may cause the tree to sway, and the climber will freeze into immobility, crying out in fear. Far below he may hear the slow chanting of an elder, calming him, and reassured he will continue the climb.

Once they have decided that the nest is worth robbing, two small baskets of leaves are prepared. Into one smouldering wood is placed along with some wet leaves to make plenty of smoke, but the climber still smears his face with ash to protect himself from the inevitable stings. Onto his back he straps an axe and climbs up, trailing a long line of thin knotted vines. As he approaches the nest, he stops and hauls up the smouldering basket. Placing it beside the entrance hole he blows smoke into it. Furious bees shoot out and sting his largely unprotected body, but they do not sting too often and anyway, as the day is now well advanced, most of the workers are out foraging for pollen and nectar. The smoke helps to keep some of those bees now outside the nest at bay and reduces those inside to a stupor.

Unfortunately the nest is not at the entrance but may be some distance down inside the hollow trunk. The pygmy taps at the bark, judging from the sound the exact position of the nest. Bracing himself against the trunk, he begins to hack away at the bark,

On a simple harness of vines, a pygmy braces his feet against the tree while cutting into the bark to get at honeycombs concealed within the hollow trunk.

sending pieces of wood splintering out into space, spiralling down towards the ground. Eventually, he breaks through into the cavity and more angry bees buzz round his face, but intent on his purpose he reaches in and grasps the honeycombs, stuffing them into his mouth, grubs and all, with muffled whoops of joy, chewing the wax and sucking at the delicious mixture, honey dribbling down his chin. After months of a comparatively tedious diet such a sweet sensation on his tongue is the finest luxury the forest larder can provide.

The group below begins to shout their impatience, waiting with large trays made of leaves. Once he is sated, the honey gatherer tosses pieces of comb down towards them and as they fall, those below laugh and jostle for position to catch them. With a 'splat', a piece lands on the lucky one's leafy plate and he eagerly grabs at it, plunging the sticky mess into his mouth. Another piece falls from the sunlit forest roof, hard to see coming through the leaves. It hits a small branch and spins through the air, showering golden droplets of honey, lit by the sun. With a thud the comb lands on the ground and all pounce for it amid much laughter. The children are quick at finding the combs, picking out grubs and noisily sucking them into their mouths. Honey guides, small birds of the understorey, also partial to bee larvae, hear the commotion and fly in, in the hopes of picking up some leftovers. Clouds of small black trigonid bees swarm over the pygmies in search of sweat and sweetness. Eventually the second basket, shaped like a bucket, is hauled up and into this the remaining honeycombs within the nest are placed and lowered to the ground. Then the climber descends. Squatting on the forest floor, each with a large green leaf tablecloth spread before them, the pygmies consume as much honey as they can eat. The remains are placed in a large tree bark tub and, almost drunk with pleasure, the pygmies carry it off back to the village to divide it amongst their families.

The effort of climbing trees like this cannot be an everyday business so to catch animals that run through the tree tops, other methods must be used. Many tribes use bow and arrow but as many others have developed another means of reaching into the forest roof, the blowpipe. Few people are more adept at using it than the nomadic Penan of Borneo, like Leloh, my guide. Their camps or *sulaps* are designed to last only a few weeks and are soon absorbed into the decaying litter of the forest floor, leaving little evidence of their presence when the hunters have moved on. Once, whilst peering into the canopy to search for leaf monkeys, I became aware that it was I who was being watched. Slowly turning round, I found a small group of Penan watching me a short distance away, almost blending with the trees and bushes. A small, well-built man stood holding his tall blowpipe to one side, a sharp spearhead bound with rotan vines to its top. Nearby were several women, naked save for a simple necklace of beads and a once colourful sarong. Some carried children at their hips; other children clung nervously to their

mothers' sides, peeping out from behind them. There was a moment's silence whilst we stared at each other awkwardly until the ice was broken with a few polite nods and some simple words of greeting, and then they were gone, vanishing quickly into the forest.

I knew the group to be that of Nyapun, who lived about five hours' walk from our base camp on the Melinau river. Two months passed before he showed himself by walking into the camp one day, though without doubt he had watched us from the forest many times before without our knowing. The day he brought his family to the camp was a time of special enchantment I shall never forget. Only he had ever seen white people before. His wives and their little children all with nervously smiling faces, squatted on the intricately woven rush mats that we had spread on the bamboo flooring of the longhouse we had built, just set back from the Melinau river. Trilling frogs and crickets filled the warm night outside the long verandah, accompanied by the hiss of the tilly lamps hanging from the roof. It must have been a daunting experience for the gentle Penan, to be surrounded by a motley group of poorly shaven and faintly smelling scientists dressed in a curious collection of mil-dewed trousers, expedition sweatshirts and heavily booted feet or alternatively Malay sarongs and traditionally paisley patterned shirts, depending on whether the wearers chose to 'blend' with the country they were in or not. Small geckos shimmered across the *atap* walls, snapping at moths recovering from their exhausting skirmishes with the glowing lamps. A tiny pet mouse deer picked its way amongst the feet of those who had gathered in welcome, and eventually the evening's dancing could begin.

The music, alas, came not from native instruments but from a cassette purchased in a town downstream; a sign of the times, but the effect to me was nonetheless delightful. The two women slowly danced round and round, their feet barely moving as they bobbed gently up and down to the sound of the music, arms held out, hands flicking forwards and backwards in front and behind them. It was a dance representing the search for food in the forest, running swiftly through the undergrowth. Then they rubbed their hands between their thighs and wriggled their hips, signifying the grinding of plant fibres. Later it was Nyapun's turn; with his *parang* placed on the floor, he crouched and bobbed gracefully around it in a hunting dance, holding his arms out like the wings of a bird flying over the forest, eyes alert and searching. Both were dances of great simplic-ity, a reflection of their lives, at one with the forest.

The next morning I went in search of monkeys, accompanied by Leloh and his blowpipe. After six hours' hard walking we reached a limestone cave overhung with small stalactites around which vines and creepers spread their clinging tendrils and dropped curtains of leaves down towards the ground. Here centuries of Penan hunters must have spent the night warmed by a small fire, as we did. At one side of the cave in a sheltered corner Leloh had made another small fire, and round it had placed four thin sticks. On these something

like bark was balanced, into which he placed some sap he had collected from an ipoh tree. It would be a long night of waiting, for he was making poison.

There are many kinds of poison known to the tree people. Such knowledge is an integral part of their lives, for with poison they can hunt and even defend themselves against their enemies. In South America *Strychnos* plants yield curare, a rapidly acting poison that relaxes muscles, making it hard to breathe, leading to eventual suffocation. The Yanomami always use it on their long arrows to kill birds and monkeys because it makes them release their grip in the agony of death, and so fall to the ground. Doctors in our operating theatres have also found such an effect to their advantage

In the dark understorey of the Amazon forest, a Waorani hunter searches the canopy for a bird or monkey with which to feed his family. The poisons which tip his lethal blowpipe darts are made from toxins wiped from the backs of sweating frogs.

and administer modern drugs derived from curare to quieten our muscles, making it easier for anaesthetized breathing to be carefully controlled by a machine.

Animals, too, can be sources of lethal poison. Further inland from the site of our first walkway in Panama, the Choco Indians tip their darts with secretions wiped from the back of sweating frogs. They search for just two highly coloured poisonous species which they keep in tubes of cane, feeding them until they need their poison. Then they remove a frog and pass a piece of wood down its throat and out through one of its legs; they may even warm the unfortunate amphibian beside a fire. This torture causes a froth to appear on the frog's back which is infused with the deadly poison, something the frog would ordinarily produce to ward off the attentions of less formidable predators than the Choco. Arrows and darts are dipped into the froth and will remain potent for many months. One frog may donate sufficient poison for fifty such weapons. Further south the Indians seek the poison of another frog, *Phylobates terribilis*. These bright yellow frogs contain in their skin one of the most toxic substances known to man; even to handle them is dangerous so there is no need to subject *terribilis* to the ordeal its relatives face. It is sufficient merely to wipe a dart or arrow across its back. On entering the blood stream of another animal the poison quickly sends nerve impulses into disarray and muscles into spasm. The heart fails and the creature soon falls from the forest roof and into the hunter's possession.

Leloh was shaving a spicule of wood he had removed from his bamboo quiver. It was now late into the night and rain was falling heavily outside the cave. The night frogs delighted in it and sang with even greater gusto to their mates. Water dribbled down the stalactites at the cave entrance. The main fire was out, but shadows from the smaller one flickered across Leloh's face as he squatted beside the slowly steaming bark. He was using steady strokes with a small knife blade on a thin, slightly curved handle, the wood end of which he balanced against his thigh. All through the night he tended the fire and looked into the sizzling mixture inside the bark. At its base, a dark tarry liquid had collected and into this he dipped the sharply pointed spicules. Tipped with this poison they could kill a bird or monkey within a matter of minutes. Occasionally he took out thicker darts to which a small sharp arrowhead was fixed; these too were dipped into the poison. The Penan use them to kill larger animals on the forest floor, such as pigs which they would then chase with small hunting dogs, until the poison began to work and the pig, perhaps old and tired, turned to face them. Then he would spear it with the blade on the end of his blowpipe.

Leloh was not fond of scrambling up vines of unknown strength, though occasionally forest people will climb up them with their blowpipes to get a better view. The mammals and birds of the canopy are vigilant, so the silence of a blowpipe is preferable to the twang of a bow and can give a crucial advantage. For me to go

hunting with him would have been an absurd nuisance, though Leloh would undoubted have accepted my company politely. The Penan, like most forest people have the unnerving capability of being able to walk over even dry leaves and twigs with almost no sound at all, but even after several months of diligently searching for monkeys and gibbons it was hard for me to approach without them noticing me first. The best I could do was to intercept their route and then remain still until they passed by. Provided I could remain absolutely still, concealed amongst the vegetation, and preferably stop breathing too, the monkeys occasionally came unbelievably close, a superb reward after months of watching mere silhouettes in the canopy. Then it is only the excited pounding of blood in your ears which seems certain to reveal to them that man is watching.

Holding the long ebony tube to his lips, Leloh could fire a dart with accuracy high into the tree tops to pierce a roosting pigeon or a sitting monkey. Leaf monkeys, in particular Hose's leaf monkeys, were highly prized not only for their meat but also for the green bezoar stones they contain in their livers, which can be sold to the Chinese for high prices to be ground into potions. But should the monkey troops fall below a certain number, the Penan will usually leave them to recover. The Penan occasionally helped in the collection of specimens by reversing the dart before firing it, sending its pith-weighted end speeding up to dislodge a small creature, such as a lizard, high in the trees, which would fall, stunned, to the ground to be examined, marked and released before it had time to wake up.

In parts of South East Asia, the blowpipe may not always have been the favoured weapon of tree people. Amongst Malaysian Negritos, or *Semang* as these pygmy aboriginals are often called, there is a considerable body of evidence that suggests that until the turn of the century, the bow and arrow was the principal hunting weapon. Now few are skilled with it, a change most likely caused by the introduction of muskets into the region in the 1800's. Armed with this new weapon, the pygmies quickly hunted out the larger animals of the forest floor such as sambar deer, seladang, a kind of forest bison, and even rhinoceros. Faced with a scarcity of prey, the hunters turned to squirrels, monkeys and birds in the canopy as a source of food and to the blowpipe as a superior hunting weapon.

The arrival of the shotgun is often the first of many great changes to the forest nomads' lives. Increased hunting pressures from expanding human populations shoot wildlife from the forests and into the mouths of hungry children, and the old taboos and practices which kept the forest people in harmony with their surroundings slowly begin to break down.

A great change is coming to the gentle Penan. My presence alone, along with the other *orang puteh* or white men who had come up their river, was part of that change. They will never be the same again. The coming of the 'New Way' is irresistible and indeed many tribal people desire it. Who would deny the advantage of an out-

board motor to those dependent upon rivers for transport. Digital watches, cassette radios and television are as alluring to them as they are to us. I was dumbfounded on my arrival from the other side of the world to find myself in a small village on the banks of the Baram river, after a considerable journey by Land Rover and river boat, to find myself watching an episode of *The Rockford Files* which I had missed the week before in England. The Top Twenty hits, just a few weeks older than our own, blared from a modern radio nearby. But more often the benefits from contact with the Western world bring a double-edged sword which in the past has been sorely struck.

Between 1957 and 1963 tuberculosis, influenza and smallpox were deliberately introduced into tribal villages in the Matto

For the Aucas, poison darts provide access to the canopy bounty, otherwise out of reach. Such traditional methods will rarely result in the loss of too many howler monkeys from the Ecuadorian rainforest, but the introduction of shotguns and a swelling population of hungry settlers quickly alters the balance.

Grosso of Amazonia by pioneers and game hunters. Tribal groups in South America have been bombed to make way for the Trans-amazonian Highway, had their food laced with arsenic, and been the objects of man-hunts in Paraguay during which surviving parents were killed and the children sold off. The list of atrocities is extensive. More insidious has been the gradual erosion of cultural identity, and loss of faith in elders and leaders to negotiate land rights with developers and governments who regard them as 'minors', often holding their views in contempt, preferring to 'integrate' them into the dominant culture as quickly as possible. It is a form of gentle genocide. Once dependent upon goods the forest cannot provide, the tribal people are locked into a cash economy in which labouring, often for logging companies which have taken over their ancestral lands, is their only source of funds with which to buy the materials they now need. Unused to this new way of life, they quickly fall into debt and demoralization.

Yet there is much that we could learn from them. Hunter–gatherers and those tribes that practise a slash and burn agricultural system are the only humans on earth who seem able to exploit the forest without destroying it. Over-hunting is rare where traditional methods are used and by felling a little bit of forest over a large area in which to grow rice or maize, the shifting agriculturalist does not return too often to the same area, giving the forest time to regenerate. Far from being primitive systems, they are better than anything 'modern' man has been able to devise.

The future of the tree people and the canopy under which they live rests with the governments that purport to own them. But all the world has a stake in the future of these forests, and in the uses to which the remarkable knowledge of their peoples are put. In the centuries to come it may not be their lives which are at immediate risk, but our own. That variety is the spice of life is a truism, yet it has its foundations in fundamental laws of nature. A world in which supercultures dominate and absorb all others is as unstable as a world dependent on nature bankrupt of genetic diversity. Without freedom of choice, natural selection is made sterile and evolution is brought to an end.

Most of the world's tree people will be gone in another generation, not because their forests will have vanished but because their culture will. Proximity to the modern world and the follow-on effects of numerous pioneer farmers, exploiting the forest without the knowledge to ensure its survival represent the least controllable elements in the changing face of the forest.

Along the roads the loggers leave behind, the sound of cheerful human voices follows. On old carts drawn by mules or oxen, and on impossibly overladen trucks, pioneer farmers begin to arrive in their thousands with their wives, children and simple possessions. They often come from lands far away where the soil is productive and the human population explosive. Many come from fertile homelands lured by the heavily advertised government promises of their very

Western banks pour millions of dollars into Indonesia's transmigration programme to move landless poor from overcrowded Java to less populated islands. New homes result, but often on poor soil and at the expense of virgin forest, whilst much already cleared land available for cultivation exists elsewhere. Such resettlement schemes are often abandoned, but by then the damage to the forest is done.

own plot of land in the new frontier. On television, radio and posters the message is clear. An agricultural revolution is being wrought in the new 'Wild West' and the unproductive, unappetizing, unloved forest is being rolled back.

Over-population is ultimately the forests' greatest threat for it is this which fuels the quest for more land. Yet there is no shortage of land in the areas from which the forest has already been removed; per head of population there is more in Brazil than in the United States. But the reforms which could provide for all are not welcomed by those who own the land and in Latin America ninety-two per cent of arable land is held by just seven per cent of the land-owners.

As the pioneers arrive in thousands, they clear and burn the forest and those that arrive late move into areas nearby, that were untouched by loggers and zoned for watershed protection or an Indian reserve or perhaps a national park. And as each year more arrive, slowly the forest becomes a patchwork and the clearings coalesce. The Indians that lived there before are pushed aside but occasionally fight back, kidnapping children and even killing settlers in desperation that their plight should be heard. But it is an unequal contest and they are soon overwhelmed and demoralized, though the stronger tribes retain some dignity in the few extensive reserves. The pioneers, alas, have no tradition of sustainable use of

the forest as practised by the indigenous Indians, and their efforts to raise crops and families soon reap only disappointment from the infertile soils. With nowhere else to go they must move on, often abandoning the government schemes altogether, and repeating the process and clearing new areas, rapidly accelerating the rate of devastation. The landless poor of one area move, to become the landless poor of another. Between them they account for greater destruction than all the logging companies put together.

Our connection with this destruction is more intimate than you might think. Multilateral-Development Banks fund many of the government schemes to move the landless poor and so help them bring the forest to its end. Converting the forest to cattle ranching is another popular, but short-lived scheme, again backed heavily by the World Bank and Inter-American Development Bank.

Edible plants are soon eaten out giving way to unpalatable weeds and within five to seven years the ranches are abandoned and a new area of forest must be cleared. Nonetheless, good profits are realizable in the short term and in politically volatile countries, that makes for good business. It is no surprise that the proximity of Central America to the United States has fostered the destruction of the forest there as the majority of the cheap beef reared on the deforested lands is exported to the USA to swell the hamburgers of the fast food industry. Though this trade represents less than two per cent of American beef consumption, it has resulted in a quarter of all the tropical forest in Central America disappearing from the world for ever. The long term cost to the Central Americans for our cheap beef continues to remain outside the hamburger giants' equations.

In some parts of this tale of destruction there appear to be hopeful signs of change. The international agencies which indirectly fund the destruction of the canopy have in some cases instigated environmental impact studies prior to the loans being agreed and refuse those which appear to call for agricultural development on tropical forest soils unable to sustain it. In addition, safeguards for Indian populations are sometimes written into agreements between governments and development consortia and there is a growing tendency to link loans to conservation activities such as protection of watersheds. By declaring forests surrounding irrigation schemes as nature reserves, their sponge effects can ensure that irrigation channels remain full when rain fails to fall. But the reality of the situation is that infringements of such conditions rarely result in loans being withdrawn and the staff employed to examine the impact of new developments is pitifully small. But it is a step in the right direction and the enormous extent to which environmental degradation has been unwittingly funded by the Western taxpayer is drawing such agencies into an increasingly uncomfortable light in the eyes of the public, forcing them to consider the notion of working conservation in with development more seriously.

What can mere individuals do to stem this global tragedy? At one

end of the spectrum are decision-makers in government, international aid agencies and industrial giants; at the other are those who seek to play their part by unravelling another piece of the tropical forest jigsaw. These are the people who dedicate their lives to understanding the most complex ecosystems on earth, to deciding how large the forests that remain should be, what benefits may accrue to man, how to cultivate a tree so that more may be grown, or how to find out what is there before it has all gone. Some have chosen to explore the part of the forest that is least known and may therefore have most to offer. These are another kind of tree people, the arboreal naturalists. For them the challenge is to understand the forest before it has vanished, and they are rapidly running out of time.

A great change is coming to the forest. By the time this Penan child is old, his Bornean homeland will have altered beyond all recognition.

10 | Above the Future Forest

For the animals, the first inkling of the change to their forest may be the sound of a powerful bulldozer. Even mighty trees, tall as houses, are no match for its blade. With tracks churning the thin red soil, the shining steel pushes into the bark and without deep roots to grip, the forest giant topples as easily as a pencil on a tabletop. Many others will fall with it, bound by clinging creepers and vines. Once the beast has passed, the birds and animals can rest again but their normal routes may soon be divided by a chasm through which the sun burns to a new road below. Shade-loving creatures retreat deeper into the forest and monkeys chatter and scramble near its edge, unable to reach favourite fruit trees on the other side, their routeways and home ranges cut asunder. And as more roads appear they find themselves living in diminishing islands of trees, unable to escape.

Then the loggers come, cutting into the forest down the lines of their concession, and more besides to which they are not entitled, to provide timber for building, wood chips or perhaps fuel. In the past rainforests could not easily be made into paper, but new technology has changed all that; most hardwoods now can be reduced to neat piles of chips in minutes. Those logs destined for sawmills are chained onto the backs of groaning lorries, and disappear from the forest in a noisy cloud of diesel fumes. Of the half that will be exported fifty-three per cent go to Japan, thirty-two per cent to Europe and fifteen per cent to the USA.

Soon the smell of smoke begins to fill the forest. Aircraft may suddenly appear above the cringing creatures in the fractured canopy, dropping firebombs through the tattered branches. Defoliants may have stripped many trees bare already, poisoning many of the animals in the process. The timber, dried in the sun, quickly burns into a firestorm consuming all those remaining creatures that are unable to flee. Eventually the roaring flames will subside, the green canopy will be gone and emerging from the smoke will be a silent wasteland.

The green tropical forest canopy still covers some eleven million square kilometres of the Earth's surface. But in recent years the rainforest has begun to diminish rapidly in many areas through man's growing need for firewood to prepare food, timber for construction and space to grow crops or graze cattle. Some forty per cent of the global coverage has been lost since this exploitation began. It will never return again, as it takes hundreds of years for true rainforest to regrow once it has been cut down and develop-

Within a forest firestorm there is small chance of escape for most canopy creatures. Progress clears the way for farmland but often a desert is the result. In our own lifetime we will see most of the world's rainforests vanish. Will our children ever forgive us?

ment rarely allows it such respite. Far from it, the destruction proceeds apace. Some forty hectares of virgin rainforest will have disappeared forever, during each minute that you have been reading this book. An area roughly the size of California disappears each year.

To exploit them is not a sin. The countries in which they are found often are poorly developed and need agricultural land to feed rapidly expanding populations. They also need foreign exchange to pay for roads, hospitals and irrigation schemes. Selling their wood is no more wrong than Western countries exploiting their oil. In both cases the resource will eventually run out. But unlike oil, rainforests contain the world's genetic deposit account for the future. By destroying them we are changing the course of evolution irrevocably, and faster than has ever happened before. They harbour countless benefits for an increasingly impoverished world which have only recently begun to be realized – new kinds of foods, cures for cancer and numerous other diseases, as well as insecticides to save our crops, to say nothing of their magnificent timber resources or the numerous animal and plant species that delight every child's eye. Not since the dinosaurs vanished from the world has such a change occurred. To continue the destruction without thought for the future and the great changes we are making to our planet, that is a sin. All perhaps would be well if rainforests could be regrown, but to date few rainforest trees have been cultivated successfully under the conditions commerce dictates. Our capacity to recreate a virgin forest once cut is currently nil. And there has been little pressure to do so: it is simpler to cut from the wild.

What will happen? Will we suffocate for lack of oxygen? Will the 'greenhouse effect', caused by the burning of fossil fuels and the forest's timber, raise global temperatures, melt the ice caps and drown coastal cities? Will the earth's climate change and rain cease to fall on the American grain belt, turning it to desert?

At present it is impossible to say, but can we afford to take such risks? I suspect that human nature is such that it will continue to ignore the prospect of such speculative catastrophies and concentrate, quite naturally, on the delight produced by a cheap hamburger, the durability of hardwood window-frames, the colour of our television's veneer, the chewing qualities of gum, the blessings of anti-cancer drugs, the pill, and rubber, not staying to imagine a world without green forest filled with noisy monkeys, clouds of feeding birds and brilliant butterflies.

All of these quantifiable benefits, and thousands more, have been bequeathed to us from rainforests, with many others potentially to follow.

Perhaps the greatest benefits within the forest that have so far remained almost totally unexploited lie in the realm of pharmacology. Millions of plants have been at war with animals for centuries and have so produced countless substances in their defence, along with many others that enable them to survive in the rainforest's

In the vanguard of change, bulldozers push new routes into the forest. They sound the death knell for the animals and plants of the jungle, as well as the tribal way of life which depends on them. Ultimately, the whole world suffers, because we depend on these forests ourselves to maintain the atmosphere we breathe.

When retiring to bed with a mug of cocoa, few people would think of its origins inside the cacao pod deep within the rainforest. From the pill to anti-cancer drugs, numerous other benefits have accrued to us from these valuable environments, with more being discovered each year which could form the basis of billion-dollar industries in the future. Preserving the natural laboratory which made them makes sound economic sense.

unique environment. These are known as phytochemicals. Very often the scientist is at a loss to conceive new compounds even from computer programmes, and turns to the plant kingdom for inspiration. Many of the new compounds which go to work in our hospitals and on our fields have their origins in the natural world. Increasingly in the last few years the full measure of the quantity of remarkable phytochemicals that exist in tropical forests has begun to be realized, and with that realization has come awareness of the tragic loss to humankind entailed in forest destruction, and the fact that tree peoples' traditional knowledge of plants and their uses is lost with them.

In the past we owed our health to our knowledge of how plants could help us. Most modern drugs were developed from them – today almost fifty per cent of our medications are still derived from plants. The USA imports millions of dollars' worth of medicinal plants each year. There is a one-in-ten chance that the next time you enter a chemist for a prescription you will leave with a product conjured from a rainforest phytochemical. Many of our steroid hormones, including ingredients for the pill, are synthesized from the Mexican yam. Perhaps most celebrated of all are the anti-cancer drugs, developed from the rosy periwinkle, whose delicate pink flowers, found in the understorey of tropical forests, were used by tribal people as an oral medicine. Vincaleucoblastine and Vincristine are two drugs developed from it which now result in ninety-eight per cent remission in certain forms of acute leukaemia, and eighty per cent remission in treating Hodgkins disease, a cancer of the lymphatic system. Almost three-quarters of the plants known to possess some form of anti-cancer property originate in the lowland tropics, yet even now only a tiny proportion have been screened for their potential. Almost in despair the noted Brazilian phytochemist, Otto Gottlieb, wrote in 1981: '... almost nothing at all is known about the chemical composition of 99.9% of our flora'. How many more botanical superstars would be found, if only there was the will to look.

The remarkable thing is that much of the work involved in sorting out the most useful plants for humans has already been done by the forest peoples. Yet in the developed world the science of ethnobotany remains in its infancy. Peruvian Indians use the blood-red latex of the *Croton* tree to rid themselves of stomach cancer. The dried flower clusters of *Philodendron dyscarpium* are used by the women of Makuna and Kubeo Indians to prevent pregnancy. The *Tachigalia* tree, which has such a strange suicidal flowering cycle, is known as the 'no children tree' by the Bara-Makus nomads of Amazonia. Deni Indians in Brazil drink a tea brewed from the liana, which also gives them poison for their arrows, to induce temporary sterility. Scientists extend the list each year but it barely keeps pace with the rate at which such knowledge is being lost forever, along with the tribal traditions which have sustained it through successive generations.

It may be a tribute to the selective abilities of the Western digestive system that a mere twenty species of plant stand between us and starvation. This extraordinary dietary dependence is the result of years of selective exploitation of marketable foods discovered in colonial, usually tropical, dependencies. Once coffee, cocoa, rice and corn became established in the Western diet, it was hard for new species to make it to the table. As a result the countries in which they grew became dependent on exporting them to bring much-needed foreign exchange. Less than six per cent of the food eaten in the United States comes from food plants which originated there. This fragile existence on so few plants suits multinational companies which control the trade, though it is but a fraction of what the world has to offer. Increasingly, though, manufacturers must turn to wild plants to derive more productive crops to fuel the Green Revolution. A 'wonder' rice bulging with grains and resistant to pathogens does not always remain so. Infusions of wild germplasm are occasionally needed to top up the laboratory strains with a genetic tonic. The increased productivity adds about seven hundred million dollars a year to the value of American food crops. To destroy the greatest storehouse of genetic diversity on which future known and untried food crops may depend must be the height of human folly.

In the future perhaps the best reason for studying insects in rainforests will not be because of their intrinsic interest to entomologists or their harm to man, but because of their potential benefits. Yields of oil from oil palms in Malaysia improved to the value of one hundred million dollars in less than two years when a small beetle introduced from Cameroun took over the job of pollinating them. Entomologists believe that for every insect pest there is another insect to tackle it and it is certain that many will be found in the canopy. The search for these insecticidal insects has only just begun and, like bio-engineering, could become a billion-dollar business. Some years ago citrus growers in Florida spent thirty-five thousand dollars on importing three types of parasitic insects to control fruit pests. Now these parasites save the industry thirty-five million dollars per year. American farmers presently apply about four hundred thousand metric tons of chemical insecticides to their crops each year, ten times as much as in 1950, but they lose twice as much food to insects now as they did then. All over the world insect pests are becoming resistant to almost everything we can throw at them. Sooner or later, it will pay us all to turn to the insect world and work with it, to find a way out of the mess.

Industry is at last beginning to learn from the tree people. Natural pesticides occur in abundance in rainforests, though few have been tried commercially. *Lonochocarpus* plants were long known to Amerindians as a good source of poison to stun fish. Now the active ingredient, *rotenone*, is one of the world's most valuable biodegradable pesticides. Even petroleum can be made from trees. *Copaifera* trees produce an oil so volatile it can be poured directly into

diesel engines, and at least one research institute runs its fleet of Toyota trucks on it. When fossil fuels become uneconomic to extract, could the vast tracts already denuded of forest be put to use to fuel the world? Perhaps a little optimistic but many products currently derived from crude oil could be manufactured from this extraordinary tree and others like it.

Whilst there is little public awareness of the origins of these products, many of which are now the basis of billion-dollar industries, it is hard to remain oblivious of the starving millions in Africa and elsewhere, of the floods that carry away so many thousands of lives, of the cattle dying on the Latin American grasslands, of the scarred landscape that almost inevitably appears once the forest has gone, without wondering if these things are not related to the damage we are doing to the green canopy. It appears that the forest engine is rapidly falling apart; perhaps a new and improved model would more adequately fit our needs. If rainforest could be regrown once cut perhaps all would be well; if sufficient forests could be protected for posterity the gene bank would continue to pay interest, and we could enjoy the animals too. It is time to call in the biological mechanic to explain what we should do. Now the awful truth dawns upon us. The mechanic does not know what to do either.

One of the greatest difficulties facing the conservation lobby lies in placing a value on forests which appear to be doing very little of economic value. A tropical forest is a bit like a huge electricity generator. A small input of energy, say a drum of fuel, keeps the machine going for a long period during which time the electricity it produces can be put to a great many uses. If the generator is destroyed, and the drum of fuel is put to the match, very little can be done with the short-lived heat it produces. The same is true of a rainforest. It manages to use the sun's energy, plus a little bit of oiling with nutrients from the atmosphere, and by feeding upon itself, runs very efficiently. Once the forest is removed, the energy from the sun has no engine to work on and the baked soil soon grinds to a halt without regular lubrication with artificial fertilizer. Were I to examine the engine amidst the noise and clatter of its moving parts, with no knowledge of such machines, I would have no idea what it was doing or how it worked. The electricity it produced would be invisible and its valuable effects often in use a long distance away from the machine itself: we rarely think of the generator when turning on a light. The value of rainforests in maintaining the world's climate is also hard to see, as are their effects in preventing floods far away from where the forests themselves exist. These are so-called downstream effects, and may not be noticeable to the people who should be responsible for keeping the forest generator going. They have more tangible problems to deal with, such as paying off foreign loans and raising standards of living. Set against a large capital account which apparently fails to pay any interest, conversion to agriculture, even though short-lived, seems a better option. So the destruction proceeds apace.

Worldwide, there are perhaps fewer than twenty-five scientists who have sufficient knowledge, and are competent, to undertake large-scale development-orientated studies of tropical ecosystems. Those who can walk into a rainforest and confidently identify all the plants there can be numbered on one hand. How can this be? Set against the vast sums being used to destroy rainforests for short-term gain, the mere forty million dollars annually going towards research into what they consist of and how they work is derisory compared with their potential benefits. Half the biologists studying them are still trying to attribute names to the animals and plants there, let alone discover how they inter-relate with each other. The world of science is being asked how to create plantations using trees whose growth requirements are unknown, and to advise on the setting-up of nature reserves with no idea of how big they should be to sustain the animals that live in them. Alas, it is no use complaining that more time is required; the best that can be hoped for now is an inspired guess. It does not always work.

At Jari river in Brazil the American industrialist Daniel K. Ludwig carved out the largest rainforest plantation of all time. At a cost of eight hundred million dollars an area half the size of Belgium was cleared of forest animals and Indians in the 1960s, and planted with fast-growing Caribbean pine, eucalyptus and Asian Gmelina trees. The latter trees did not do as well as expected on the poorer soils,

Pine trees for the planting at Jarri river in Brazil. Plantations can never replace what was there before as we do not know or understand the complex structure of a rainforest, but if economically successful they could reduce pressure on virgin forest itself.

and political pressures forced Ludwig to sell the enterprise before its true potential could be realized. The eucalyptus and pines, though they have grown reasonably well, are now threatened by pests and diseases which thrive in the monoculture plantations. Much larger plantations are planned for Amazonia in the future. It remains to be seen if they prove economic.

Agronomists and foresters are now beginning to agree that the agricultural approach most likely to succeed is one which mimics the diversity and interdependence of the forest itself. Plans to grow a wide variety of crops with trees, or agroforestry, as is successfully practised on infertile soils in some parts of the world, are gaining acceptance. Village schemes to create mosaics of forest, providing wood and food crops are also being funded by the World Bank, ironically alongside their financial support of the destruction such schemes are designed to replace.

It may well be possible to select fast-growing plantation hardwoods, and the race is on to find them. As there has been relatively little attempt to breed new strains of rainforest tree more suited to man's needs than the generally slow-growing hardwoods, efforts in this direction could prove of great value. Nations that were once timber exporters to the world, faced with the realization that they will soon need to import the very trees that once grew in abundance within their own borders, are becoming anxious to find a home-grown solution to their problem. As the loggers move on they are often required to leave sufficient trees behind to enable the forest to restore itself, or even to plant new trees so that plantations may grow; but the cost is high and though government regulations look impressive on paper there are so few officials to check on them in the 'wild frontier' that few companies take much notice. If there is a fuss, a blind eye can usually be bought. So whether a forest is clear-felled for paper or merely selectively logged for the finest trees, it is rarely given a chance to recover and the outcome is usually the same. The edge of the 'New World' advances.

In financial terms the UK is the third largest user of tropical hardwoods in the world. The USA is the largest importer of plywoods, almost half of it consisting of shredded rainforest trees. Possibly an effective way to reduce extraction of trees from these forests is to persuade individuals to boycott hardwood timber products. Hard-hitting campaigns are remarkably effective at changing the public's attitudes to what they buy, as Canadian fur sealers know to their cost. Governments could also discriminate against timber imports unless they were harvested from sustainable sources. In time such restrictions on importation and use could help to develop sustainable plantations. But the best that can be expected is a new forest with a canopy quite unlike that which grew there before. The only hope for natural rainforests and their inhabitants is protection within large, adequately buffered, reserves.

In response to the public outcry and scientific dismay at the rape of the world's rainforests numerous large areas of protected forest

have appeared on maps within government offices. Developing nations have few funds to police them, however, and they are often gradually eroded. But that they exist at all is a step of great value. Many nations in which rainforests are found have publicly stated their commitment to a conservation strategy, and intend to set aside as much as five per cent of their total land area as permanent nature reserves. In a country such as Indonesia, that five per cent embraces a great deal of forest. As the pressure increases from international agencies such as the World Wildlife Fund and UNESCO's Man and Biosphere Programme, there is hope that a sufficient proportion, representative of the world's remaining rainforests, will survive in perpetuity, but there is often much political resentment in the rainforest countries about what is seen as a new form of colonialism. Most of the advisers, whether bankers or botanists, who presume to tell them what they should do with their forests, do not come from within their own borders; international meetings held to iron out plans to preserve rainforests are often unattended by many of the countries in which they grow.

A key factor is to determine how large a reserve should be in order for it to survive indefinitely. When only islands of forest remain, a process known as ecosystem decay occurs, and even if the remaining forest covers many square kilometres, for some reason, certain of the animals that formerly lived there either die or desert, and the forest gradually becomes poorer in species. The trees also suffer from our ignorance of their needs. Practically nothing is known about how different species survive together in the forest, how their composition may alter through time. One thing is certain. They have not always been where they are now.

During the Pleistocene era, when the world was cold and dry glacial conditions prevailed, the great forests shrank and existed as isolated islands for millions of years. During this time new species evolved peculiar to each fragment and when warm conditions returned the forests expanded to their present range. The intermingling of so many different species may be a reason for the extraordinary diversity of life in rainforests today. The original 'refugia' from which this expansion occurred are likely to be forests of great value as it was here that so many species existing today evolved. Ultimately, an understanding of how the forest expanded and now sustains itself is to be found in the mechanisms by which trees reproduce themselves, and how one species gives way to another through time: the dynamics of the forest. In Panama such an experiment in tropical dynamics is underway on Barro Colorado Island, situated in the Panama Canal's Gatun Lake.

Working from the Smithsonian Tropical Research Institute's station there, Dr Stephen Hubbell and Dr Robin Foster have identified the species and position of every single tree in fifty hectares of forest on the island. This is a huge task because of the enormous numbers and variety of species involved, as well as saplings which have yet to grow beyond the thickness of a human

finger. A similar scheme is soon to be under way in Malaysia. The information is plotted onto a computer so the touch of a button reveals a tree-map showing the distribution of any species in the area in relation to the shape of the land surface, soils, moisture, temperature and other factors. Gradually a picture of the requirements for their survival may be built up over years, as the changing composition of the forest area is charted, but there is one crucial gap in the data which at present cannot easily be filled: the knowledge of how and when each tree produces its flowers, who comes to pollinate them, when leaves and new shoots appear, and when fruits are spread amongst their branches. To discover these things has been next to impossible because over half the trees on the island are canopy species, and what is going on in their crowns is largely invisible from the ground. Yet as we have seen, it is here that they hold their breeding systems and genes flow between them on the bodies of bees, birds or bats, and it is here that numerous other interactions occur with the sun, with climbing vines and epiphytes, with other neighbouring trees, and with the animals that depend on them for fruit, seeds or leaves. It is to learn how the canopy sustains itself as well as seeking other knowledge, that the arboreal naturalists of the future must climb.

Around the world there are growing numbers of arboreal naturalists, people who have decided to take their lives into their own hands because of their fascination with the natural world and how it works, and because of their love of forests. But there is a deeper felt mission. They know, as do many others, that the forests are doomed and that they have before them a quest of impossible proportions, that of understanding the most complex exhibition of life on earth, perhaps the greatest experiment in evolution the planet has ever spawned. It is a daring prospect to explore nature in the heartland of natural selection, to examine the patterns and processes of an environment which has reached a climax of living on this fragile earth. It is hard to believe that mere accident, moulded by a length of time beyond the imagination of our short-lived human minds, could realize such diversity. Tropical nature has a face which at times appears familiar but like a mask it can be peeled off, revealing many players beneath, so that as fast as one is removed, a new character is exposed, taunting the human clown into tearing off another layer, all the time wondering if at last the truth will be revealed.

Andrew Field picked up his small backpack with the day's needs: notebook, water bottle, something to eat, and the climbing ropes. In a week he would be going home to England and four years of study in the Venezuelan forest canopy would be at an end. There was just one more tree to climb to take some final collections and then it would be back to Richmond to write it all up and submit the results for a doctorate at the University of Reading. Stepping out of the research station at Rancho Grande, he waved, said he would be

back later that night, and was swallowed up in the forest of the Henri Pittier National Park.

It had all begun in Hawaii, years before. After graduating from Durham University, the lure of exuberant tropical life on that Pacific island had cast its spell over him. Few naturalists, once addicted, can resist it. Some months as a forest guide in Ecuador and a growing desire to do something in the battle to save the world's rainforests, convinced him that investigating how they worked was where his immediate future lay. Finally he found himself in Caracas, capital of Venezuela, an extraordinary city nestling like a new Manhattan in the jungle, surrounded on all sides by magnificent forested mountains. Some distance inland was the old, isolated research station at Rancho Grande. Few scientists now made use of the somewhat tumbledown building, but at least it was a base from which to work. Little was known about the natural history of the area and no attempts had been made to explore the crowns of the large tropical trees. Field determined to discover how particular trees were pollinated, and immediately began thinking of ways to get up amongst their branches of flowers.

First he tried erecting aluminium ladders but soon realized they were expensive and cumbersome to build. Reading about the new rope-climbing techniques provided the inspiration for building a tree platform and a radiating series of rope catwalks. Members of the local climbing club taught him to climb, using ropes and jumars, and in time all his own equipment arrived from England. Over the next few years he built quite a network in the trees and was able to walk with confidence amongst the branches, spending many nights up there, watching to see who would be creeping around the crowns under cover of darkness. There was a roof and a simple bed; he could spend days aloft without ever needing to go down to the ground. For exercise he could step out onto the flimsy rope bridges he had built, leading from the platform to other trees nearby. There had been no one to help. At the start it had been terrifying, suspended precariously amongst the leaves, so high above the ground, alone. The thick leaves so close gave a false sense of security. How solid they seemed, yet there would be no support from them if he crashed to the ground.

No one else knew anything much about the *Gyanthera* tree Andrew had chosen to put the platform in, but he had spent so much time there in the last few years that the tree was now like a friend. All kinds of creatures came to visit. Hummingbirds hovered in front of the flowers during the day; at night bats flapped in to lick nectar and pollen. Small marsupial frogs crept into the airborne pools in the tree's branches, to let their tiny young brood of tadpoles wriggle out of the pouches in their parent's back. Then there were the new species of beetles he had found, and always that delightful view out over the forest. He had learnt so much about how the tree was pollinated and how the wind dispersed its seeds on flimsy, papery wings. But it had been lonely.

David Attenborough coming to use the tree, along with a BBC film crew making *The Living Planet* series, had been a high point. Seeing the filming in progress and everyone hanging on ropes as the world's most famous naturalist explored his tree, was an experience Field would never forget. He longed to involve himself more in the world of television and popular natural history. He had even thought of writing a book about life in the rainforest roof, based on his work there. Perhaps the magazine articles he had written and the audio-visual slide show he devised for the Venezuelan Conservation Society would help to heighten interest in the forest canopy. The nature trail at Rancho Grande he had built was almost complete, too. It was so important to get local people out into the forest, to understand its beauty and intricate life forms. Perhaps then they would take greater care of it.

It was a twenty-minute walk from the research station to his house in the trees. For this last trip Andrew took a different route into the forest, to the big tree he had chosen to climb. Eventually, pushing through the shrubs, he stepped over dry leaves to the base of the trunk and looked up into the huge branches, darkly silhouetted against the bright sky. Having chosen a tree limb strong enough to take his weight, he put the pack down and pulled out the powerful catapult his mother had sent him from England. Tying some nylon line to a stone, he raised his arm, pulled back the rubber thongs and sent the stone hurtling up through the leaves. It took several goes to get it over the right branch. Walking to the other side of the tree he located the thin nylon line, followed it down to where the stone had fallen, and attached the climbing rope to the line. The rope looked a little worn but it always took so long for things to arrive in Venezuela, and money was so tight. His grant was almost through but that would barely pay for the flight home. After a few minutes he had pulled the rope over the limb, and made it fast. He clipped on the ascenders and stepped into the stirrups, letting his weight be taken by the harness on the rope. With steady movements, he began to climb.

No one at the research station knew exactly where he had gone to climb the new tree. When Field failed to return in the evening as planned, they thought perhaps he had decided to spend the night in the forest, nothing unusual about that. Time passed. They spent two days searching in the forest before they found him. Judging by the extent of his injuries, he had fallen from a great height, and must have died instantly.

A fate such as Andrew Field's could so easily be suffered by me or anyone else prepared to work in the canopy. The dangers of working there cannot be over-estimated. Great care must always be taken with the personal discipline that safety demands, but equipment can still fail despite close scrutiny, and ultimately there is always an element of chance that cannot be calculated. Andrew Field is not the only person to have fallen and there will be others. Fortunately his biological collections and labours have not been

Arboreal naturalists such as Andrew Field dedicate their lives to finding out how the forest functions. His group of walkways in the Venezuelan forest canopy provided a first glimpse of the natural world to be found there. Tragically, in 1984, he fell to his death. A nature trail at Rancho Grande is a memorial to his work.

wasted and are now lodged at Venezuelan Institutions and the Royal Botanical Gardens at Kew in England. Should you visit Rancho Grande you will be able to walk along the delightful nature trail there, now named after him.

The introduction of modern climbing techniques to the study of the rainforest roof has led to a growing number of people across the world experiencing for the first time the delights and dangers of inch-worming their way up into the canopy. As each new individual brings his or her mind to bear on the complexities of animal and plant life there, a greater understanding will follow. If their efforts are not to be wasted we must pay heed to them. Scaffoldng towers and more sturdy structures have sprung up in Australia, or Africa and Latin America from which just a small part of the forest can be examined.

Many animals, such as primates, which inhabit the canopy, act as reservoirs for diseases which can be transmitted to man via mosquitoes. Knowledge of where these mosquitoes live and how they breed is therefore of vital importance in understanding how such diseases as malaria and yellow fever enter the human population. Using the scaffolding tower built by the East African Virus Research Institute in Uganda, it was discovered that the yellow fever virus is passed by a particular mosquito which begins biting monkeys at dusk, just after they have settled in the canopy for the night. When these monkeys raid human plantations, the virus is picked up by local mosquitoes and is so transmitted to man. Migrant workers returning to towns enable yet another mosquito to transmit the disease between humans there.

Only female mosquitoes need blood, the males prefer nectar or rotting fruit juices. By placing human bait at different heights up the scaffolding tower, it proved possible to discover the levels at which the females feed and at what time of the day or night. One feed will give one mosquito enough protein to lay up to a hundred eggs. Many arboreal mosquitoes lay their eggs in a water-filled tree hollow; some will hover in front of this curving their abdomens towards it and firing eggs into it like a pea-shooter. Water-filled bamboos also positioned at varying levels on the tower to provide egg-laying sites revealed that different species of mosquito bred at different heights in the forest, too. Such information is vital in understanding how best to combat the diseases such biting flies transmit.

Numerous other disease-transmitting flies, such as tabanids, also inhabit the canopy. Some have brilliant green eyes and may be as large as a bee, delivering painful bites with annoying persistence. Whilst sitting on a canopy platform small sandflies, the like of which I rarely saw on the ground, settled on my exposed skin and drove their tiny stylets through it. One of these sandflies, with attractive white spots on its wings, almost trebled its body size in less than ninety seconds before drunkenly flying off, bloated and red, leaving a spot of blood on my skin as its calling card.

As man has felled the forest, animals which inhabit the canopy and their disease-bearing flies have come down with it; indeed there is speculation that the virus which causes AIDS, known in monkeys, may have been brought into contact with humans for the first time in this way.

On the Ivory Coast, French researchers are studying the pollination of *Terminalia* trees from platforms high in their branches, and others are doing similar work in the forests of Gabon. The engineering teams of Operation Drake proved that lightweight aerial walkways could be built between the crowns of emergent trees to enable humans to walk amongst them. Those in Panama, Papua New Guinea, and Sulawesi provided a brief opportunity to peer at canopy leaves, watch bees at flowers, and snatch unknown bats from the air. Though these walkways no longer exist, others are being erected elsewhere through the expedition which follows in its footsteps, Operation Raleigh. This giant venture, in which four thousand young people are taking part, has fostered a new series of walkways, the first in Costa Rica close to an international research station at La Selva, whose scientists can now use it. Others may follow in northern Australia, and West Africa. Bioresources, founded by the conservation organization, Earthlife, and headed by Dr Conrad Gorinsky, has embarked on a worldwide long-term programme beginning with Operation Raleigh's Venturers to help record information on traditional uses of tropical forest plants in the twenty countries it visits. Gorinsky believes the stored data will be of immense use to industries worldwide. At worst it may become a Domesday Book that future generations may weep over: 'You mean they let that go extinct, and that?'

Don Perry also has plans to construct a new rope web in Costa Rica from which to suspend himself, and perhaps others, amongst the crowns. Photographers and film-makers now use similar techniques and endure enormous hardships to bring the magic of the canopy into our homes. Phil Agland, a founder of Earthlife and maker of the award winning film *Korup* spent thousands of hours perched uncomfortably on canopy platforms, filming the animals around him. It took six and a half weeks of waiting to obtain footage of white-nosed monkeys pollinating the pentadesma tree. It is now quite possible to construct a complete network of lightweight bridges reaching many trees over a large area and this, combined with an extensive rope web, could provide access to all parts of the forest on a much greater scale than has hitherto been possible. There would be no lack of users; only those who can provide the funds are faint-hearted.

Like the animals of the forest before him, the arboreal naturalist is evolving as each new technique allows a greater reach into the forest, but all the climbing ropes, walkways and rope webs in the world cannot overcome man's greatest limitation. He cannot fly. One area yet remains beyond his touch, the air zone immediately above the canopy, and the outer fringes of its leaves. Only the

A meeting of two primates in the forest canopy. Film-makers such as Wolfgang Bayer have done much to bring the unique world of the rainforest roof into our homes, often risking great danger in the course of their work.

smallest, most dextrous mammals can venture there to lick nectar from flowers, or bite the choicest buds, and man is not amongst them; he can merely delve into just a few tree crowns in an ocean of forest and on the meagre knowledge he gleans from these must base his crucial predictions. This outer zone is also the realm of bats and birds and flying insects which can float on the wind and journey with ease from tree to tree. Here hornbills and toucans fly between the crowns and birds of prey can soar for inspection.

In Sulawesi I was interested in plotting the exact position of our walkway from the air so that I might place it on the map for later reference, should anyone choose to return to that same spot. The walkway was the longest we had built, with one section measuring seventy-five metres from tree to tree. Few crowns obscured our view of the sky but to make sure its position would be visible from the air, I arranged for some large orange balloons to be flown from the main anchor trees. Taking advantage of a visit by the local Indonesian Governor, I borrowed his pilot and helicopter to do a quick flight over the walkway site, which was some distance from the base camp where the helicopter had landed. Below, the forest stretched like a mottled blanket. Time and time again we circled the area where the walkway should have been but it remained invisible, nor could I see the balloons. That brought home to me the reality that all our efforts amounted to just a tiny pathway between a few tall trees, which were themselves swallowed up in the enormity of the forest roof. To sample a much greater area of the canopy, dipping into the crowns of many species, hundres of metres apart, to investigate the creatures and strange plants that live there and then move on to compare these with others elsewhere, must now be the goal of future arboreal naturalists. But how to do it? The answer is simple: a hot air balloon.

The turbulence from helicopter rotor blades has the unfortunate effect of frightening or blowing away all the animals and many of the leaves from a tree crown, but a balloon would have a much less disruptive effect. All the equipment necessary for a hot air balloon could be transported in a large pickup to a carefully picked launching site. Lifting off from a forest clearing during the calm of dawn, the balloon would float slowly over the crowns. No doubt monkeys would scatter at the sight of this extraordinary flying beast and its occasional noise but flying birds might be less afraid. The opportunities for photography and filming would be as never before. With judicious use of gas, the balloon's height above the canopy could be accurately controlled, enabling it to rise gently over an emergent tree. Then, either as the air in the balloon cooled and became less buoyant, or by releasing some from a valve in the envelope, I could float down the other side. As flowering tree crowns drifted by, grappling irons could be thrown into the branches, carefully bringing the balloon to a halt. Now, anchored above a tree, the balloon could be winched down into it, whilst ensuring that sufficient lift was maintained to hold it aloft. Reach-

OVERLEAF
Spurred on by the excitement of early discoveries, increasingly adventurous canopy explorers are planning for the future. Microlight aircraft and hot air balloons are already in use, and a special airship is poised to float off the drawing board and out over the forest.

ing from the basket, I could pluck samples at will and might even be able to scramble out amongst the branches on ropes or a sturdy supporting net placed over them for the purpose, before returning to weigh anchor and float on across the forest roof. If all this seems an unlikely tale, at the Institute of Evolutionary Science at Montpellier in France, plans for just such a venture are already well under way.

In October 1986, Professor Francis Hallé and his colleagues will float across the canopy of the forest in French Guiana on the north-east coast of South America. The project has been three years in preparation, inspired by the pioneering work of Marcel and Annette Hladick, who managed to study lianas and trees in the forest roof of Gabon in West Africa by using a tethered, hydrogen-filled balloon. The mini blimp was held in position by a cable attached to the side of a vehicle which they drove along a forest track. A large-format polaroid camera slung beneath it enabled them to obtain detailed photographs of the canopy, from which they managed to make some of the first descriptions of its architecture.

The new plan is much more ambitious, a floating platform in the sky. Large rubber tubes, similar to those of an inflatable dinghy, will be blown up on the ground creating a huge raft about the size of a tennis court, with taut netting for the floor stretched between the tube framework. With propane burners blazing, an enormous hot air balloon will be inflated in the centre, and carrying its piloting crew of two, the giant raft will rise over the forest and float over it, searching for a suitable crown to land in. Then the raft will be anchored to the trees with guiding ropes, assisted by helpers on the ground. Slowly releasing air from the balloon, the rubber framework will settle into the branches and, if stable enough, the giant balloon can be deflated.

Scientists on climbing ropes will ascend to the raft for as long as they wish, days and nights, gaining unique access to the flowers, leaves and smaller creatures that have either not taken flight or have resumed their lives despite this strange craft in their midst. Then the scientists will descend, the balloon will be reflated and the raft will float on to a new location.

Tests in France, using a helicopter to deposit the raft into the trees, have proved the idea can work but the rainforest canopy will be a different matter. It will be a potentially dangerous mission, since should anything go wrong once above the forest, the balloon may crash into the canopy far from any routes along which help could come. But in October in French Guiana the winds are light and predictable, and offer the best chance of success.

That is the Achilles heel of hot air balloons: they are at the mercy of the wind. Above the canopy raging storms can blow up with surprising speed and then depart as quickly. In that time a balloon could be blown far off-course; even light air currents could play havoc with a tethered balloon. Greater manoeuvrability has been achieved by arboreal naturalists who have taken to wings.

Ultralight aircraft, developed from hang-gliders, make ideal vehicles for photographing the rainforest roof. They are simple to fly, relatively cheap and need only small rough grass airstrips. Once airborne, it is possible to skim the canopy surface for five dollars an hour. Alfred Vooren has done just this in the Ivory Coast's remaining forests. His pioneering work is part of a silvicultural project in UNESCO's Man and Biosphere pilot programme for the area called Project Tai. In conjunction with the renowned biologist, Roelof Oldeman from Wageningen University in the Netherlands, Vooren has been taking stereo-photographs of selected canopy trees. These produce a three-dimensional image of the crowns from which it is hoped to determine the trees' ages from the patterns formed by their branches. They hope, too, to be able to discover how many of the trees are dying, and why.

Photographs of the canopy from above are often hard to obtain: aircraft come expensive and suitable airstrips are few and far between. Yet much can be revealed from such photographs: it is even possible to identify many species of trees from the air by the colour of their flowers, leaves and branches. As the arboreal naturalist is slowly climbing up from the forest floor, another way of looking at the canopy is coming down to meet him, this time from outer space. Landsat satellites are one of the many 'spy-in-the-sky' devices now orbiting the earth, their purpose entirely peaceful. Their multispectral scanners can cover the entire planet's surface every eighteen days. The images they return can pick out buildings, crops, logged areas, even different types of forest, so that maps of rainforests and how they are changing can be made from space, and the rate of destruction monitored year by year. Before ever leaving London I was able to see a complete vegetation map of the proposed nature reserve at Morowali in Sulawesi using images beamed from space to compile a digital view of the canopy on a computer monitor. The patterns the scanners produced were then 'ground truthed' in the jungle itself when we visited the reserve to see exactly what kind of forest the digital view represented.

Landsat imagery is still barely accurate enough to distinguish between forests made up of even quite different species of trees, as the green leaves do appear very similar when viewed from space. Also, tropical areas are often covered by cloud and the canopy is therefore hidden. Now various forms of aircraft-borne radar which can 'see' through cloud promise a better view; even laser beams operated from space may be used to reveal the contours and thickness of the canopy over large areas more accurately than ever before.

No amount of peering into the canopy from space, however, will replace the value of exploring its animals and plants in situ. At present no system exists which enables the arboreal naturalist to inspect closely the colourful tree frogs peeping out from bromeliad pools and then to float over tree tops across a valley to another chosen tree, to observe bees entering its flowers. To find ways of

studying large areas of the forest canopy on a regular basis remains an exciting challenge and in the next decade exciting new plans will find their way off the drawing board and into the trees.

Whilst watching the Superbowl Championships on television I was amazed at the way in which camera shots could be taken high above the stadium and then dropped down amongst the players, following them across the field with incredible speed. No crane or balloon is involved. At each corner of the stadium, large towers are erected. At the base of each is a precisely controlled winch from which cables run up the towers and meet in the middle over the pitch. At this point a camera, stabilized with a gyroscope, is placed. A computer controls the winches and thus the tension on each cable, and at the simple movement of a joystick, the camera can be moved in any direction in three dimensions with enormous speed. I see no reason, apart from its cost, why such a system could not be adapted to reach across a valley filled with tropical forest. High resolution video pictures could then be beamed from all parts of the canopy day and night. By up-grading the system it may even be possible to adapt it to carry a human being, who could move to any position above the forest by use of a simple switch. If that is too ambitious, perhaps it would be a simpler affair to adapt the rope web system, and suspend the arboreal naturalist, perhaps in a lightweight gondola, which could run along the ropes in a similar way to a small cable car on the ski slopes.

Large helium-filled balloons are now available which can be deflated and carried in the back of a small truck. Stabilized video cameras can be operated from them to provide unshakeable views: they are being used now to film motor races and other sporting events. Perhaps the helium balloon is the answer to the greatest challenge of all, the construction of an airship specifically designed to explore the forest roof.

Whilst using a large dirigible owned by Goodyear to investigate atmospheric pollution above industrial areas in the Mediterranean, I began to wonder whether airships or similar lighter-than-air craft could be adapted to provide a means of exploring the canopy. Such a craft would be powered by two quiet engines and be capable of carrying several people and their equipment anywhere over the rainforest within reasonable range of its base. The finance and technology would be no different from those required for the creation of a new vehicle for plumbing the ocean depths. Unpredictable wind conditions over the forest would, at certain times, make operation of such a craft extremely difficult but I have no doubt that modern technology has the capability to come up with solutions. Operating in conjunction with an existing forest research programme, the machine could systematically photograph the forest roof with cameras using special infra-red film to reveal vast amounts of information on the stage of flowering, fruiting and leaf production at present totally unobtainable on any significant scale. It could float over specific trees from which regular samples could

be taken, whilst at the same time sensors could reveal the meteorological conditions in different parts of the forest which appear so important in determining where many of the insects and other animals live, and when trees flower or fruit.

The need for such a vehicle to enable humans to explore this last biological frontier is undoubted. Then, as each year passes, and more arboreal naturalists have the good sense to suspend themselves from ropes or walkways in the canopy, and perhaps even float above it, our knowledge will expand. Already, in the few short years that have seen the beginnings of man's efforts to return to the trees, so much that was unknown about our natural world has been revealed, along with the sure knowledge that wise, sustainable use of these forests and the enormous genetic resources they contain makes sound economic sense. Growing public awareness and concern for the fate of the world's rainforests must push an increasingly irresistible tide of persuasion across the world, while the jungle is still with us.

A tropical rainforest is similar to a clock. Perhaps the mechanism that makes it work is too complicated to understand yet, but unless we continue to explore it there will be no hope of effecting repairs should the clock break down. One thing is certain. There is no need to understand how the clock works in order to tell the time, and time has all but run out for these once vast forests. The speed of their demise gives evolution no chance to soften the blow so that their countless life forms can adapt. The world's most intelligent ape is cutting off the branch on which it is sitting. It was within the canopy's branches that our intelligence and plundering nature were born. In the canopy we learnt to choose between poisonous leaves, to hunt for insects, and to recognize the colour of a ripe fruit. From damp moss and clear water within the hanging gardens we could quench our thirst. There too we learnt to fear the shadow of passing eagles and called out to warn families and offspring in the first beginnings of language. Our abilities to climb along arboreal highways enabled us to search widely for the resources we needed in order to survive and our minds blossomed in response to the opportunities the forest provided. Our departure from the canopy to become an exploitative ground-living ape, increasingly beleaguered by our ever-increasing numbers, has not altogether robbed us of our connection with the world in which we once lived, and deep down we all know that unless a more balanced use of the natural riches available to us eventually emerges, there will be a change, but it will not be one of our choosing.

The rainforest counts its life in millions of years and this is not the first time that it has been in retreat. In time the green canopy may one day begin to spread across the earth again from those fragments humankind allows to remain, but the planet will be a quieter place: so many creatures will have been lost. Man, too, perhaps; certainly those animals that survive to repopulate the canopy may have little enough to fear from him by then.

Once a great Maya civilization existed here at Tikal in what is now Guatemala. Though nine centuries have passed, the re-grown forest is still different from the virgin forest left undisturbed by the Mayans and, so far, by others.

In the preservation of the enchanted canopy we have an awesome responsibility, governing the fate not only of half of all the creatures and many of the plants that share this planet with us, but ultimately ourselves as well. The discovery that nature's last frontier is richer than was ever before dreamed is a message of hope, a gift for us to enjoy, and use wisely.

Bibliography

Ayensu, E. S. (Ed.) *Jungles.* Crown, New York; 1980.

Bates, H. W. *The Naturalist on the River Amazonas.* John Murray, London; 1864. Reprinted by the University of California Press, Berkeley.

Darwin, C. R. *The Movements and Habits of Climbing Plants.* John Murray, London; 1876.

Elrich, P. and A. *Extinction – The Causes and Consequences of the Disappearance of Species.* Victor Gollancz Ltd, London; 1982.

Forsyth, A. & Miyata, K. *Tropical Nature – Life and Death in the Rainforests of Central and South America.* Charles Scribner's Sons, New York; 1984.

Hanbury-Tenison, R. *Mulu – The Rainforest.* Weidenfeld and Nicolson, London; 1980.

Hingston, R. W. G. *A Naturalist in the Guiana Rainforest.* Longmans, Green, New York; Edward Arnold, London; 1932.

Huxley, A. *Green Inheritance.* Collins, London; 1984.

Mabberley, D. J. *Tropical Rainforest Ecology* Tertiary Level Biology Series. Blackie, Glasgow; Chapman & Hall, New York; 1983.

Mitchell, A. W. *Operation Drake – Voyage of Discovery.* Severn House, London; 1981.

——. *Reaching the Rainforest Roof – A Handbook on Techniques of Access and Study in the Canopy.* Leeds Phil. and Litt. Soc./ UNEP; 1982.

Myers, N. *The Sinking Ark.* Pergamon Press, Oxford; 1979.

——; *Conversion of Tropical Moist Forests.* National Academy of Sciences, Washington, DC; 1980.

——. *A Wealth of Wild Species – Storehouse for Human Welfare.* Westview Press, Boulder, Colorado; 1983.

Richards, P. W. *The Tropical Rainforest: An Ecological Study.* Cambridge University Press, England; 1952.

Skutch, A. F. *A Naturalist on a Tropical Farm.* University of California Press, Berkeley; 1980.

Wallace, A. R. *The Malay Archipelago.* Macmillan & Co, London; 1969.

——. *A Narrative of Travels on the Amazon and Rio Negro.* Ward, Lock & Co, London; 1889. Reprinted by Dover Books, New York; 1972.

Whitmore, T. C. *Tropical Rainforests of the Far East.* Clarendon Press, Oxford; 1975.

Whitten, T. *The Gibbons of Siberut.* J. M. Dent & Sons Ltd, London; 1982.

Photo Credits

10–11 Robin Hanbury Tenison, RGS

15, 54, 106, 155 Jean-Paul Ferrero, Auscape International

16, 35, 78 G. I. Bernard, Oxford Scientific Films

18–19 Bruno Barbey Magnum

22 above, 81, 100 right, 111 Densey Clyne, Mantis Wildlife Films, Australia

22 below, 100 left, 130 K. G. Preston-Mafham, Premaphotos Wildlife

24 Max Nicholson

30, 217, 221 Andrew W. Mitchell

31 Rob Fitzgerald, Orpix

36, 41 Francis Hallé, Institut Botanic

37 Eric Hosking

38–9, 60, 69, 191 Wolfgang Bayer Productions

42 Tony Beamish, Ardea London Ltd

43, 68, 90, 153 Michael Fogden, Oxford Scientific Films

49 Francois Gohier, Ardea London Ltd

50, 52 K. Wothe, Bruce Coleman Ltd

55, 183 Alain Compost, Bruce Coleman Ltd

62–3 P. K. Sharp, Oxford Scientific Films

67, 95, 96, 125, 127, 176–7, 192, 200 Michael Fogden

72–3, 141, 244–5 E. S. Ross

74 Daniel Barthelemy, Institut Botanic

75 above and below D. H. Thompson, Oxford Scientific Films

86 C. R. Huxley

88 Liz and Tony Bomford, Ardea London Ltd

91 G. K. Brown, Ardea London Ltd

94, 110 Michael Fogden, Bruce Coleman Ltd

99 above, 173 Stephen Dalton, NHPA

99 below G. I. Bernard, NHPA

104, 124, 159 Frithfoto

109 Keith and Liz Laider, Ardea London Ltd

113, 184 Rod Williams, Bruce Coleman Ltd

115 Dieter and Mary Plage, Bruce Coleman Ltd

120, 202–3, 207 John Wright

128, 148–9, 222, 229 Loren McIntyre

135 E. A. MacAndrew, NHPA

136 T. W. Davies

139 Donald R. Perry, Camera Press

147 M. K. and I. M. Morcombe, NHPA

150–1, 186 Tom McHugh, the National Audubon Society Collection, PR

156 Delacotte

160 Merlin D. Tuttle, Bat Conservation International

Index

References in *italics* are to illustrations